The Twitter Job Search Guide

Find a Job and Advance Your Career in Just 15 Minutes a Day

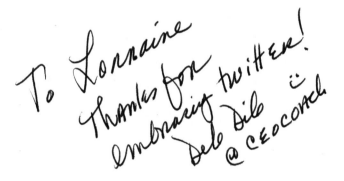

Susan Britton Whitcomb
Chandlee Bryan
Deb Dib

jist Works
America's Career Publisher

The Twitter Job Search Guide

© 2010 by Susan Britton Whitcomb, Chandlee Bryan, and Deb Dib

Published by JIST Works, an imprint of JIST Publishing
7321 Shadeland Station, Suite 200
Indianapolis, IN 46256-3923
Phone: 800-648-JIST   Fax: 877-454-7839   E-mail: info@jist.com

Visit our Web site at **www.jist.com** for information on JIST, free job search tips, tables of contents, sample pages, and ordering instructions for our many products!

Please call our Sales Department at 800-648-5478 for a free catalog and more information.

Trade Product Manager: Lori Cates Hand
Interior Designer and Page Layout: Toi Davis
Cover Designer: Honeymoon Image + Design
Proofreaders: Chuck Hutchinson, Jeanne Clark
Indexer: Cheryl Lenser

Printed in the United States of America

15 14 13 12 11 10   9 8 7 6 5 4 3 2 1

Library of Congress Cataloging-in-Publication data is on file with the Library of Congress.

We have been careful to provide accurate information in this book, but it is possible that errors and omissions have been introduced. Please consider this in making any career plans or other important decisions. Trust your own judgment above all else and in all things.

Trademarks: All brand names and product names used in this book are trade names, service marks, trademarks, or registered trademarks of their respective owners.

ISBN 978-1-59357-791-9

Dedication

For #jobseekers. Our heroes. We salute you!

Contents

Section 1: How and Why Twitter Can Help You in Your Job Search   **1**

Chapter 1	**What You Want It to Be**	**2**
	Like Twitter, This Book Is for Everyone	*3*
	You Can Do This, Even if You're Not a Techie	*3*
	What's Inside The Twitter Job Search Guide	*4*
	How to Use This Book	*5*

Chapter 2	**Ten Truths About Twitter to Benefit Your Job Search**	**6**
	1. Find Connection, Support, and Strength	*7*
	2. Tap into a Wealth of Free Job Search Information	*8*
	3. Locate Job Leads	*8*
	4. Connect to the Hidden Job Market and Insider Contacts	*9*
	5. Broadcast Your Brand and Drown Digital Dirt	*9*
	6. Expand Your Network—Fast	*10*
	7. Cultivate Serendipity	*10*
	8. Get Real-Time Responses That Will Expand Your Thinking	*11*
	10. Foster a Forum for Sharing, Learning, and Laughter	*12*
	Twitter's Growth Is Good for You	*13*

Chapter 3	**For the Skeptics**	**14**
	Responses to Nine Common Complaints About Twitter	*15*
	The People You Want to Know Are on Twitter…	
	Shouldn't You Be There, Too?	*20*

Chapter 4	**How Twitter Differs from Other Social Media**	**21**
	Twitter Transformed the Rules of Engagement	*22*
	The Power of Twitter	*22*
	The Big Three: Facebook, LinkedIn, and Twitter	*23*
	A Power User's Perspective	*25*
	Looking Ahead	*27*

Chapter 5	**Twitter Secrets from Successful Job Seekers**	**28**
	Twitter for Job Search Myth-Busting	*28*
	Learn from the Landed	*29*
	Meet Our Baker's Dozen of "Branded and Landed" Experts	*31*

Section 2: Get Branded to Get Landed   **34**

Chapter 6	**Employers Are Googling You: A Crash Course on Managing Your Online Identity**	**35**
	Your Digital Footprint	*36*
	Build and Manage Your Brand on Twitter and Beyond	*36*
	Seven Steps to Dissolve and Deflect Digital Dirt	*39*

Chapter 7	**Your Brand and Twitter**		**41**
	The PB&J (Personal Brand & Job) Brand Sandwich		*41*
	Personal Brands Reflect and Connect		*42*
	The Brand to Land™ Plan to Get Hired Faster		*43*
Chapter 8	**Ten Steps to Mining, Defining, and Refining Your Brand**		**47**
	Step 1: Take Stock		*47*
	Step 2: Look Outward		*48*
	Step 3: Look for Personal Patterns		*48*
	Step 4: Look for Work Patterns		*48*
	Step 5: Tie Patterns to Accomplishments to "Then What?"		*48*
	Step 6: Analyze Accomplishment Themes		*49*
	Step 7: Analyze for Buying Motivators		*49*
	Step 8: Start Developing Your Brand Statement		*50*
	Step 9: Say It in Your Voice		*50*
	Step 10: Craft the Value Proposition		*50*
Chapter 9	**Your Branded Value Proposition (BVP)**		**51**
	The Employer's Eternal Question: What's in It for Me?		*51*
	Three Key Questions to Identify Your BVP		*53*
	Twitterizing the Pitch		*54*
	If You Need More Help		*54*
Chapter 10	**Sound Bites with Teeth: Writing Your 160me™ Twitter Bio**		**56**
	Say It Short, Say It Sweet		*56*
	Your Twitter Bio: We Call It the 160me		*58*
	The Four-Step Pitch Process for Job Seekers		*59*
	The Goal? A Follow, a Click-Through, a Call!		*60*
Section 3: Twitter Basics			**63**
Chapter 11	**What's in a Name: Choosing Twitter Account Settings to Boost Your Online Presence**		**64**
	Power SEO for Twitter		*64*
	Six Steps to SEO Success with Twitter		*66*
	Other Settings		*74*
Chapter 12	**Branding Your Twitter Account with a Customized Background**		**75**
	Modifying Twitter's Standard Backgrounds and Colors		*76*
	Displaying a Custom Background		*77*
	Creating Your Own Design		*80*
	Tailor-Made Designs		*82*
	Resources		*83*
Chapter 13	**The Art of Following and Being Followed**		**85**
	Creating Connections, One Follower at a Time		*86*
	The Who, What, When, and Where of Attracting Followers		*87*

Chapter 14	**How to Speak in Tweets: The Language and Style of Twitter**	**90**
	Twitter Terminology and Shorthand	*90*
	On the N.O.S.E.: A Four-Point Model for Writing Great Tweets	*93*
	Sources to Create Great Content	*96*
Chapter 15	**The Art and Science of the Retweet**	**97**
	The Incredible, Flexible Retweet	*97*
	The Art and Science of Getting Your Tweets Retweeted	*100*
	Five Ways to Retweet and Boost Your Job Search	*101*
	Thanking People for Retweets	*102*
	Great (and Not So Great) Retweets	*103*
Chapter 16	**Tweeter Beware: Staying Out of Legal Hot Water**	**104**
	A New Challenge for the Courts	*104*
	Your Tweets Are Showing	*105*
	From Digital Dirt to Legal Hurt: How to Protect Yourself	*106*
	Who Owns Your Tweets?	*107*
	Kodak's Pioneering Social Media Guidelines	*107*
	Legalese and Parting Advice	*109*

Section 4: Job Search, Twitter Style   **111**

Chapter 17	**Job Search Advice from the Trenches**	**112**
	Ten New Rules for a New-Economy Search	*112*
	The Psychology of the Search	*117*
Chapter 18	**Recruiters Reveal Job Search Secrets**	**120**
	Recruiter Tweets	*120*
	A Recruiter Sounds Off on Resumes	*124*
Chapter 19	**Turbocharge Your Resume with Tweets**	**125**
	What Is a Twit-Fit Resume? Why Use One?	*126*
	Ten Steps to a Twit-Fit Resume	*126*
	We Twit-Fit Pizza Guy's Resume	*128*
Chapter 20	**Cover Letters Are Just 10 Tweets**	**132**
	Does Your Cover Letter Pass the Yawn-Meter Test?	*132*
	For Cover Letters, as for Twitter, Brevity Rules	*133*
	The Case for the 10-Tweet Cover Letter Technique™	*133*
Chapter 21	**Using Twitter to Help Ace the Interview**	**139**
	Pre-interview Research	*139*
	Interview Advice	*140*
	Follow Up	*142*

Section 5: The New Networking   **143**

Chapter 22	**Jump into Twitter to Jump-Start Your Network**	**144**
	Twitter and Networking = Career Momentum	*145*
	It's All About the People	*148*

Chapter 23   Leveraging Twitter Throughout Your Job Search
and Networking   150
Connecting the Real with the Virtual   *151*
Ten Ways to Use Twitter to Integrate the Real and
the Virtual   *151*
Go Virtual to Get Visible   *153*

Chapter 24   Twitter Networking: A Safe Space for Introverts; a
Party for Extroverts   155
Top 10 Twitter Tips for Introverts   *156*
Top 10 Twitter Tips for Extroverts   *157*

Chapter 25   Niche Market Networking on Twitter   159
Mind Your Ps and Qs (Positions, Quality, and Quantity)   *159*
Five Strategies for Niche Marketing on Twitter   *160*
Make Your Network Aware of Your Niche with Twitter   *161*
Who You Are Is as Important as What You Do   *162*
Niche Market Networking Checklist   *162*
Niching and Networking: A Career-Long Strategy   *163*

Chapter 26   Discretionary Authenticity: How to Share, How
Much, and with Whom   164
What Not to Share: The Blacklist   *164*
How to Share   *165*
How Much to Share   *166*
With Whom to Share   *166*
A Three-Point AIM Model for Appropriate Sharing   *167*
Twitter Tips for Discretionary Authenticity   *168*

Section 6: Conducting Your Twitter Job Search in 15
Minutes a Day   169
Chapter 27   Maximize Twitter in Just 15 Minutes a Day   170
Strategies for Optimizing Your Time on Twitter   *170*
Your 15-Minute-a-Day Schedule   *171*

Chapter 28   Using Twitter for Job Leads, Feeds, and Advice Needs   175
Sources of Job Leads: Search Engines for Job Listings   *176*
Hashtags: Organizing Information, People, and Leads   *177*
Sources of Feeds: General Directories of Employers and
Job Postings on Twitter   *179*
Advice and Trends from Job Search Experts and Recruiters   *180*

Chapter 29   Twitter Lists: Streamlining Tweets and Optimizing Your
Experience   181
Use Lists to Save Time and Boost Job Search Efficiency   *182*
Getting Started: Using and Maintaining Lists   *183*
A Final Word on Lists   *187*

Chapter 30   Research on Twitter: Finding People, Positions, Places
to Work, and Other Puzzle Pieces   188
Poke and Pry with Purpose: Twitter's Advanced Search   *189*

		Tap Google, Bing, and LinkedIn to Augment	
		Twitter Searches	*190*
		Explore Other Twitter Tools for Finding Stuff	*191*
		Research, Social Media Style	*192*

Chapter 31	**Twitter APIs: There's an App for That!**	**194**
	Desktop Twitter Clients	*195*
	URL Shorteners: 140-Character Conservation Tools	*196*
	Finding Conversations on Twitter	*196*
	Finding New Friends with Shared Interests	*196*
	Timing Is Everything: How to Get Your Tweet Across	
	at the Right Time	*197*
	Backing Up Your Tweets	*198*
	Technical APIs	*199*
	Mobile Apps	*200*
	Want the Latest and Greatest?	*201*

| Chapter 32 | **Parting Tweets of Wisdom from Savvy Job Seekers** | **202** |

| **Section 7: Appendixes** | **206** |

Appendix A	**140 Tweet Tips from Career Experts**	**207**
	Using Twitter in Your Job Search	*207*
	Using Twitter for Networking and Visibility	*210*
	Using Twitter for Personal Branding and Social Media	*211*
	Using Social Media for Your Career	*212*
	Using Twitter: General Tips	*212*
	Job Search Tips: In a Nutshell	*213*
	Networking Tips	*215*
	Personal Branding Tips	*216*
	Resume Tips	*217*
	Interviewing Tips	*217*

| Appendix B | **Chapter Contributor Bios** | **218** |

| Appendix C | **The Distinguished (Baker's) Dozen: Stories from** | |
| | **Successful Twitter Job Seekers** | **226** |

| **Index** | **236** |

Foreword

Sitting in Chicago's O'Hare International Airport, all were frustrated. My flight was delayed for at least two hours and the terminal bustled with disgruntled fellow passengers. One young man looked especially downtrodden—suit disheveled, shirt coffee-stained, tie twisted—as he flopped to the soiled carpet with his bags.

The man—let's call him "Steve"—opened his backpack and pulled out an equally battered laptop. As he flipped it open, something caught my eye. It was a sticker placed over the manufacturer's logo which stated, "follow me on Twitter," and included his "@" username. Curiosity piqued, I grabbed my iPhone, logged into Twitter, and decided to see what Steve had to say.

It will sound grandiose, but Steve's life was about to change.

You see, Steve had flown to Chicago on his own dime to attend a much-heralded job fair. With only two years of postgraduate work experience, Steve thought he would truly differentiate himself if given a chance to interact with a recruiter face-to-face. Instead, he found himself in endless receiving lines each hundreds of job seekers long. The recruiters were exhausted, the open positions were few, and the competition was fierce. After 10 hours and nearly $1,000 in expenses, Steve had secured a grand total of 10 minutes of recruiter face time. Ten minutes.

Steve shared much of this story via his Twitter account. After a few minutes, I "tweeted" that I'd love to buy him a coffee while we waited for our flight. He looked up to find me standing 10 feet away.

Long story short, we connected. And by connecting with me via Twitter, Steve was able to locate an unadvertised position within 10 miles of his home. He was hired on the spot and has worked there ever since.

Steve's case is not unusual. Thousands of individuals have realized that Twitter is a powerful tool for job seeking. But therein lies the problem: There are tens of millions of active and passive job seekers, yet only a small fraction are leveraging what Twitter has to offer. That is about to change.

In *The Twitter Job Search Guide,* authors Susan Britton Whitcomb, Chandlee Bryan, and Deb Dib have demystified this essential job search and career management tool. And better yet, these experts have taken a perceived limitation of Twitter—namely its 140-character limit per message—and turned it into a lesson in concise and critical thinking.

In an era where self-professed experts are seemingly around every corner, trust, credibility, and value are often waylaid. Susan, Chandlee, and Deb have applied decades of "offline" expertise to ensure your "online" time is well spent. There is no mystery. There is no trickery. There is only practical, no-nonsense advice that pours freely from three of the market's most highly respected career thought leaders.

In Twitter-worthy style, let me summarize what you're about to experience:

Congratulations. You have joined a unique group of individuals who "get it." Revel in your newfound knowledge.

This book will fundamentally change the way in which you look at yourself, your career opportunities, and the proper role of technology.

There is no BS or fluff. Every word is purposeful and every chapter is essential. Don't skip anything.

Much like Twitter, this book is what you make of it.

Fifteen minutes a day is all it's going to take. Fifteen minutes was all it took for Steve and me to connect. Fifteen minutes was all it took for Steve to connect to an unadvertised job opening. And 15 minutes into his interview, Steve knew the job was meant for him. Twitter is open 24/7 and the clock is running. Get to work.

—**Mark Stelzner (@stelzner), Founder, JobAngels (@jobangels)**

About This Book

Twitter.

Of all the sites associated with social media, none may be more embraced or reviled, used or abused, comprehended or confused.

What *is* clear is that Twitter is one of the most innovative and useful devices for job search and career management, and—as of this writing—one of the tools least used by those who need it most.

In *The Twitter Job Search Guide* we are on a mission to change that! In this book you'll find a wealth of information on using Twitter to build your personal and career brands; grow your network; increase your visibility; attract attention as a subject-matter expert; expand your knowledge of your industry, profession, and target companies; and have some fun on a personal level as well.

And we'll show you how you can do all that in 15 minutes a day!

The Twitter Job Search Guide is divided into seven sections. Whether you are a Twitter neophyte who needs a deep-dive into the Twitterverse or a seasoned user who'd like some new tips, you'll find value in each section.

In section 1 of the book you'll learn why Twitter is a very special and unique job search tool. We cover untold truths about how Twitter can revolutionize your job search and answer concerns that a skeptic might have. You'll learn how Twitter differs from—yet can be integrated with—other social media. Most importantly, you'll see the power of Twitter in action when you meet our baker's dozen of job seekers who share their Twitter job search success stories.

Section 2 begins with the critical career importance of controlling your online reputation in the age of Google, and then moves on to explore the process of building and managing your brand so that you can use Twitter to successfully expand your visibility in a way that is authentic and compelling. You'll learn 10 steps to "mine, define, and refine" your personal and career brands and how to showcase the power of your brand through an employer-attracting branded value proposition. The result will be communicated in your 160me™ Twitter bio.

Before you can search for a job on Twitter, you'll need to know how to use it. Section 3 is our "Twitter FAQ" manual. This how-to section jump-starts Twitter newbies and has enough useful tips to keep even seasoned Tweeters interested. From choosing your Twitter handle and customizing your Twitter background to writing engaging, on-brand tweets, you'll learn what works, how to choose your strategy, and how to execute it. Twitter is all about community—we teach you how to follow (and choose whom to follow), how to be followed, how to engage your community, and how to avoid common pitfalls and legal hot water.

Once you know your brand and value; have your Twitter handle, account, and 160me bio; and are fairly adept at the Twitter basics, you're almost ready for your Twitter job search. Before you jump in, it's wise to review the foundational concepts of job search. These are critical to success when using any methodology, and are even more important in Twitter, where every word counts. In section 4 we've taken these concepts and updated them to be applicable to today's social media environment. You'll find 10 essential steps for Twitter-style job search and interviewing, as well as our Twit-Fit process for developing resume content and 10-tweet cover letters. Finally, revel in the wisdom of our Twitter-friendly panel of recruiters who divulge their favorite job search secrets.

Twitter has opened the door to a whole new level of networking by lowering the barriers and enabling dialogue between people who would previously have been separated by gatekeepers, distance, anonymity, shyness, or even fear of rejection. In section 5 you'll learn networking and niche-ing, Twitter style, and how to leverage both throughout your job search and career development. Whether you are an introvert, extrovert, or somewhere in the middle, networking with Twitter can comfortably fit your style and help you shine.

Section 6 will equip you to "plan your work and work your plan" on Twitter—in just 15 minutes a day. We've compiled a comprehensive library of tools, tips, and strategies that—after your initial learning curve—can help you focus your efforts and develop your network in a surprisingly limited time, leaving you free to manage the other areas of your job search!

Finally, section 7 is where successful Twitter job seekers and the Twitter careers community speak. We asked hiring managers, career coaches, resume professionals, personal branding strategists, and job seekers who use Twitter to share their best job search, branding, networking, interviewing, and Twitter tips. We received more than 400 and, in honor of Twitter's famous character limit, selected 140, which you'll find in appendix A. (You'll find the others on *The Twitter Job Search Guide* Web site at www.twitterjobsearchguide.com.)

Be sure to check out the bios of all of our chapter contributors (appendix B); we predict you'll be impressed with the depth and range of their experience and expertise. They exemplify the sharing you'll find within the Twitter community and we are grateful for their wisdom.

We saved the best for last: our successfully employed job seekers! Join them as they tell of their experiences in using Twitter as part, or sometimes all, of their job search strategies. These savvy searchers range from college students to seasoned executives and admin professionals to intellectuals, located in small towns to metro centers on multiple continents. Each has a unique story with a common path to a happy landing: Twitter.

Acknowledgments

The seed for this book was planted in Coleman Falls, Virginia, where Wendy Enelow, a prolific author in her own right, hosted a gathering of career thought leaders at her "gentleman's farm." Many ideas were birthed that day, including the idea of Susan, Deb, and Chandlee collaborating on this book. To Wendy, who brought us together, and to our other thought leader colleagues Louise Kursmark, Beverly Harvey, Cindy Kraft, Donna Moniot, Elisabeth Sanders-Park, and especially to Jan Melnik (she knows why!), who encouraged us in the process, we thank you.

No book is ever the work of one writer, or in this case, three, and such is the case with *The Twitter Job Search Guide*. Social media has enabled us to bring together the insights and experiences of more than 100 career experts, staffing and recruiting professionals, and successful job seekers in this book (see the appendixes). We are honored and humbled by your willingness to share your insider secrets. You have made this book what we could never have done on our own.

To our chapter contributors, many of whom are respected authors and all experts in their fields, who gave not just their wisdom, but their most precious commodity: time. The writing, rewriting, and ruthless editing to help keep us under our page count is deeply appreciated. We thank you: Jason Alba, Laura Allen, William Arruda, Jacqui Barrett-Poindexter, Kim Batson, Rob Blatt, Nancy Branton, Sue Brettell, August Cohen, Kirsten Dixson, Alison Doyle, Wendy Gelberg, Robyn Greenspan, Katharine Hansen, Mark Hovind, Susan Ireland, Susan Joyce, Michael (Animal) Keleman, Abby Kohut, Cindy Kraft, Jessica Lee, Jeff Lipschultz, Jan Melnik, Chris Perry, Lindsey Pollak, Karla Porter, Barbara Safani, Dan Schwabel, Marshall Sponder, Mark Stelzner, Donna Sweidan, Wendy Terwelp, Harry Urschel, and Bill Vick.

To our colleagues and "tweeps" who contributed more than 400 tweet tips to this book, applause! Your active presence on Twitter has raised the visibility and credibility of the careers industry, supported job seekers in countless unseen ways, and underscored the importance of proactive career management for all.

On behalf of job seekers everywhere, we thank you: Walter Akana, Renee Alfieri, Deborah Bashaw, Kim Batson, Laurie Berenson, Kathy Bitschenauer, Bridgette (Weide) Brooks, Dawn Bugni, Randi Bussin, Katie Canton, Claire Chapman, August Cohen, Mack Collier, Paul Copcutt, Kellye Crane, Janet Cranford, Annemarie Cross, Jean Cummings, Robert Dagnall, Sharon Delay, Kevin Donlin, Robyn Feldberg, Tom Fitch, Megan Fitzgerald, Louise Garver, Wendy Gelberg, Meg Giuseppi, Beverly Harvey, David Heiser, Shannon Kelly, Erin Kennedy, Myriam-Rose Kohn, Cindy Kraft, Michelle La Faunge Berns, Andy Lee, Maureen McCann, Jan Melnik, Cheryl Minnick, Meg Montford, Joan Olson, Cindy Pace, Chris Perry, Kris Plantrich, Barb Poole, Julie Rains, Brian Ray, Jane Roqueplot,

Teena Rose, Andrew Rosen, Barbara Safani, Elisabeth Sanders-Park, Andrea Santiago, Ebony Scurry, Phyllis Shabad, Laura Smith-Proulx, Susan Strayer, Billie Sucher, Stacy Swearengen, Donna Sweiden, Wendy Terwelp, Rosa Elizabeth Vargas, Charlotte Weeks, Daisy Wright, and Stephanie Zonars.

Our Twitter job seekers—Biana Bakman; John Bordeaux, Ph.D.; Mark Buell; Kelly Giles; Doug Hamlin; Jen Harris; Desiree Kane; Jon Lazar; Michael Litman; Stephen Moyer; Warren Sukernek; Jamie Varon; and Shannon Yelland—thank you for pioneering and paving the way. Your adventurous and innovative spirit in finding new ways to use Twitter will rewrite the job search how-to books.

To Mark Stelzner, founder of @jobangels, you are an example of what we admire most: compassion with action. To Jeff Pulver, thank you for allowing access to your 140 Characters Conference in Los Angeles—the experience was foundational to grasping the broad application of Twitter; and to Alexis Stack, for making the introduction. And to the social media team at Eastman Kodak, thank you not only for sharing your social media best practices in the book, but for leading the way in the first place. Thanks also go to Sam Horn, veteran author, wordsmith, and alliterative genius—your guidance and cheerleading are cherished.

The terrific team at JIST Publishing who recognized the skyrocketing importance of Twitter and went to bat to make this the first-to-market print book exclusively dedicated to Twitter and the job search. And to Lori Cates Hand, visionary, editor extraordinaire, and savvy social media and Twitter user, thank you for breaking new ground on a three-author project that involved two first-time authors and more than 100 contributors!

To our families, your patience, patience, and patience (and more patience) allowed us to write this book in record time. To our clients, coworkers, and colleagues, thanks for your support and for bearing with our deadline pressures.

From Susan: To my husband Charlie, thank you for being Charlie, and remembering to feed our kid (and her friends) when I would forget. To Emmeline, thanks for leaving "daughter love notes" for me to find at 4am on my computer screen as I sat down to work many mornings. To my mom, my heartfelt thanks for teaching me how to be organized and meticulous in my writing, way back in high school. And to my team at The Academies: Lyndsey Lehman, who is much more than a Business Manager to me, I love you (and forgive you) for making me migrate to a Mac in the middle of a book deadline; Teri Meeks, who came on board in the middle of this project and got a quick initiation into the myriad behind-the-scenes details of publishing a book (and handled it like a pro); and to Academies directors and instructors Nancy Branton (Leadership Coach Academy), Beverly Harvey (Job Search Academy), and Kim Avery (Career Coach Academy), for your patience as coach training projects got put on hold during the deadline and stepping up to the plate to help lead, thank you!

From Deb: To my husband Doug, who had the original idea for my careers business back in 1989. You're my soul mate, my not-so-silent partner, and my cheerleader. Thank you for always believing in me. To Patrick and Jessamyn, who still remember our mad dash to the post office many years ago (pre-Internet!), in the snow, to make a submission deadline for the first book in which my work was featured. You've supported me through the crazy times of building a business from home while raising you, and have grown to be exceptional adults. I am proud to be your mom. To my parents and favorite librarians, Emily and Ray Wile. Your passion for books made reading my life's blood. To Mark Hovind, who encouraged me to "write tight"; to Jason Alba, who taught me Twitter as a NOOB; and to Pat Schuler, my coach and guiding light. You are each a glimmering facet in the prism of my career. And to my clients, who make my work a joy. Thank you for "doing Capitalism right." You inspire me.

From Chandlee: To my family and my cheerleaders, Anna and Amelia Bryan, Eric Bricker, Robin Cecola, Sheila Curran, Lindsay Doering, Leslie Haynsworth, Ken Hendra, Anne Janeway, Chrissy Jisha, Lauren Ryan, Carolyn Sprague, Marcjana Turns, and Lily Williams. To friends at Dartmouth, Columbia, and Penn with special thanks to Peggy Curchack and the late Mary Morris Heiberger. To my high school English teacher Mr. Gasque and to Symphony Space. To my prolific father and my proofreading mother, you are now allowed to read what I've been working on—but please hold your tongue with revisions! And finally, to the NYC Job Seekers MeetUp group for asking great questions and giving me a broader perspective.

And finally, from each of us to each other: The opportunity to collaborate on this project, though a mountain of work, has been an indescribable blessing and a blast. This quote from Harry Truman sums it up: "It is amazing what you can accomplish if you do not care who gets the credit."

The Web Site: www.TwitterJobSearchGuide.com

Twitter, like all technology, is advancing at warp speed. There will undoubtedly be changes and additions to what we've written before the book even hits the bookshelves. For that reason, we've created www.TwitterJobSearchGuide.com. Visit the site for updates, plus several hundred additional tweet tips from our career experts, and additional training tools. You'll also find a media page, information on booking speaking engagements, and our upcoming engagements.

And don't forget to follow us on Twitter:

> http://twitter.com/SusanWhitcomb

> http://twitter.com/chandlee

> http://twitter.com/CEOCoach

See you there!

SECTION 1

HOW AND WHY TWITTER CAN HELP YOU IN YOUR JOB SEARCH

1. Twitter Is What You Want It to Be

2. Ten Truths About Twitter to Benefit Your Job Search

3. For the Skeptics

4. How Twitter Differs from Other Social Media

5. Twitter Secrets from Successful Job Seekers

CHAPTER 1

TWITTER IS WHAT YOU WANT IT TO BE

*"We defined a mere 1 percent of what Twitter is today. The remaining
99 percent has been, and will continue to be, created by the millions of
people who make this medium their own, tweet by tweet."*

—*Jack Dorsey, creator, cofounder, and chairman, Twitter, Inc., in his
foreword to the book* 140 Characters: A Style Guide for the
Short Form *by Twitter cofounder Dom Sagolla*

There is no shortage of information at our fingertips today. It's estimated that a
week's worth of content in *The New York Times* contains more information than a
person was likely to come across in a lifetime in the 18th century.

But with this superabundance comes conflicting advice, especially around job search.
How do you find what you need to know, who you need to know, who needs to
know YOU, *and* sort it all out?

In a word, Twitter.

Twitter is what you want it to be. It can be a one-stop shop for today's job seekers
or just a small but important strategy in your campaign. You get to decide how you
will use it. There's no one-size-fits-all Twitter strategy.

Should you opt to lean into the Twittersphere, you can find insight, encouragement,
connections, job leads, and company insider information—in bite-sized messages of
140 characters or fewer.

Throughout this book you'll see tips called "Need to Know." If you're new to
Twitter, there's a language of sorts to learn—acronyms, terms, and phrases that
you'll need to know to use Twitter. You'll find explanations in these boxes. Here's
the first…

Need to Know: Twitter limits messages to 140 characters, including spaces. All
messages are referred to as "tweets."

You can also find masterful advice from some of the world's most respected career experts on everything from how to start your search to how to negotiate salary. It's a genuine goldmine at your fingertips.

And yet, many job seekers are hesitant when it comes to Twitter—and with good reason. A recent *Time* article said it best: "The one thing you can say for certain about Twitter is that it makes a terrible first impression." And opinions abound about Twitter's time-sucking, what-I-had-for-breakfast, too-confusing-to-use reputation—so many, in fact, that we've devoted a whole chapter to presenting our counter-position on how Twitter can help (see chapter 3).

With all the misinformation surrounding Twitter, we wouldn't blame you if you were skeptical. But the fact that you're reading this book means that at the very least, you are curious.

We encourage you to keep an open, inquiring mind and consider what Twitter can do for you. We believe Twitter has the potential to become one of your most effective, quick, and easy-to-use job search tools. We're excited to show you how to make that happen.

Like Twitter, This Book Is for Everyone

The Twitter Job Search Guide was written with a wide variety of people in mind, much like how Twitter works for a wide variety of users: students and emerging professionals building their brand, career-minded professionals (from support staff to sales reps and supervisors to C-suite execs), as well as the many career experts who help people navigate the job search journey.

Regardless of your background or circumstances, the principles covered in this book will work for you; they are universal.

You Can Do This, Even if You're Not a Techie

Some of you may already be power users of Twitter who picked up this book to glean new ideas for a job search. Others are either not yet on Twitter or just getting started.

We can help you through your Twitter entry process. We've been there. We were once Twitter NOOBs, too.

Need to Know: *NOOB* is Twitter shorthand for "Newbie."

We're not ashamed to admit that we don't know any computer programming languages, and we're not always the first ones on the block to own the latest tech toys. But our admitted lack of tech expertise helps us explain Twitter in layman's terms—and proves that you can do this, too!

In fact, like many (perhaps most) of our readers, we don't claim to be social media experts. We have embraced Twitter and other social media because we recognize the incredible value it brings to our personal and professional lives.

> **Need to Know:** SearchEngineWatch.com defines *social media* as "A category of sites that is based on user participation and user-generated content."

The opportunity to build relationships through social media—via approachability, authenticity, and collaboration—is priceless. And the wealth of knowledge available through social media—with immediacy, accessibility, and freshness—is icing on the cake.

If you're a NOOB, give yourself permission to test Twitter. Fair warning: At first glance, Twitter looks disorganized, random, even useless. (It's like arriving in a foreign country and not knowing the language.) We encourage you to look past that. Stay awhile and explore—wade in slowly and test the waters. You'll experience what millions have come to realize: Twitter is terrific.

What's Inside *The Twitter Job Search Guide*

We've designed this book to do five things:

1. Teach you everything you need to know to jump into Twitter prepared with a compelling personal brand, a strategy, and the tools to make your experience as effective as possible—in just 15 minutes a day.

2. Teach you new, easy-to-master, Twitter-inspired processes for building your resume and cover letter. You'll also find strategies for creating a concise bio, along with "sound bites" to help communicate your value in the short form employers expect online. (We affectionately refer to this as a "Twitpitch" and a branded value proposition.) And we'll share how to carry your value proposition/Twitpitch across other social media and many other forms of career communication.

> **Need to Know:** A *Twitpitch* is a 160-character bio used in your Twitter profile.

3. Give you inspiring, relatable, real-world stories of people who've used Twitter effectively to build online visibility, create a vibrant network, research companies, and, yes, even get a job.

4. Show you how to communicate on Twitter to add new relationships and deepen established associations. These relationships, or your "tweeps" in Twitter parlance, can be your open door to uncovering new career opportunities, gathering market intelligence, and gaining all-important job endorsements.

5. Share the wisdom of more than 50 experts in social media, personal branding, job search coaching, resume writing, and more. These folks are leaders in their fields, they know what works, and we're bringing their best to you.

How to Use This Book

We know there are as many ways to read a "how-to" book as there are readers. Some people like to skim chapter headings; others dip in here and there; still others read cover to cover. Whatever your style, you'll find the information in this book easy to access and easy to use.

We encourage you to begin at the beginning—it's tempting to jump to the section on how to use Twitter, but if you do, you might miss foundational information on which your effective Twitter presence must be built.

Some exceptions:

- If you are already convinced Twitter is the best thing since sliced bread, skip chapter 3.
- If you are not in active job search mode, you can skip the chapters on resumes and cover letters.
- If you have unlimited time and love falling into an Internet black hole, you can skip section 6 on managing your Twitter time in just 15 minutes a day.

Twitter is designed for short communication: All messages are conveyed in sound bites of 140 characters or fewer. That's 20 characters fewer than a text message. In keeping with this format, we've endeavored to make this book as "twittified" as possible, meaning our content is aimed to be short, fluff-free, useful text. It's an easy read, with lots of places to stop and peruse a tip sheet, a real-world story, or an interesting quote.

Our wish for you is that, upon completion, you have a useful new tool that makes your job search more effective and even—dare we say it—more fun!

CHAPTER 2

TEN TRUTHS ABOUT TWITTER TO BENEFIT YOUR JOB SEARCH

"The qualities that make Twitter seem inane and half-baked are what makes it so powerful."

—*Jonathan Zittrain*

The truth about Twitter is that there are dozens of ways it can enhance your job search and career. In fact, you don't even need a Twitter account to benefit from what it has to offer (although we highly recommend getting one).

Twitter is scalable, allowing you to participate as much or as little as you wish. You may choose to explore Twitter as a passive participant, becoming active as you begin to develop ideas for injecting Twitter into your job search. Here's how passive and active participants can benefit:

- **Passive participant:** At this level of engagement, you can choose to use Twitter purely as a tool to uncover job leads posted by recruiters who tweet or read job search tips from the many career experts using Twitter.

- **Active participant:** As an active user, you can elect to position yourself as a standout candidate or subject-matter expert. Those in this category answer others' questions, respond to on-brand tweets, retweet relevant tweets, share online resources, and point people to their blogs.

> **Tip:** Of course, not all job seekers have blogs, but having an active, information-rich blog is a great way to raise visibility within your industry and attract interest from recruiters and employers. As an alternative to writing your own blog, consider commenting on blogs relevant to your industry.

Whether you're a passive or active user, you can find a style that works for you and solutions that will support and enliven your job search.

Here are 10 to start.

1. Find connection, support, and strength
2. Tap into a wealth of free job search information
3. Locate job leads
4. Connect to the hidden job market and insider contacts
5. Broadcast your brand and drown digital dirt
6. Expand your network—fast
7. Cultivate serendipity
8. Get real-time responses that will expand your thinking
9. Research breaking news or corporate culture
10. Foster a forum for sharing, learning, and laughter

Here they are in greater detail.

1. Find Connection, Support, and Strength

The world of job search can be a lonely place. Job seekers need answers, support, and hope. Twitter is a place where you can find all of this, and more.

Beyond answers (more on that in truth #2), you'll find a community that cares.

Stay-at-home moms (and dads) who tweet have caught the media's attention because of the new sense of community created by these parents. Individuals affected by cystic fibrosis are a growing community on Twitter. People with the disease can't be in the same room with one another because of the potential for additional complications caused by contact. Yet they can congregate on Twitter.

These people, and many other previously isolated groups, now have a vehicle for real-time connection to share tough trials, as well as memorable moments, with others who understand. The same is true for job seekers.

For most people, job loss is a time of trial. For some, it is a true crisis. Finances, self-esteem, and purpose are threatened; insecurities are exacerbated by sudden separation from coworkers, customers, and friends. Psychologists attest that isolation is an incubator for depression.

Whether you've lost your job, are in a position that isn't working, are thinking of switching industries, or are just "testing the waters" for an upward move, connecting with others on Twitter will keep your spirits up and your hopes kindled, and can even help chart your course.

In addition to looking for help, be aware of opportunities where you can be of assistance to others—doing so will make you feel productive, empowered, and fulfilled, even if you might be feeling a bit scared, frustrated, or uncertain.

Tip: Humans come together in public places in times of crisis or joy. When 9-11 terrorists shattered our sense of security, people came out of their homes and workplaces looking for community. Strangers became acquaintances, and acquaintances became friends. When World War II ended, Times Square and town commons across America were packed with celebrants. Twitter is a virtual space of strangers waiting to become friends. With an estimated tens of millions of users, there is always someone to connect with.

2. Tap into a Wealth of Free Job Search Information

Some of the best and brightest minds in job search and career management are on Twitter and available with a simple search. Experienced career coaches, recruiters, resume writers, and human resource professionals can answer specific questions. Links to blog posts and other resources give more in-depth information.

Following job search and career coaching thought leaders is commensurate to having free consulting at your fingertips. Twitter's List functions allow you to quickly follow a list of recommended experts. Twitter's hashtag (#) system also allows you to easily get related tips all in one place.

Need to Know: A hashtag—represented by the pound sign (#)—is a way to aggregate tweets pertaining to a topic. Placing # before a keyword in a tweet allows that tweet to be searchable in that category. As a job seeker, some of the hashtags you might be interested in searching for include #resumes, #networking, #jobseekers, #jobs, #career, #careercollective, #mcm, and #careercoaches. You'll find more on hashtags in chapter 28.

3. Locate Job Leads

As mentioned earlier, you can search for and follow recruiters and staffing managers who regularly tweet about fresh, live job openings. There are also new job sites popping up that interface with Twitter, such as TweetMyJobs.com and TwitterJobSearch.com.

In the past, your primary venue for getting in front of recruiters was to e-mail your resume using a distribution service. Recruiters receive hundreds of resumes in their inboxes from these services, so your chances of being seen were slim to none.

Tip: Send a message to a recruiter who has tweeted relevant job postings. You'll have a much better opportunity to stand out from the crowd of candidates. Your message might sound like this: "Just e-mailed my resume for product mgr. opening. I've helped similar co's gain double-digit market share. Will follow up early next week." Note that the key here is the hint of value to come and initiative to follow up.

4. Connect to the Hidden Job Market and Insider Contacts

You can tap the hidden job market as never before using Twitter. Search Twitter or sites related to Twitter for the names of hiring managers, influencers, potential coworkers, or people in the news affiliated with your target employers and see who comes up (more on this in chapter 30). Or use LinkedIn to find company and insider contacts, and then follow them on Twitter.

> **Tip:** Twitter allows you to create relationships with people simply by reading their tweets. Knowing how they think, understanding their values, and getting a glimpse of their personal lives enables you to create deeper connections and relationships when it comes time to network or interview.

5. Broadcast Your Brand and Drown Digital Dirt

The people with the pen are the people with the power. Twitter allows anyone to take up a virtual pen and exercise the right of free speech—it's the First Amendment on steroids. Never before in all of history has there been a vehicle that so thoroughly democratizes the dissemination of information.

Twitter is the perfect platform to broadcast your brand, convey a strong value proposition, and allow your voice to be heard (more on branding in section 2). It gets your message out in a targeted, efficient manner.

> **Need to Know:** A *personal brand*, often referred to as simply "your brand," is the thing that is your unchanging center. It's your promise of value, the wellspring from which your talent flows. It's not spin; it's not fake; it's authentically you. Your *value proposition* is what your brand looks like in the world of work—it says what you are known for doing, what happens when you do it, and why an employer should care.

With so many industries negatively impacted by the recent economic downturn, thousands across the globe are faced with retooling their career brands—transferring skills into a new role or industry. For those with several decades of experience who feel typecast in an old profession, this can be a daunting task.

Take heart—no matter how old you are, there is always an opportunity to reboot, reinvent, and rebrand yourself. Even Michael Milken, once dubbed the "Junk Bond King," made a comeback after a stint in federal prison. A cover article by *Fortune* magazine called him "The Man Who Changed Medicine" for his positive influence on medical research.

More than 80 percent of recruiters these days use Google to find information on candidates as part of their research and evaluation process. Unfortunately, 30 percent of those candidates are not considered because of negative or unflattering information found online.

> **Need to Know:** *Digital dirt* is bad or negative press about you that comes up when your name is typed into a search engine.

Your Twitter account and status updates (tweets) will show up in Google and Bing searches, enabling you to communicate a precision brand. And, if you're dealing with digital dirt, your tweets can help bury those links.

6. Expand Your Network—Fast

Twitter is the fastest way to grow a large and diverse network in your area of expertise. It is asymmetrical, in that you can follow almost anyone on Twitter that you want (except the small number of people who protect their tweets).

> **Need to Know:** Twitter's model encourages and enables you to *follow* any user whom you find interesting, including prospective employers, recruiters, and networking contacts.

Other social media sites operate symmetrically: You and your contact both agree that you will connect. LinkedIn suggests that you connect only with those you know well, and the Facebook model is based around the concept of "friends" who must first approve your request to connect.

No matter how job search technology changes, one fact remains constant: Purposeful, generous networking continues to be the most effective way to find new opportunities and build your career. See chapter 22 for more ideas on networking.

7. Cultivate Serendipity

"Luck is what happens when preparation meets opportunity," said Seneca. Twitter enables you to intersect with far more possibilities than you could on your own.

A case in point: Susan was looking for speakers for her monthly Thought Leader Forum offered through Career Coach Academy. When reviewing her Twitter stream one day, she found a white paper on how to leverage Facebook and, seeing value in the information, retweeted it.

> **Need to Know:** A retweet (RT) is to Twitter as forwarding is to e-mail. It's sending a tweet that you've read and liked on to your network, while attributing the tweet to its original author. (Learn more in chapter 15.)

The Twitter user who originally posted the tweet sent her a private thank you. Conversation ensued. She learned that the individual, @GLHoffman, was not only an author, but the brains behind the popular new site LinkUp.com. Susan ended up finding the speaker she needed, and GL found another audience to tell people about his work.

> **Tip:** A serendipitous retweet can become a new, win-win business relationship that likely would not have happened through some other social media site.

8. Get Real-Time Responses That Will Expand Your Thinking

"Twitter is a tickertape of collective thoughts…they stream in front of you in a way that is strangely relaxing," says Terry Starbucker in his blog at www.TerryStarbucker.com. A tweet to all your followers or a question directed to someone in particular can yield immediate, up-to-date information. If you're scheduled for an important networking meeting or interview and need information quickly, you can get it.

Twitter also exposes you to diverse perspectives that expand your thinking. In the way that taking a vacation to a foreign country expands your viewpoint, Twitter expands your perspectives for possibilities.

> **Tip:** Communicating with others from across the globe (without the time and expense of travel) brings new ideas, insights, and innovation.

9. Research Breaking News or Corporate Culture

These days, bloggers and microbloggers are breaking stories before CNN does.

> **Need to Know:** A Twitter user is a microblogger. Similar to blogging, microblogging "allows the sending, or 'publishing,' of brief text updates that can be viewed on the Web by a mobile or computer user."

If you're writing a cover letter or preparing for an interview, a Twitter search on the company name can reveal information that other candidates won't yet have. Bingo—you now have an edge over your competition.

You can follow executives to get a real feel for corporate culture. For example, tweets from Zappos' CEO Tony Hsieh (his Twitter handle is @zappos) give wonderful insights into the fun but down-to-business flavor of the successful online shoe company.

Need to Know: A Twitter *handle* is the name you choose for your Twitter account. It's how you are known and followed on Twitter. The "@" is customarily used with your handle. For instance, Susan is @SusanWhitcomb, Deb is @CEOCoach, Chandlee is @Chandlee (more on Twitter handles in chapter 11).

Tip: The surest way to find someone on Twitter is to enter the full URL with the Twitter username (assuming you know it). Searching for a name or username by itself does not always bring up complete results. For example, if you were looking for one of the authors, you'd enter http://twitter.com/SusanWhitcomb, http://twitter.com/CEOCoach, or http://twitter.com/chandlee.

You can also uncover potential problems or office politics at target companies and decide whether that will impact your desire to work there.

Tip: Sharing breaking news with your followers—news that is relevant to your industry—can also position you as an "A" candidate in the eyes of recruiters and hiring influencers.

10. Foster a Forum for Sharing, Learning, and Laughter

Our knowledge is the "amassed thought and experience of innumerable minds" (Ralph Waldo Emerson). Twitter aficionados understand that the whole is greater than the sum of its parts. One plus one on Twitter can equal millions.

Twitter is an opportunity to participate in the knowledge stream of your field and contribute to a body of knowledge that is dynamic and growing. You can tweet live from a conference you are attending, engage with people and debate ideas, exchange helpful tips and resources, and more.

As you do, a dual dynamic occurs: You position yourself as a knowledgeable resource in your field, and at the same time, your (and everyone's) contributions raise the knowledge, understanding, and cohesiveness of the entire community.

Tip: You can also find some good laughs on Twitter—something every job seeker needs! Whether you want a list of comedians (check out WeFollow at http://wefollow.com/twitter/comedian) or simple everyday people who make you giggle, you can find them on Twitter. A couple of our favorites are Tim Siedell (@badbanana) and Tom Bodett (@TomBodett). View their Twitter streams and see if you don't guffaw.

Twitter's Growth Is Good for You

There you have it: ten reasons to use Twitter in your job search and career.

But stand by—given Twitter's exponential growth and the open-source environment for new applications, there will undoubtedly be more "truths" unfolding over time…truths that will make your job search and career management even more effective.

If you're still not convinced of Twitter's value, turn to chapter 3. If you're on the bandwagon, jump to chapter 5 to learn how everyday job seekers found jobs using Twitter.

FOR THE SKEPTICS

Tweeting is not just for birds and nerds!

Do you remember a world without the Internet? Without Facebook, LinkedIn, or YouTube? Without text messaging? Without smart phones? Without instant connectivity?

All these technologies are about communication, yet many didn't exist until just a few years ago. Facebook was founded in 2004, LinkedIn in 2002, and YouTube in 2005. Now all are household names and we can't imagine doing life or business without them! Twitter is fast joining the ranks of these "indispensible" communication tools.

Jeff Pulver, Internet protocol pioneer and founder of the 140 Character Conference, says, "…the worldwide adoption of Twitter in various segments of society in the 21st century is as big as the introduction of the telegraph and/or telephone in the 20th century…. I believe the change we are experiencing is deep rooted…. Twitter provides a platform for people to listen, learn, and connect with others who share that common experience."

Do you want to be left behind, or do you want to be among the millions using Twitter to share information and viewpoints while raising their visibility and building a following that attracts opportunities?

> **Note:** If you're an "early adopter" and Twitter is already an integral part of your life, you can skip this chapter! Then again, we've threaded many useful tips throughout, so you'll likely enjoy reading on.

We're here to debunk the myths surrounding Twitter, and to encourage you to spread your wings into the Twitterverse and soar to a successful job search.

Responses to Nine Common Complaints About Twitter

Have you said this (or something like it)? "I don't tweet; Twitter is for twits!" Here are some of the leading myths and arguments for not using Twitter, and our thoughts that dispel them.

1. Something that has such short messages can't be useful; and, anyway, no one writes anything interesting.

Try telling that to anyone who does text messaging!

Your mind thinks in shorthand for texting and your mind can do the same for Twitter, in 140-character precision that forces clarity. If you can get your message across in a text, you can do it in Twitter.

For many people today, text messaging is their main form of communication, more common to them than using e-mail or the phone.

> **Tip:** Twitter is like texting, but your messages go to a community of readers rather than to an individual.

Twitter is teeming with information and "learning junkies." You can learn about emerging trends; research companies; delve into the hidden job market; connect with recruiters; build relationships with like-minded people in the arts, sports, and business; or access thousands of blog posts related to your interests. Options for learning (and helping others learn) are endless.

If you need immediate information, post a query on Twitter and you'll likely receive what you need. Want to know what's happening in the world, in real time? Follow "trending topics" on Twitter and join the dialogue. The Twitterverse hears what's happening as it happens, before it even hits the newswires—from earthquakes, to the unrest in Iran, and more. That immediacy is unprecedented in the world of communication.

2. I just don't have time.
or
I'll have to be on it all the time.

Tweeting effectively doesn't have to take much time. In fact, we believe that with a little up-front time invested in learning the right strategies and tools, you can tweet in as few as 15 minutes a day.

That's less than two hours a week to propel your job search! Compared to the time most people spend posting resumes onto "black hole" job boards, 120 minutes or less of weekly Twitter time promises a healthy return-on-investment in terms of visibility building and networking.

> **Tip:** Using "tweet later" programs, you can compose and schedule your tweets and move on with your day. Your tweets will be tweeted without you, giving you a consistent presence without the need for much Twitter time (more on that in chapter 27).

3. No one I care about is on Twitter. Twitter is for kids.

Recruiters, human resources professionals, business leaders, Fortune companies, CEOs, business leaders, motivational speakers, marketers, scientists, celebrities, students, professors, authors, entrepreneurs, politicians, and more are on Twitter.

In October 2009, the Pew Internet & America Life Project study found that "Some 19 percent of Internet users now say they use Twitter or another service to share updates about themselves, or to see updates about others. This represents a significant increase over previous surveys in December 2008 and April 2009, when 11 percent of Internet users said they use a status-update service" (http://pewresearch.org/pubs/1385/who-uses-twitter-tweets).

> **Tip:** Despite media hype to the contrary, Twitter is used for business, science, and politics, as much as or more than it is used for "social" purposes.

A recent 140 Character Conference in Los Angeles represented a widely diverse group of Twitter evangelists, including the following:

- Al Seckel (@insightfultoo): cognitive neuroscientist
- Mariel Hemingway (@Marielhemingway): actress and cookbook author
- Anita Campbell (@smallbiztrends): CEO, Small Business Trends
- Arianna Huffington (@ariannahuff): Cofounder and Editor-in-Chief, The Huffington Post
- Chief Dan Alexander (@bocachief): Chief of Police, Boca Raton, FL
- David Sarno (@dsarno): Internet business reporter, *LA Times*
- Jon Klein (@jonklein): President, CNN
- Marc Sirkin (@autismspeaks): Chief Community Officer, Autism Speaks
- Mark Victor Hansen (@MarkVHansen): Motivational speaker and founder, *Chicken Soup for the Soul* book series
- Porter Gale (@porterVA): VP Marketing, Virgin America
- Tom Jolly (@TomJolly): Sports editor, *New York Times*

4. No one will read my tweets.

People who are just "everyday Joes" can build a list of thousands of followers, solely by being interesting, informative, or unique. The Twitterverse is a vast and hungry place—hungry for knowledge and hungry for connection. Provide quality in either and you'll develop a following.

> **Need to Know:** "Followers" are your Twitter community, people who have chosen to add you to the group of people they like to read. However, don't expect to gather hordes of followers immediately. Building a reputation takes time.

You can tweet about your subject-matter expertise, passions, and even current events. The goal is to have a few pages of useful, fascinating tweets before you select whom you will follow. When those you follow (or those who find you) check out your profile page, they will be enticed to follow you.

> **Tip:** Many people use Twitter's search function to seek tweets and tweeters in subject areas of interest. Write good tweets in your area of expertise and these people will find and follow you.

5. No good companies or recruiters are on Twitter.

Tell that to Zappos, Ernst & Young, Comcast, Apple, Microsoft, Google, Southwest Airlines, Accenture, KPMG, ADP, Allstate, Burger King, Delloite, Expedia, ECOLAB, EMC, Hershey, Hyatt, Intel, Mattel, the Mayo Clinic, MTV, Raytheon, Razorfish, Sodexo, Adidas, Thomson Reuters, UPS, Verizon, Warner Bros., IBM, Best Buy, CitiGroup, Lowes, Ford, Coca-Cola, the U.S. Department of State, and many more. The list continues to grow.

Companies are flocking to Twitter to build product and employment brand awareness, monitor and manage customer service in real time, search for talent, and create relationships that will lead to perfect fits for future positions. Many companies now monitor their brands on Twitter, watching for both positive and negative comments. Consumers have had complaints immediately addressed after posting them on Twitter. No company likes a complaint going viral (rapidly spreading to an ever-widening audience on the Web).

> **Tip:** Corporations aren't the only players in the game. Small companies and nonprofits are benefiting from exposure on Twitter as well.

The *Wall Street Journal* profiled such a match in "A New Job Just a Tweet Away" (September 8, 2009). "In June, Rob Totaro landed an interview for an account-manager job at Potratz Partners Advertising, a small agency in Schenectady, NY, after learning about the position on Twitter. In the meeting, he joked that he wasn't sure he could work for a firm that supports the Red Sox, which he had discovered from reading tweets the company posted about a recent employee outing to a ball-game. 'It was a great ice breaker,' says Mr. Totaro. He got the job."

6. I just now figured out how to use LinkedIn. I don't need to use another social media tool, and it's too hard to learn another program!

LinkedIn is a must-have presence for job search and career-building. No dispute there. But LinkedIn doesn't lend itself to real-time conversation, and it limits your reach to your network.

Twitter is built to create conversations and relationships. It's not one-to-one; you can follow agreement without limitation, and anyone can follow you. You can make friends and contacts faster, with greater ease and deeper connection. Twitter has the energy of immediacy, and we think it's just more fun than LinkedIn.

With our Twitter tutorial (see section 3), you can be up and running with a Twitter account and Twitter basics in about 15 minutes (chapter 11). Invest an hour in getting up to speed (chapters 13 through 15), and you'll be conversant in what you need to know to be an effective Twitter user.

> **Tip:** Practice makes perfect, so be sure you actually use Twitter after your instruction. "Use it or lose it" applies here!

7. I can build my network the old-fashioned way. And anyway, if I'm not looking for a job, I don't need Twitter!

Harvey Mackay's *Dig Your Well Before You're Thirsty* is the seminal book on networking. Written when the Internet was young, before social networking, and before Twitter, it stands the test of time because it works.

> **Tip:** Many of "Mackay's Maxims" easily cross borders from traditional networking to Twitter:
>
> "It's great to be liked. You'll have a network you can always use. Once. It's even greater to be needed. You'll have a network you can always use. Period."
>
> "If everyone in your network is the same as you, it isn't a network, it's an anthill."
>
> "Getting through the fence to the top dog is easy, if you know the gatekeeper."

We are passionate advocates for the power of networking and for the power of Twitter to help. We're not suggesting you avoid in-person networking. We are suggesting that Twitter makes it far less time-consuming and far more fun to comply with "Mackay's Maxims."

What does Harvey Mackay think about Twitter and networking? Why not ask him? You can follow him on Twitter: @HarveyMackay.

8. My company won't like it.

Fair enough. This can be true, and it's wise to be careful.

When you are employed, you are not just you. You are representing your company's brand, and you are privy to proprietary knowledge. There is a fine line between representing yourself and crossing into territory that reflects upon your company.

Dan Schawbel, personal brand guru for Gen Y, defines "10 Ways to Get Fired for Building Your Personal Brand," one of which includes attracting the wrong attention to your company's brand because of your own (www.personalbrandingblog. com/10-ways-to-get-fired-for-building-your-personal-brand/).

The immediacy of Twitter makes it very easy to tweet without considering your impact. "Common sense is encouraged!" says Schawbel. "The sad thing is I firmly believe we're going to see more cases of carelessness in the coming years, as more people use social networks, more access social networks from their mobile phones, and the lines between work and life balance are blurred. Try putting yourself in your employer's shoes the next time you post on Facebook or tweet."

> **Tip:** If you are employed and find a new job, in your excitement, don't announce it on Twitter before you resign from your current position!

We'll show you how to navigate Twitter so your company won't mind.

9. I don't feel the need to share my personal life, and I don't want everyone to know what I'm doing.

We agree. In business, "social media" isn't necessarily "social"! You can choose to make Twitter an exclusive vehicle for business networking and visibility building. Develop your Twitter presence as one that supports and accelerates your professional brand, thought leadership, and stature as an expert.

Some Twitter users find they enjoy the connection Twitter provides and want an increased ability to tweet at a more personal level. They often create multiple handles for business and personal tweets.

However, connection is not just about knowledge. Chemistry and affinity are important as well, and those connective traits are best expressed in tweets that reveal the non-business side of you. So get a little personal about your favorite sports team, television show, or movie. Brag about your kids a bit, or talk about the sunrise.

> **Tip:** If you are a single-account tweeter, as most users are, we suggest a 75:25 ratio of professional to personal tweets.

When using Twitter to express your brand in job search, always remember that your best strategy is content and connection.

The People You Want to Know Are on Twitter... Shouldn't You Be There, Too?

In a recent poll conducted by LinkedIn, more than 3,900 LinkedIn users responded that Twitter "was the most important new platform for brands to master," choosing Twitter over Facebook, the iPhone, and even LinkedIn itself (http://polls.linkedin.com/poll-results/35931/uxtqg).

The people who cared most about Twitter mastery included business development, marketing, and creative workers, as well as C-level and senior-level executives and business owners at medium- to large-sized companies—just the people a job seeker should want to reach!

CHAPTER 4

How Twitter Differs from Other Social Media

*"The ability to learn faster than your competitors may
be the only sustainable competitive advantage."*

—*Peter Senge*

Social media has forever changed the way we receive and communicate information.

Unlike traditional media that is distributed through journalists and media conglomerates, social media can be disseminated through the general public—users like you and me. The broadcasting of information and opinion has been democratized.

This participatory process is a key characteristic of social media, a phrase that didn't even exist a few years ago. Today, you have an equal voice in contributing to the overall dialogue and determining what will be hot or not.

THE TREND OF SOCIAL MEDIA? SPEED!

Never in the history of mankind has a trend reached such large numbers so quickly.

- It took radio 38 years to reach an audience of 50 million.
- Television did it in 13 years.
- It took the Internet four years to reach an audience of 50 million.
- The iPod did it in three years.
- The behemoth of all social media sites, Facebook, took just two years.

See the video "Did You Know?" at www.mixx.com/videos/2969509/
youtube_did_you_know for more fascinating details like this compiled by Karl Fisch, Scott McLeod, and Jeff Bronman.

Twitter Transformed the Rules of Engagement

In June 2009, Twitter earned the honor of a *Time* magazine cover, the equivalent of a gold medal in popular culture, with its story on "How Twitter Will Change the Way We Live."

The article by Steven Johnson describes how Twitter transformed a forum on the future of education from a six-hour static event to a dynamic exchange that continued on for months with input from both invited guests and the Twitter community at large.

Johnson eloquently described the phenomenon:

> *Injecting Twitter into that conversation fundamentally changed the rules of engagement. It added a second layer of discussion and brought a wider audience into what would have been a private exchange. And it gave the event an afterlife on the Web. Yes, it was built entirely out of 140-character messages, but the sum total of those tweets added up to something truly substantive, like a suspension bridge made of pebbles.*

The Power of Twitter

Twitter provides you with a semblance of omniscience and omnipresence. Twitter gives you the ability to hear what others are thinking on an inestimable range of topics, and to "be there" as part of the conversation, even if you're situated on the other side of the world.

The ability to have your finger on that "suspension bridge of pebbles," or what social media guru Chris Brogan calls "the informational pulse," is the power of Twitter.

Celebrity journalists report that Twitter has greatly improved their access to celebrity news and events. Before Twitter, journalists had to call publicists for the celebrity's comments. With the arrival of verified celebrity accounts on Twitter, journalists can contact the celebrities directly by tweet alone.

How does this relate to your job search? Consider those coveted hiring managers as the celebrities. In the past, you had to go through the maze of gatekeepers to get to the cloistered person in charge of hiring decisions. Now you can have access to this person with the click of a Follow button.

The ability to level the playing field—placing you nearly peer-to-peer with influencers, leaders, and hiring authorities—is the power of Twitter.

> *"My experience has shown me that the people who are exceptionally good in business aren't so because of what they know but because of their insatiable need to know more."*
>
> —*Michael Gerber*

And you can do so much more, particularly when you combine Twitter with other social media sites that connect you to preexisting networks of colleagues and friends.

The Big Three: Facebook, LinkedIn, and Twitter

When it comes to the social media sites that relate to job search, the most popular are Facebook, LinkedIn, and Twitter.

Facebook is the largest, recently topping 65 million users in the United States alone (worldwide numbers are estimated at more than 300 million). LinkedIn is a close second, adding approximately one million users every two weeks, with more than 50 million users at the time of writing (half of whom are in the United States).

Of the two, LinkedIn is the most widely accepted business networking tool. Its many features, including the ability to see your network within "three degrees," make it a popular destination; however, as with Facebook, your participation is restricted by group and individual connections.

On Twitter, this boundary does not exist because the choice of where to "follow" or "be followed" is less restrictive. You can block other Twitter users from following you, but the default (unless you have protected your tweets from the public) is to allow them to follow you.

Although Twitter keeps its total number of user accounts close to the vest, you can track the number of tweets—and the numbers are astounding. According to Mashable.com, a popular Internet blog dedicated to the latest in social media, in a joint article with CNN, users send out approximately 25 million tweets per day, and have sent more than 5 billion since Twitter's launch. (Sites like www.tweetspeed. com and www.twittercounter.com also provide interesting statistics.)

Table 4.1 provides a comparison of Facebook, LinkedIn, and Twitter.

Table 4.1: Comparison of Facebook, LinkedIn, and Twitter

	Facebook	LinkedIn	Twitter
Used for	Personal	Business/professional	Either (as a user, you get to define how you'll use it)
How to Establish Connections	Opt-in: Your friends must approve your request to connect.	Opt-in: Your business associates must approve your invitation to connect. In some cases, you may not be able to invite someone to link to you unless you have some prior connection.	Opt-out: You can follow virtually anyone you want (the majority of Twitter users do not block access).

(continued)

(continued)

	Facebook	LinkedIn	Twitter
Timeline/ Immediacy	Real-time	Static	Real-time
Types of Conversation	Personal and professional	Professional	Anything goes
Open or Closed Networking System	Essentially closed, limited to groups and individual contact.	Essentially closed, limited to groups and individual contact.	Not limited. It's "open networking" where anyone can connect.
Potential to Engage in Conversation	You can engage in conversation only with people who have accepted your invitation to be "friends." (Allows limited messages to people outside your network.)	You can engage in conversation only with groups you belong to on LinkedIn or through one-way discussion in Q&A forums. (Allows limited invitations to people outside your network but will block you if they find you abusing the feature.)	You can start a conversation with anyone. Also, Twitter's hashtag system makes it easy to find, follow, and engage in topics of common interest.
Other Bells and Whistles	Loaded with flair and giveaways, from Farmville to Mafia Wars to Pillow Fights.	Lots of add-ons, including ability to search jobs function, share PowerPoint slides in the SlideShare add-on, read and write book reviews, engage in Q&A, and carry on discussions in groups.	Nothing but 140-character status updates (although the many sites built to complement Twitter, such as SocialOomph. com, offer bells and whistles).
Profile	Your profile can include data about your marital status, movie favorites, and much more.	Your profile isn't 100 percent complete until you outline what you've been doing the last 10 years.	You get 160 characters to describe yourself. That's it!
Sponsors	Contains advertisements on the site.	There is no advertising on the site, although companies pay to list job postings.	There is no advertising on the site.
Job Search Component	None (at time book went to press).	LinkedIn has a job function that helps you identify insider contacts for opportunities.	Nothing on Twitter proper; however, new application sites are popping up, such as twitterjobsearch.com and tweetmyjobs.com.

	Facebook	**LinkedIn**	**Twitter**
Paid or Free	Free	Free with upgrade available	Free

A Power User's Perspective

Everyone on Twitter was once a NOOB (Newbie, in Twitter-speak). Some people never move past their initial exploration. Some use Twitter sporadically. Some weave it into their daily communications. And a select group of visionaries bring Twitter usage to a whole new level—that of Power User. How? Chandlee interviewed social media content strategist Rob Blatt to find out.

An award-winning new media producer and the founder of New York–based Blattcave Productions, here's how Rob's contact information and Twitpitch look on Twitter. Notice that there is no ambiguity as to who he is or what he does, and that he's for hire!

I'm for hire! Content strategist, A/V producer and Emmy and Oscar winning audio engineer. Blubrry.com Community Advocate. Tweets are CC BY-NC-SA licensed.

Here are Rob's insights on the differences between Twitter and other social media sites.

Q: What sets Twitter apart from other social media?
A: Twitter is very lightweight: There's no resume or interests. You only get a 160-character bio, a link, and a background. There are no gimmicks such as giving away "ice cream," "throwing sheep," or quiz results that you can use to annoy new friends.

You can make friends and new connections faster on Twitter than you can on Facebook or LinkedIn. On Twitter, the barrier to entry in developing a relationship is low but the potential for return on investment is high: Following someone is as easy as a click; approval of followers is rarely required. On other sites, users have to approve connections (LinkedIn) or friends (Facebook) before you can engage in regular one-to-one contact. This facilitates engagement.

Q: How does Twitter facilitate engagement?
A: Twitter expands your network—instantly. You can have conversations on Facebook as well, but when you post a status update on Twitter, anyone can read it, respond, and provide advice.

For example, if I get stranded in the Las Vegas airport, I can tweet about that and ask for suggestions on where to get the best sandwich in the airport, where to find free Wi-Fi or a power-charging station, or simply find out if other flights to my city are being delayed. In rare instances, I've heard of travelers who've scored free Wi-Fi, travel bonuses, and airline incentives through interactions with airline and airport staff on Twitter.

When you set up your Twitter account properly, you can receive Direct Messages from anyone following you. You can set up these messages to be received by SMS, or text messages, via your cell phone. Therefore, the connections you make have the potential to be extremely personal.

> **Need to Know:** A *direct message* (DM or D, for short) is a private message sent only to you, as opposed to the public messages or tweets that Twitter is known for. You must be following a person for him or her to be able to "direct message" you.

Q: How do you use Twitter?

A: I use Twitter as a way to disseminate publicly personal information about myself and my interests.

Q: What is publicly personal information?

A: I define publicly personal information as things I want other people to know about me: I have three dogs (one of whom was adopted from Puerto Rico), my wife and I saved a baby squirrel, I have a taste for wheat beer, and just as important as that: I have a podcast.

I am a content strategist. I have an interest in business. If I read that you are sick or that you had a leaky apartment, I'll know that information about you—and I can ask you about it the next time I see you. Everything that I put on my account is a conversation starter, and you can feel free to engage me by asking.

Q: Rob, in 36 months you've written over 15,000 tweets—that's 1.5 times the content of *Moby Dick*—140 characters at a time. How much time do you spend on Twitter a day?

A: I spend an average of 30 minutes a day on Twitter, broken up into ten-second to two-minute intervals. Here's how:

- **Scan TweetDeck:** I monitor Twitter at a glance through TweetDeck, an application that allows me to monitor tweets from a desktop. TweetDeck allows me to organize my Twitter followers by category—friends, professional colleagues, mentions, and interests. I take a quick look at what people talk about, respond to items as appropriate, and get back to my production work.

- **Check text messages:** I have set my preferences in Twitter so that I receive Direct Messages by cell phone via SMS. Generally, most people who send me Direct Messages are people that I've communicated with in the past. I live in Brooklyn, New York, and have many Twitter friends whom I only communicate with through Direct Messages—I don't know their phone numbers, and I don't need to.

- **Check my e-mail:** There are a number of services you can use to monitor your Twitter mentions and messages without ever logging in. I use Nutshell Mail, which sends me notifications on new followers, people who've stopped following me, @replies, and Direct Messages in three-hour increments. I've already received the Direct Messages—except the ones that were sent to me overnight when my phone is off—but I monitor the @replies and followers lists to respond to others.

  Using Nutshell Mail saves time that I might otherwise spend checking new followers and following up throughout the day. This also helps me keep my e-mail box clean as I don't receive messages every time I receive a new follower or Direct Message.

> **Need to Know:** An @ *reply* is a tweet that starts with an @ and then a username. For example, starting an update on Twitter with **@CEOCoach** means that I am addressing Deb directly. Although I'm writing to her, all followers will see the tweet, like a group conversation.

Q: What impact has Twitter had on your life?

A: The personal: I have made friends across the country and around the corner that I know I will have for life through Twitter. As nerdy as that sounds, I am absolutely sure of that. My wife Amber and I have had people from across the country, the UK, and Australia attend parties that we've thrown.

The professional: I have received job leads that have come through Twitter. It has been the easiest way to let people know that I was—and am—available for work. Twitter has also allowed me to showcase my skills in social media. Currently, I freelance for a company that hired me, in part, because of my knowledge of social media that has come through my use of Twitter.

The dream come true: I am a lifelong fan of comics, and I received a free pass to cover the New York City Comicon (Comic Convention) for ABC News Radio. I got the free pass after asking the question on Twitter, "Who can get me into Comicon for free?"

Looking Ahead

Throughout this book, you'll receive comprehensive and tangible tips for how, like Rob, you can establish your online presence, brandish your brand, and forward your job search. Be sure to visit chapter 23 for specifics on how to use and integrate LinkedIn, Facebook, and Twitter for a triple scoop of success. Who knows? Perhaps someday you'll be a passionate Twitter power user, too!

CHAPTER 5

TWITTER SECRETS FROM SUCCESSFUL JOB SEEKERS

"Twitter's going to become more and more valuable as a job-hunting tool because you can build up a job-search network in an afternoon and effectively create a whole self-presentation in the Twittersphere. And anywhere there's a place for lots of people to network and talk and share interests, the opportunities will follow."

—*Rodney Rumford, cofounder, TweetPhoto; author,* Twitter as a Business Tool*

We've said it already: Twitter can help you land your next job and manage your career. In this chapter, you'll learn how successful job seekers used Twitter to navigate their job search process—and to come out on top in a challenging economy.

Twitter for Job Search Myth-Busting

Before we begin, let's dispel several myths about using Twitter for your job search.

- **Myth:** There's one right way to use Twitter for your job search.

  Myth-buster: There's no "one size fits all" rule for using Twitter for your job search. Use the best approach that fits your needs. (It's also up to you as to when and how you disclose that you are actively seeking employment.)

- **Myth:** Twitter works for job search only in certain professions: You need to be a public relations guru, a tech savant, or someone experienced in using social media to land a new job through Twitter.

  Myth-buster: Nonsense! Employers and hiring managers across industries and professions—from the National Hockey League to Tasty D'Lite—are finding new ways to integrate Twitter into their communication strategies.

  From Fortune 500s to mom-and-pop companies, organizations are finding new ways to increase consumer interest and advertise through Twitter.

---

*"Twitter Has Potential for Job Search" (www.nj.com/business/hireme/index.ssf/2009/10/twitter_has_potential_to_help.html)

Police departments share public alerts and safety tips through Twitter. Nonprofit organizations and schools use Twitter to disseminate knowledge, share best practices, gather community support, and raise awareness of resources and needs.

Politicians, government officials, and NGOs are increasingly using Twitter as a tool for public policy and diplomacy, from Congressmen to the White House to the Consulate General of Israel and Canada's National Aboriginal Health Organization.

Through showing your ability to use Twitter, you can connect with companies and organizations and strengthen your viability as a candidate (unless, of course, you are applying for a position that requires top-secret security clearance or your tweets cross socially inappropriate lines).

- **Myth:** Twitter can only help you meet people online.

  Myth-buster: Your Twitter job search is not limited to online connections. Although several Twitter accounts interact with users through "bots" (automated code that generates responses to users), the majority of Twitter handles are used and maintained by real people.

  Relationships that begin electronically can translate into powerful connections in person. Many Twitter users regularly broadcast local networking and professional events. You can expand your circle both on- and offline through "tweetups" (community gatherings), charity fund-raisers (Twestivals), and other events you learn about through Twitter.

Learn from the Landed

In researching and writing this book, we talked to many successful job seekers who landed jobs through Twitter. Although Twitter can help anyone get landed, we learned that individuals in social media, marketing, and other communications-related positions are most likely to *advertise* their success on Twitter. This makes sense, especially given that communications professionals can demonstrate their knowledge or expertise in using social media by using it!

We also learned that there is no magic recipe for job search success—on or off Twitter—but there are some common steps that virtually any job seeker can use.

Five Twitter Best Practices

In the course of our conversations, five best practices emerged. They include the following:

- **Active participation is essential. If you build community, help will come.** All of the successful job seekers that we talked to used Twitter to build community and expand their networks. They used Twitter not only to ask for help, but also to engage with others.

- **Be upfront about interests and career objectives.** We talked to several job seekers who searched for new positions after being laid off. While their individual approaches varied in terms of when and how they chose to advertise their availability, a common theme emerged: Successful job seekers were specific about what they wanted. They let others know their skills, strengths, and preferred job function.

- **Acknowledge that the job search is a relationship-building process—not an "I-need-a-job" transaction**. The job search is like dating; it takes time to build a relationship. If you ask for a long-term commitment (a job) the first time you meet someone, chances are good that you will be disappointed.

  And so it is with Twitter—building a strong network that can generate job leads takes time. You may find job listings overnight, but it takes time to grow connections with hiring managers and influencers. In job search, as in dating, your chance of success will increase if you take the time to get to know people before you make requests.

- **Be transparent in expressing appreciation and progress.** While some job searches require confidentiality (especially if you are currently employed), many of the job seekers we spoke with used a very transparent approach. This included posting regular updates on the status of their job search, as well as shoutouts to individuals who had helped them.

- **Be clear about your brand.** Our job seekers had a distinct brand that helped their networking contacts and prospective employers get a quick picture of who they are, how they work, and how their talents would bring value to the table.

Five Jump-Start Tips for Job Search Success

The jump-start tips we've identified include the following:

- **Get career advice**: Hundreds of employers, recruiters, and career experts share advice on how to find job leads through Twitter. There are many "hot lists" of people to follow on Twitter. Here's one:

  101 Job Search Experts on Twitter http://tweepml.org/101-job-search-experts/ (Courtesy of @drewpeneton)

- **Find job listings:** See chapter 28 for a list of sites that share job search leads.

- **Create a global network:** Use Twitter lists and directories to create a community of shared interests.

  Search by job field/industry sector (for example, pharmaceutical, consumer goods, health care) and job function (for example, accountant, real estate broker, golfer).

> **Tip**: If you can't find what you want in a directory, a simple Google or Bing search will frequently result in the answers you need. Try searching with the phrase "top Twitter users to follow in" and then insert your subject area.

- **Be yourself: Monitor—and engage in—the community conversation:** On Twitter, there's a frequently spoken rule for active participation: Don't proclaim yourself an expert; show what you know by being yourself, sharing your interests, and expressing appreciation of others. We'll show you how to do this in section 3.

- **Take your relationships offline:** During the course of our research for this book, we met job seekers who found their next jobs through networking contacts developed through Twitter. Use Twitter to find out about "tweetups" and other events in fields of interest—and don't be afraid to show up alone (chances are good that you'll make new friends).

  Can't attend an event? Ask for the hashtag to follow on Twitter search, and then reach out directly to people with whom you'd like to connect. See chapter 28 for more information on how to do this.

Meet Our Baker's Dozen of "Branded and Landed" Experts

In this book, you'll meet individuals who used Twitter to land their dream jobs. Along the way, you'll see that both conventional and unconventional approaches resulted in leads, interviews, and job offers. You'll also see that you can use Twitter at any stage throughout your search process—from sourcing leads and applying for jobs to networking, informational interviewing, and getting the best advice on how to make your decision after a job offer is extended.

FOOD FOR THOUGHT

As you read the strategies of our "cast of characters," ask yourself the following questions:
- Which of these techniques would be easiest for me to adapt?
- Which techniques would help me differentiate myself as a candidate in my field?
- Which techniques should I use?
- Do I have a follow-up plan to handle interest after implementing my strategy?

Here are our walking examples of how to do it. A synopsis of who they are and what they did is included below. Read their extended stories in appendix C.

- **The Philanthropic Social Butterflies**
  Biana Bakman (@bianalog) and Jon Lazar (@JustJon)
  How two New Yorkers parlayed their philanthropic activities into job connections.

- **The Cross-Platform Campaign**
  Desiree Kane (@dbirdy)
  How an executive assistant used her tech savvy to showcase her skills and land a new job, earning 25 percent more compensation.

- **The Straight-Path Approach: Applying for Jobs on Twitter**
  Doug Hamlin (@doughamlin)
  Monitoring job leads posted on Twitter and inquiring within results in a job offer for a great position.

- **The Hire-Me Campaign**
  Jamie Varon (@JamieVaron)
  How a recent graduate from California used Twitter to demonstrate her value proposition to employers, became an overnight Internet sensation—and created her own opportunity in Rome.

- **The Networker**
  Jennifer Harris (@JenHarris09)
  Advertising interests and availability to meet for coffee yields quick results after a layoff.

- **A Serendipitous Search Leads to Significant Success**
  John Bordeaux, Ph.D. (@JBordeaux)
  A knowledge management expert finds that an "agenda-less" approach to job search leads to a purposeful professional path.

- **The College Senior at a Crossroads Finds the Right Path**
  Kelly Giles (@kellygiles)
  A college senior uses social media to decide whether or not to go to law school—and attracts the attention of a startup.

- **The Hunted**
  Michael Litman (@litmanlive)
  A London-based young professional engages the Twitter community through innovative approaches to making "live" connections—and is sought out for a job.

- **A Communications Pro Leverages His Twitter Stream**
  Mark Buell (@mebuell)
  A targeted, strategic approach to engage key industry stakeholders yields interviews, while sharing samples of his Twitter stream helped win the offer.

- **The Direct Marketer**
  Shannon Yelland (@Shannonyelland)
  Total transparency about job search objectives and search status yields a winning offer.

- **The College Intern with an International Audience**
  Stephen Moyer (@Stephen_Moyer)
  A soon-to-graduate college senior followed and engaged thought leaders worldwide and became an emerging thought leader and sought-after talent in the process.

- **The Integrated Marketing Campaign**
  Warren Sukernek (@warrenss)
  A strong Twitter community, active blogging, and focused networking yield four job offers within three weeks after a layoff.

If your circumstances are different from people on this list, be encouraged. Many of the strategies they used have universal application across industries and professions. Regardless of your job target, the important common theme that must be present for your success, both on Twitter and in your job search, is a strong brand. Turn to section 2 to learn how to get branded to get landed.

SECTION 2

GET BRANDED TO GET LANDED

6. Employers Are Googling You: A Crash Course on Managing Your Online Identity

7. Your Brand and Twitter

8. Ten Steps to Mining, Defining, and Refining Your Brand

9. Your Branded Value Proposition (BVP)

10. Sound Bites with Teeth: Writing Your 160me™ Twitter Bio

Employers Are Googling You: A Crash Course on Managing Your Online Identity

Featured experts: Kirsten Dixson, online identity expert and coauthor of* Career Distinction: Stand Out by Building Your Brand *(@kirstendixson) and Robyn Greenspan, Editor-in-Chief of ExecuNet (@RobynGreenspan)

"Today, if you don't show up in Google, you don't exist. Whether you are applying for a new job, being considered for a board position or trying to get a date, you can count on being googled. So knowing what Google says about you and proactively managing your personal brand online is critical to success."

— *William Arruda and Kirsten Dixson, coauthors,* Career Distinction

You've heard that—at some point during the job search process—hiring managers, recruiters, and future colleagues will be typing your name into Google or their favorite search engine. Your search results may determine whether a recruiter reaches out to you, a networking contact goes to bat for you, or an employer extends an offer. Given the extent to which people use search engines as research tools today, building and managing your identity online has become a critical component of your ongoing career marketing efforts.

In this and the following four chapters, you'll learn the following:

- Why managing your online identity is important in a job search (chapter 6)
- Why having a brand is the best way to build a positive online persona (chapter 7)
- Ten steps to create your brand (chapter 8)
- How to transform your brand into a branded value proposition, or "BVP" for short (chapter 9)
- How to condense your brand into a 160-character Twitter bio, the social media equivalent of the "elevator pitch" (chapter 10)

Let's start with your online identity.

Your Digital Footprint

In a 2009 survey of 2,600+ employers by Harris Interactive® on behalf of CareerBuilder.com, 45 percent of employers surveyed said they go to social networking sites such as Facebook, LinkedIn, MySpace, and Twitter to research job candidates, a big jump from 22 percent in 2008. Other studies show even higher percentages, such as the ExecuNet study, shown in table 6.1, outlining the number of recruiters who use search engines to vet candidates.

Table 6.1: Recruiters' Use of Search Engines

	2008	2007	2006	2005
Percentage of recruiters who said they have used search engines to uncover information about candidates	86%	83%	77%	75%
Percentage of recruiters who have said they have eliminated a candidate because of information they found on the Internet	44%	43%	35%	26%

Source: Online reputation management research originated by ExecuNet and tracked since 2004

Of course, as many people do, you can choose to ignore your online identity. The consequences of doing so can range from neutral (you're invisible) to toxic (you're tainted). It's like turning your back on the ocean—the surf can lap at the shore behind you, or it can crash your career in a wave of digital dirt that requires disaster recovery.

> **Need to Know:** *Digital dirt,* a term that originated from research reports by the business network ExecuNet, is information about you found online that could negatively impact your career. It can range from an ill-advised tweet, to a questionable YouTube video, to "college fun" photos on Facebook, to bad media interviews, to negative press, and more. You are being watched!

Build and Manage Your Brand on Twitter and Beyond

To help you be proactive about controlling your brand on Twitter, we tapped online identity and branding expert Kirsten Dixson, coauthor of *Career Distinction: Stand Out by Building Your Brand* (Wiley, 2007) and cocreator of the Online ID Calculator™, to collaborate on this chapter.

We asked Kirsten how job seekers could manage their online identity using Twitter. She recommends three key steps that are applicable to Twitter and other social media sites:

1. **Establish your baseline.** When you google yourself right now, what comes up?

2. **Develop your messaging.** Know what you should be communicating before you start.

3. **Devise your communications plan.** To ensure consistency and regular visibility, create a plan for what you will do and exactly when you will do it.

Kirsten will walk you through each of these steps in more detail.

1. Establish Your Baseline

Before getting active with Twitter or other online efforts, the first priority is to take a step back and assess your overall online identity.

Enter your first and last names in quotes into a search engine (for example, Kirsten would enter her name as "Kirsten Dixson" at Google.com or Bing.com). Answer these questions: How many results do you get? How many of those Web pages actually pertain to you? Do the references to you on the Web communicate a positive, negative, or neutral image of you? How consistently do those results communicate what you want to be known for—your personal brand? Knowing where you stand right now will help you determine exactly how much work you have to do and your next steps.

THE DIGITAL SCALE

from www.onlineidcalculator.com; used with permission

Kirsten Dixson and William Arruda have developed the Online Identity Calculator™, available free at www.onlineidcalculator.com. The tool measures the effectiveness of your online identity, from digitally disguised to digitally distinct. Take a moment now to go to www.onlineidcalculator.com to evaluate your digital results, which can range from wonderful to disastrous:

- *Digitally Distinct:* This is the nirvana of online identity. A search of your name yields lots of results about you; and most, if not all, reinforce your unique personal brand.

- *Digitally Disguised:* Your vanity search does not match any documents. There is absolutely nothing about you on the Web.

- *Digitally Dabbling:* There is some information on the Web about you that supports the personal brand you're trying to communicate, but not a ton of it.

- *Digitally Dissed:* Entering your name into a search engine yields little about you on the Web, but what exists is either negative or inconsistent with how you want to be known.

(continued)

(continued)

> • ***Digitally Disastrous:*** There is much information about you on the Web,
> but it has little relevance to what you want to express about yourself. This
> can be a challenge since it can be difficult to get irrelevant information to
> disappear. The information may also include results about someone else who
> shares your name.

2. Develop Your Messaging

Now that you know where you stand on the digital scale, consider your personal
brand—that is, your reputation both online and in the physical world.

Strong personal brands are known for *some*thing, not 100 things, so aim to have an
overarching theme for the majority of your Twitter communications. For example,
if you are a project management professional with a strong reputation for mentoring
other PMPs, your tweets will center on pointing people to various PMP resources,
notices about local chapter meetings, and the like. (See chapter 14 for suggestions
on the content of your tweets.)

Take stock of your strengths, particularly those that are unique to you, as well as
your personal and professional goals. You'll want to create a concise Twitter bio (see
chapter 10) that makes it clear what your followers can expect when they read your
tweets. Your bio should also be consistent with your other online profiles, such as
your LinkedIn profile.

> **Tip:** Claim your name on Twitter and other social media sites. The site www.
> namechk.com allows you to see whether your name is available at a number of
> popular social networking sites.

3. Devise Your Communications Plan

To maximize the value you get from using Twitter, Kirsten recommends integrating
it into the overall marketing mix of your job search campaign.

First, select all the communications vehicles that will be effective in reaching
your target audience. Your list might include any or all of the following: Twitter,
Facebook, LinkedIn, a blog, industry event appearances as a panelist or speaker,
professional association board membership, press quotes, a branded e-mail signature,
and so on.

It's important that you like your selected channels to use them often enough to have
an impact. If you are deathly afraid of public speaking or if you know you'll never
have time or skill to keep up a blog, get better at it or find another way of expressing
your brand. Think about how you will integrate and cross-promote the other channels to get more bang for your efforts (more on this in chapter 23).

Once you select and integrate the tools that you will be using, create an action plan to ensure a regular drip, drip, drip of communication. Put at least one online branding activity on your to-do list each week, and always aim for quality over quantity. Track your efforts to see what is working and make course corrections as needed.

Seven Steps to Dissolve and Deflect Digital Dirt

"Eighty-six percent of recruiters said they have used
search engines to uncover information about candidates...
44% eliminated a candidate because of information they found."

—*ExecuNet research*

Digital dirt can kill your candidacy for a position. It is essential to know and take steps to control the path of your online footprints. If you're new to managing your online identity, you may find that you've accumulated some level of digital dirt. Hopefully, you're not "digitally disastrous," but if you are, we've tapped Robyn Greenspan, ExecuNet's Editor-in-Chief, to help. Here's her advice:

1. **Build an online portfolio.** Buy your domain name and set up a Web site to serve as an electronic platform highlighting your skills, experience, and accomplishments. It will act as a keyword-laden showcase to display your resume, bio, and various self-marketing documents, along with links to articles you may have published, information on conference panels where you may have participated, transcripts from speaking engagements, and so on.

2. **Big blogging, little blogging.** Fresh and frequent content can quickly rise to the top of search engine results and a blog can be your forum for demonstrating your subject-matter knowledge. "Micro-blogging" in the form of Twitter, and short status updates like those found on Facebook and LinkedIn, are also being indexed by search engines, enabling you to say very little, very frequently.

3. **Prepare your profile.** Social networking sites allow users to create profile pages with the information, content, and links they want associated with their online image—often with the option of generating a personal URL that reflects a real name. The best search engine results occur when all sections of the profile are filled with keywords and completed, and visibility is further enhanced through participating in online discussion areas, forums, and groups.

4. **Tune privacy controls.** Many social media sites have settings that enable the user to control the flow of public and private information, who can view and share your content, the types of searches where you appear, and how you can be contacted. Carefully adjust settings before posting anything to avoid personal information from becoming universal.

5. **Dual digital identities.** As branding-minded individuals achieve greater comfort posting, participating, and interacting in online communities, there is a tendency to also share more personal information. Consider a boundary between the functional knowledge and professional experience you display on business networking sites such as ExecuNet or LinkedIn and information that is more appropriate for close friends. Reserve an invitation-only site, such as Facebook, as a private, digital playground.

6. **Become known for what you know.** Be generous with your time and you could wind up contributing to content published by others. Being favorably quoted, appearing on a conference panel of experts, submitting bylined articles to publications, and guest blogging all generate third-party promotions and get noticed by search engines.

7. **And just in case....** You've identified the dirt, worked hard to bury it, and were careful not to create anything else that could damage your reputation, yet there is still potentially career-blemishing online information attached to your name. If you posted the controversial information, have an honest and regretful response prepared in case it arises in interviews or employment situations. Address the circumstances, your poor judgment, and lessons learned, and move the discussion forward. Negative information about you posted by others requires quick damage control, which can range from polite requests to remove the content to full-scale PR campaigns.

CHAPTER 7

Your Brand and Twitter

"Regardless of age, regardless of position, regardless of the business we happen to be in, all of us need to understand the importance of branding. We are CEOs of our own companies: Me Inc. To be in business today, our most important job is to be head marketer for the brand called You."

— *Tom Peters in* Fast Company *(1997)*

In 1997, Tom Peters' iconic article "The Brand Called You" appeared in *Fast Company* magazine. That revolutionary article is commonly thought to have kicked off the personal branding revolution. Fast-forward more than 10 years. Personal branding is now mainstream. So is social media (but it wasn't even a blip on the radar back in 1997). And so is Twitter.

In this chapter, you'll learn the following:

- How personal branding and social media fit together
- How personal brands reflect your value and strengthen connections with employers
- The four brand essentials that can get you hired

Although it might feel like this sequence of chapters on branding is not related to Twitter, we promise you, it is! We'll tell you why.

The PB&J (Personal Brand & Job) Brand Sandwich

We like to think that personal branding, job search, and social media go together like peanut butter, jelly, and Wonder Bread. It's hard to imagine that squishy, satisfying sandwich without one of those ingredients. It just wouldn't deliver the same comfort-food experience.

Of course, detractors of Wonder Bread say it's not very nutritious—and detractors of personal branding also say that it doesn't have enough substance or depth. So what happens to your PB&J Brand Sandwich if you prefer it on seven-grain bread, with natural peanut butter and organic fruit spread? No problem. It still works, because branding reflects *you.*

Whether you like Wonder Bread or seven-grain, you can build a brand and look for a job without using social media and Twitter, but why would you want to? And you can use social media and Twitter without focusing on extending the reach of your brand; but again, why would you want to? You'd have a peanut butter sandwich without the jelly. Or a spoon of peanut butter with no sandwich (think how hard *that* is to swallow!). Both are good in their ways, but somehow miss the mark.

Personal Brands Reflect and Connect

Personal brands are about authenticity. Your brand reflects "the genuine you"—not you costumed to play the part of someone else, but you cast in the right role ... a Master F.I.T.™ role that allows you to be radically rewarded and enthusiastically engaged in work that adds value to others.

A GREAT CAREER FIT STARTS WITH MASTER F.I.T.

Master F.I.T. is an umbrella for your brand. The model, described in one of Susan's earlier books, *Job Search Magic* (also published by JIST), captures six elements essential for career satisfaction. There is an External F.I.T. and an Internal F.I.T. to consider, as described here:

External F.I.T.

- *Function:* What you do—your innate strengths, passions, talents, and skills.
- *Industry/Interests:* Where you'll do it—industry, company, specialty sector.
- *Things That Matter:* Which values and priorities are top of list (for example, compensation, organizational culture, commute, travel, good boss).

Internal F.I.T.

- *Fulfillment:* Why you work—your purpose for being on this planet! Linking your work to purpose will take your job from a career to a calling.
- *Identity:* Who are you? Identity is essential to brand; it captures who you are, how you want to be perceived, and how you bring value to your work-world.
- *Type:* How you work best based on personality type. When your work complements these preferences, you'll be energized, creative, productive, and in-demand.

You can download a Master F.I.T. form at www.susanwhitcomb.com/resources/ to complete this exercise in more detail. Consider writing one 140-character tweet for each of the six elements. The clearer you are on who you are and what you want, the easier it will be for your network to help you in your job search.

You may decide to never share this information with the outside world, but you know it's you and it's true. This is "Who you are." It's your North Star—your guide. Once you know your brand, all your decisions are brand decisions—the decisions either support your brand and authenticity or they don't. If the decision doesn't support your brand, it makes it harder to sustain success.

Your personal brand is the essence of who you are. It's who you are when you're at rest, part of how you think, and what you naturally do. It's the seed from which everything sprouts and grows. The DNA is wired into that seed and can't be changed. Think of your DNA as your "*Designed Nature and Assets.*" It is good seed. It's important and useful to the people/employers that you will encounter. In fact, it's mandatory.

Kathy Simmons (@kathynetshare), CEO of NETSHARE, Inc., a private membership organization for executives, tells us that "Your job is to determine the decision maker's needs, decide if your brand is a good fit, and then demonstrate how you can be the solution. Too many job seekers think that a multipurpose resume, while casting a wide net, is the best way to get the job—this assumes that the employer will connect the dots between their needs and your potential solutions. While this might have worked in the past, it certainly does not work anymore."

Here are a few other important things a compelling, cohesive brand can do for you:

- Controls what employers remember most about you.
- Makes you more attractive to employers, even when there are no formal job openings.
- Lowers the barriers to hiring by creating trust and conveying value.
- Elevates you from the status of commonplace commodity to one-of-a-kind.
- Guides your decisions about which leads to pursue.
- Helps employers see that you'll be a good value and a good organizational fit.

When your brand connects to your environment, you are whole and strong and you make everyone around you whole and strong. Here's a fitting synopsis from Stowe Boyd (@stoweboyd), a social media expert and presenter at Jeff Pulver's 140 Characters Conference, which illustrates that point:

> *"I am made greater by the sum of my connections, and so are my connections."*
>
> —*Stowe Boyd*

The Brand to Land™ Plan to Get Hired Faster

Our coauthor, Deb, a Reach Certified Personal Brand Strategist, outlines the four essentials of her Brand to Land Plan—and how they intersect to get you hired:

- **Personal Brand:** Your suite of *core* attributes edited down to the *one* overriding thing that defines you. It's the unchanging, hardwired, who-you-are promise of value.
- **Career Brand:** The business application of your brand—what you *do* with it in the workplace.
- **Brand Statement:** A description of what you bring to the table: what you do, *how* you do it, with whom you do it, and what happens when you do it.
- **Branded Value Proposition (BVP):** Your value in the marketplace. It says "I know what you need, I can do it, I can prove I can do it, and I can do it again!"

Everyone has a brand, regardless of his or her position, level of responsibility, education, or financial status. For example, meet our "Pizza Guy" and his brand. When we first meet him, he's just 17 years old, in high school, and a floor sweeper and counterperson at the local pizza parlor that's part of a pizza-chain franchise. He is a happy guy, is dedicated, and sets some pretty high standards for himself: Be on time, don't miss a day, keep the place sparkling, be respectful, and keep the customers laughing.

Most people would find it unlikely that a teenager in a service job could have a brand, let alone value that would impact his store. Yet he does have a brand, and it is strong and valuable. As he progresses, his brand and value help him get promoted to store manager and later rise to regional director in the company—pretty quickly, too.

Here's what the four essentials of his brand look like, at each stage of his career. Notice that his personal brand is unchanging; it's who he is, at his core. His career brand is unchanging, as well. However, as his career progresses, the manifestation of his career brand—the way he delivers value, and what that value is—changes.

> **Tip:** The wording for your brand statement should mature over the course of your career (the pizza counterperson would not use the same language in his role as a director); however, the essence of it doesn't change, regardless of the position you're in.

In table 7.1, note how Pizza Guy's four brand essentials look at three different stages of his career.

Table 7.1: The Brand to Land Plan at Different Phases of Pizza Guy's Career

Positions with Major Pizza Chain	Personal Brand	Career Brand	Brand Statement	Branded Value Proposition (BVP)
Pizza parlor counterperson	Joyful	Diligently tackles every job with buoyancy.	I tackle every job as though it's the most important job in the world. If there are people involved, that's even better!	When I make work fun, customers stick around longer and buy more, and then tell their friends, who come in, stick around longer and buy more, and then tell their friends, etc. That means more money for my boss.
Pizza parlor store manager	Joyful	Diligently tackles every job with buoyancy.	I tackle every job as though it's the most important job in the world. If there are people involved, that's even better! Customers engage, teams have fun doing more, and profits go up.	I increase store sales by as much as 37% by using my natural ebullience and diligence to create a great physical environment and rollicking, dedicated teams that get customers feeling great about buying pizza.
Director, Northeast region	Joyful	Diligently tackles every job with buoyancy.	I tackle every job as though it's the most important job in the world. If there are people involved, that's even better! Customers engage, teams have fun doing more, and profits go up.	I deliver double-digit profit increases in a bad economy by infusing contagious energy across the region, engaging teams, and attracting evangelistic customers.

In Pizza Guy's first position as counterperson, his natural ebullience and diligence made a big difference to the traffic and sales in his store. Tying his brand to value evolves him from a happy, hardworking kid to a happy, hardworking sales driver. He has effectively tied his passion for hard work and happiness to an increase in sales—not bad for a 17-year-old kid.

In his promotion to store manager, Pizza Guy's value has become more attuned to a business case. However, his value still sounds just like him, and you can see exactly how he does his job to consistently lift sales figures—using skills that most people would consider superfluous and just not important. Who cares whether he's happy and his teams are happy? Well, his customers do, and they spend the money to prove it!

In the last row of table 7.1, Pizza Guy is further along in his career than he ever expected to be, now a director of the Northeast region. He has stayed on-brand throughout his career, leveraging his unique management style to help keep the company moving forward in tough times. He's poised for the next big thing and confident in his abilities. And did you notice? His branded value proposition (BVP) is just 160 characters—perfect for his Twitter profile!

You'll come across Pizza Guy a number of times in future chapters as we follow how he creates his brand and career communications.

CHAPTER 8

TEN STEPS TO MINING, DEFINING, AND REFINING YOUR BRAND

The four brand elements we defined in chapter 7 cannot exist without a clear understanding of your brand. It's a journey that needs to be made. It's one of the most critical components of career success. Identifying your brand and tying it to your career is a maze with twists, turns, and dead ends. But there's also a prize at the end: the golden key to your career.

You do double duty when you clarify your brand. The elements can be used throughout your communications—resumes, Twitter bio, networking conversations, interviews, salary negotiations, and so on. Here are 10 steps that will help take your personal marketing message from "bland to brand" and from "which? to pitch!"

Step 1: Take Stock

Take stock. Ask yourself some of these "inside-out" (meaning how you see yourself) questions. (You'll ask outside-in questions—how others see you in regard to reputation and performance—in Step 2).

- I've always been recognized for....
- If there were one word to describe me, it would be....
- What makes me different from others who do the same job is that I....
- Throughout my career as a _____ [functional title], I've always been drawn to....
- At the heart of my experience are these three strengths....
- I am passionate about....
- I feel I am living my destiny when I....
- Boss and clients frequently compliment me for....
- I'm very good at....

Step 2: Look Outward

Ask others the same questions for critical outside-in feedback. A great tool for this is the 360Reach, a reputational (as opposed to performance-based) outside-in feedback assessment. (See "Branding Resources to Dig Deeper" at the end of chapter 9 for more information.)

Step 3: Look for Personal Patterns

For clues to your *personal brand,* analyze results and look for patterns, commonalities, and the cream rising to the top. For your personal brand, you're looking for the one linchpin lever point that underscores the heart of what you do.

Step 4: Look for Work Patterns

For clues to your *career brand,* analyze results and look for patterns about how you apply your personal brand to benefit those you work for and with (in business terms, stakeholders). Write down all the patterns you see. You can whittle them down later.

Step 5: Tie Patterns to Accomplishments to "Then What?"

For every pattern, tie it to specific outcomes (these tend to be your best accomplishments—you might already have them on your resume if you've written an accomplishments-driven resume).

> **Need to Know:** *Accomplishments,* in career terms, are things that you've done well at work—things that have made a difference to your boss, department, or employer. They have a direct or indirect, numbers-oriented, bottom-line value to employers.

Take it as far as you can. Don't just say, "it helped make things more productive." Ask: and then what? "And then, we had more orders." And then what? "We had more revenue." And then what? "We were able to increase the top line from xx% to xx% and the bottom line from xx% to xx%." And then what? "The company was able to invest in new equipment." And then what? "We went from being #7 to #2 in the marketplace."

You can stop asking the question, "And then what?" once your information is tied not only to the bottom line, but to the ultimate impact of your accomplishment.

When you are in the brand discovery process, it helps to do what career coaches and resume writers do when working with clients: create context. Place each accomplishment in the "CAR" format:

- What **C**hallenge did you face?
- What **A**ction did you take?
- What was the **R**esult?

> *"A great brand is a story that's never completely told. A brand is a metaphorical story that connects with something very deep—a fundamental appreciation of mythology. Stories create the emotional context people need to locate themselves in a larger experience."*
>
> *—Scott Bedbury, Nike, Starbucks*

Step 6: Analyze Accomplishment Themes

Carefully analyze your outcomes (accomplishments) for common themes. Look for a few strengths and skills that are present in every one of them. Whittle these down to a small cluster of themes (perhaps three).

QUESTIONS FOR ANALYZING YOUR ACCOMPLISHMENTS

When analyzing your accomplishments, consider these questions:
- What attributes/skills show up across the board on every one of them, even if other factors change?
- What type of outcome happens most frequently?
- What name or phrase would you put to it?

You should start to see clues that will lead to your career brand. For instance, you might say you solve the technology problems no one else wants to touch, or that you create new systems that save money, or you develop training techniques that enable the sales force to work more effectively, or that you invent new products using green technologies, or even that you sweep a floor cleaner than anyone else—and with a better attitude.

Step 7: Analyze for Buying Motivators

Carefully analyze the outcomes for the type of benefit (value) delivered. These are the motivators that cause employers to "buy" (hire) you. Here are some suggestions for the benefits you want to link to, taken from Susan's *Résumé Magic* (also published by JIST):

- Make money.
- Save money.
- Save time.
- Make work easier.
- Solve a specific problem.
- Be more competitive.
- Build relationships/an image.
- Expand business.
- Attract new customers.
- Retain existing customers.

Step 8: Start Developing Your Brand Statement

Link your themes to outcomes: When I do _____, _____ happens.

Going back to our Pizza Guy, he says, "When I make work fun, customers stick around longer and buy more, and then tell their friends, who come in, stick around longer, and buy more, and then tell their friends, and so on. That means more money for my boss."

This is a career brand statement. It also doubles as the start of a brief elevator pitch or Twitter bio.

Step 9: Say It in Your Voice

Write your brand statement in your "voice." This should be natural to you. Use your words, not someone else's. Practice saying it out loud. If it's not something you would say naturally, rework it until it feels comfortable.

Notice Pizza Guy's language for his brand statement: "I tackle every job as though it's the most important job in the world. If there are people involved, that's even better." It's conversational, unpretentious, and energetic, like he is.

As an adult, the essence of his brand statement will be the same, although the language will change slightly with his maturity.

Step 10: Craft the Value Proposition

Turn to chapter 9 for step 10. Your value proposition is so critical—to your job search, to your career, and to using Twitter for both—that we gave it a whole chapter. You'll see why!

YOUR BRANDED VALUE PROPOSITION (BVP)

Featured Contributor: Mark Hovind, founder of JobBait.com and a pioneer in using branded value propositions to create powerfully brief cover letters (@MarkHovind).

> *"There is only one way…to get anybody to do anything. And that is by making the other person want to do it."*
>
> —*Dale Carnegie*

What does it take to get the attention of a decision maker? Ironically, it's the thing that is usually missing from most resumes, cover letters, elevator pitches, and even Twitter Bios/Twitpitches. The answer? It's the one-two punch of a value proposition tied to a personal brand—in other words, a branded value proposition.

> **Need to Know:** A *Branded Value Proposition,* or *BVP* for short, answers the employer's question, "What's in it for me?" with a clear, concise, and compelling message that expresses tangible benefits from your services. You deliver that benefit via your brand.

A BVP is the core of your career, your trigger for Twitter, and the secret weapon most job seekers ignore (or just don't know about). It ties your past to your potential, your talent to your target, and your deeds to dollars; and it predicts that you can do it again.

The Employer's Eternal Question: What's in It for Me?

> *"You don't get paid for the hour. You get paid for the value you bring to the hour."*
>
> —*Jim Rohn*

Employers and hiring managers are selfish. They need to be—the success or failure of a company is in their hands.

Whether running Fortune companies, nonprofit organizations, company divisions, small businesses, or the corner deli, the employer craves an ideal hire. An ideal hire will meet—or even exceed—the employer's needs and desires. The individual who can best prove potential to satiate that employer craving gets the interview—and often gets the job.

A BVP answers the employer's question of "What's in it for me?" It helps the hiring decision maker understand the two elements critical to a hire:

- **Can you help the company make money?** *Money* (the dollarized value proposition) is the interview driver that gets you in the door and can get you on the short list.

- **Will you bring the right chemistry to fit within the company's culture?** *Chemistry* (the brand) is the "who you are and how you do what you do" that demonstrates fit and gets you hired from the short list.

> **Tip:** An effective BVP focuses on measurable results, primarily in dollars or percentages. It is crisp and to the point—without fluff, self-praising adjectives, generalities, or any other vague language that has built-in wiggle room.

Your BVP is your sales pitch. Here are two job search scenarios developed by Mark Hovind to illustrate this point. The first lacks a differentiated message of value or brand; the second uses a BVP as a sales pitch. As you read them, ask yourself which would most impress employers?

EMPLOYER SCENARIO 1: "NO, THANKS."

Let's look at what happens with our Pizza Guy (you'll remember him from chapter 7 as the pizza counterperson kid who rose to become regional director), who applies for a management job without the one-two punch of a BVP sales pitch:

1. He crafts a resume and letter that says what he has done. The first line in his cover letter, or the summary section of his resume, says something like, "I'm a seasoned manager with a business-to-consumer background, have an MBA, and have 15 years of experience."

2. The decision maker thinks, "So what? Who cares? Go stand in line. You can cut in front of the MBAs with 10 years of experience, but please stand behind those with 20. By the way, what does 'seasoned' mean? Are you experienced or are you ready to retire? I have plenty of people on staff with a B2C (business-to-consumer) background. Why do I need you? We're just fine."

3. Pizza Guy has hidden his potential value to the new company so well, behind meaningless facts and platitudes, that he—a valuable potential employee—can't get face time with a decision maker.

4. No value, no interview, no job.

Now, here's the sales pitch with a BVP.

EMPLOYER SCENARIO 2: "COME ON IN; TELL ME MORE."

What if Pizza Guy, in his role as regional director, stuck his head in the decision maker's door and said, "Would you like to increase your gross margins even in a down economy?

"I've already helped a top fast-food chain grow their sales 30 to 40 percent on average and double their margins in a struggling region by overhauling operations and infusing contagious delight, passion, and ownership across teams. The fun-filled loyalty program I developed to attract evangelistic customers was profiled in the *Wall Street Journal.* The jump in margins and positive press helped raise our NASDAQ price 10 points."

Now, the decision maker might respond with, "Please, come in, sit down... tell me more."

Why? Because the decision maker speaks only one language—money—and Pizza Guy spoke that language. Yet the decision maker hires with his head and his gut—and Pizza Guy sweetened the deal with his chemistry.

How did Pizza Guy come up with this language? By answering a few critical questions.

Three Key Questions to Identify Your BVP

The questions that follow will help you identify your BVP. (Before answering these questions, review the CAR stories you wrote in step 5 of the preceding chapter to help get your creative juices flowing.)

1. What is the most intractable problem facing the employers you are targeting in your search? (This may take some research and networking to answer.)
2. How have you used your brand and skills in the past to resolve similar problems? Choose the single most impressive story to describe this.
3. What was the bottom-line benefit and ultimate impact of doing so?

Draft a short story about these answers, and don't be concerned about the wording at this point. It often takes multiple drafts to condense your BVP into powerful, persuasive language. And, in the next chapter, you'll have a chance to laser it even further into a 160-character Twitter bio.

In the meantime, let's look at Pizza Guy and see how these questions helped develop his BVP as regional director.

1. *Intractable problem:*
   "Declining sales in a down economy."

2. *Use of brand and skills to resolve problem:*

"When I arrived, teams were disheartened and sloppy. Quality suffered. The stores were just plain sorry-looking. There was nothing to engage customers… quite the opposite—coming into one of our stores was just depressing. It was no wonder we'd lost substantial business.

"I knew 'job one' was infusing contagious energy and optimism across the region—along with zero tolerance for anything but the highest standards [note the infusion of brand here]. We accomplished what we set out to do: We engaged teams, became a beacon for how to do our business right, and created evangelistic customers [skills]. The fun-filled loyalty program I developed to attract evangelistic customers was profiled in the *Wall Street Journal*."

3. *Bottom-line benefit:*

"Within one year, I stabilized falling sales; within three years I increased sales 30 to 40 percent on average and doubled their margins in a struggling region. The jump in margins and positive press helped raise our stock price 10 points.

"This was done in a bad economy and within a rapidly failing unit of the company. Our best practices are now being adopted company wide, enthusiastically implemented by managers I have trained, and I'm ready to tackle the next big thing that needs doing."

Of course that's not all he did, but it's the essence of what he delivered to the company, and how he did it. Pizza Guy's BVP story is a "good read!"

Twitterizing the Pitch

When Pizza Guy needs his BVP whittled down from a mouthful to a nibble (or a tweet), he says:

I deliver double-digit profit increases in a bad economy by infusing contagious energy across the region, engaging teams, and attracting evangelistic customers.

Now that's powerful precision.

In the next chapter, you'll learn how to "Twitterize" your BVP, condensing it to just 160 characters. That's a tall order, but we've tapped networking expert Laura Allen of NYC-based 15-Second Pitch to show you how.

If You Need More Help

Brand discovery is a deeply personal and complex activity. Our intention is to give you a sense of the process and a jumping-off point to begin your journey.

We each have been through the branding process and will attest that it goes much more easily with input from a trained branding strategist. Here are some free and for-fee ideas for taking the process further or obtaining assistance in defining and creating your brand elements.

BRANDING RESOURCES TO DIG DEEPER

Read books like *Career Distinction* by personal branding experts William Arruda and Kirsten Dixson (Wiley & Sons) or *Me 2.0* by Gen Y branding guru Dan Schawbel (Kaplan). (Fee)

Enroll in Web-delivered brand training via the Reach Branding Club (www.reachbrandingclub.com). (Fee)

Engage in a brand-specific assessment like 360Reach for critical "outside-in," anonymous, reputational feedback (www.reachcc.com/360reach). (Free and fee)

Follow a few of the many (free) blogs on the subject. Some we like are

- William Arruda's Reach Brand Strategists' Blog: www.thepersonalbrandingblog.com

- FishDogs Career Branding for Social Animals: http://blog.fishdogs.com

- Chris Brogan: www.chrisbrogan.com

- Dan Schawbel: www.personalbrandingblog.com

- Networked Blog List of Top 50 Blogs in Personal Branding: www.networkedblogs.com/topic/personal_branding

Set up Google Alerts for terms like "personal brand" and "personal branding." You'll have the latest thought leadership at your fingertips. (Free)

View innovative, fun, actionable videos on all aspects of personal branding skills, techniques, and uses at www.personalbranding.tv.

Engage a Certified Personal Branding Strategist (find a list of these professionals at www.reachpersonalbranding.com). (Fee)

Follow the many personal branding strategists and personal branding experts on Twitter. A good place to start is Reach Certified Personal Branding Strategists (www.reachpersonalbranding.com/resources/reach-social-media/) or 70+ Top Personal Branding Experts on Twitter (http://tweepml.org/Personal-Branding). (Free)

Use Twitter's List feature to find brand experts that others are following. See more on lists in chapter 29. (Free)

CHAPTER 10

SOUND BITES WITH TEETH: WRITING YOUR 160ME™ TWITTER BIO

Featured expert: Laura Allen, cofounder, 15secondpitch.com (@la15secondpitch)

> *"...with your audience drowning in more noise than ever, cutting your message to fortune-cookie length may be the best chance you have at getting their attention."*
>
> —*John Tozzi in "The Escalator Pitch," Businessweek.com* *

Imagine two college students who have an idea for an online information portal. They have no experience running a company or startup. They need funding and they need investors. How will they attract interest?

With these famous eight words: "Access to the world's information in one click." With those eight words, Sergey Brin and Larry Page, the founders of Google, pitched a vision and got a listen. The rest is history.

As a job seeker, you need the same powerful simplicity. You don't get the luxury of ambiguity. You don't get to muddle through an elevator pitch or job interview if you want to get hired. You need to know, in precise, value-rich terms, *your* "eight words"—or, in the case of Twitter, your 140 to 160 characters. In this chapter, we'll outline the steps to create those critical characters that will appear in your Twitter bio.

Say It Short, Say It Sweet

Many credit social media guru Stowe Boyd with coining the term "Twitpitch." In fact, in a blog post dated April 26, 2008, titled "Twitpitch is the Future," Boyd declares that the only way that companies can pitch him is by using a Twitpitch.

> **Need to Know:** A *Twitpitch* is, to paraphrase Stowe Boyd, a 10-second-long "escalator pitch" that drops superlatives and buzzwords to get to the heart of the matter.

---

*www.businessweek.com/smallbiz/content/may2008/sb20080516_673078.htm

Laura Allen, who collaborated as our invited expert on this chapter, thought it would be appropriate to send Boyd a public tweet on Twitter and ask for his thoughts on the Twitpitch. Here is their exchange.

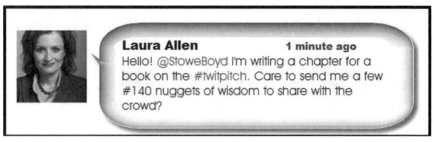

Laura Allen   1 minute ago
Hello! @StoweBoyd I'm writing a chapter for a book on the #twitpitch. Care to send me a few #140 nuggets of wisdom to share with the crowd?

Figure 10.1: Laura Allen tweets Stowe Boyd asking about the Twitpitch.

Stow's responses, in figure 10.2, should be read from bottom to top, as that is the order in which they were sent.

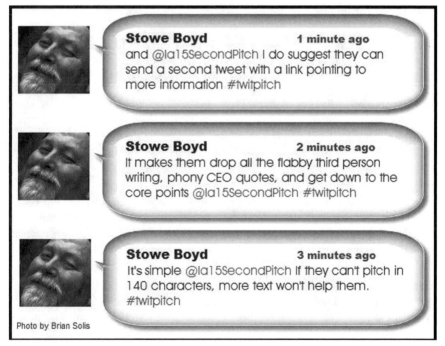

Stowe Boyd   1 minute ago
and @la15SecondPitch I do suggest they can send a second tweet with a link pointing to more information #twitpitch

Stowe Boyd   2 minutes ago
It makes them drop all the flabby third person writing, phony CEO quotes, and get down to the core points @la15SecondPitch #twitpitch

Stowe Boyd   3 minutes ago
It's simple @la15SecondPitch If they can't pitch in 140 characters, more text won't help them. #twitpitch

Photo by Brian Solis

Figure 10.2: Stowe Boyd responds on the Twitpitch.

Stowe's reply was a chilling challenge: "If they can't pitch in 140 characters, more text won't help them." Stowe doesn't have the time and energy to read a startup company's 100-page business plan. And he's not wasting time going to their Web site and reading their "About Us" pages, either.

> **Need to Know:** The Twitpitches to which Stowe Boyd refers are 140 characters long, like a tweet. The good news is that you get an extra 20 characters, for a total of 160 characters, in your Twitter bio. Bonus!

Your Twitter Bio: We Call It the 160me

Like Stowe Boyd, recruiters and hiring managers are also looking for ways to do their jobs more effectively. They simply don't have the time to read three-page resumes of each of the hundreds of candidates for each open position they need to fill. Laura, our 15secondpitch.com expert, says, "It seems probable that in the near future, decision makers will require candidates to send a short pitch before they are asked to send a full resume. You will increase your chances of success by being able to cut through the clutter and tell them exactly what makes you remarkable."

How do you cut through the clutter? Enter the 160me.

> **Need to Know:** The *160me*™ is a micro-bio of 160 or fewer characters, appropriate for your bio on Twitter. The 160me catches interest, conveys the all-important branded value proposition (BVP), and creates desire on the part of employers to take the next step and learn more about you. For our purposes, we'll use *160me, Twitter bio, micro-bio,* and *bio* synonymously throughout this book.

Is it easy to do? Laura asserts, "I could lie and say this is going to be easy, but I'm not going to do that. Boiling down your entire career into 160 or fewer characters is probably one of the most challenging tasks in your job search. Luckily, the payoff is immense, so it's really worth the time and energy to get it right."

Later we'll look at a sample 160me, but first, meet Ken. Laura connected with Ken at a networking event in New York City. Laura tells us, "I liked him right away because he looked interesting: He had long hair and a very nice suit. His appearance was a bit of a contradiction, which made me curious enough to go over to him and ask him what he did for a living."

Laura continues, "Ken told me he was looking for a business-development position at a film company or TV network. But, like many job seekers, Ken struggled to explain what he had done professionally and what he was looking for in his next gig."

Laura worked with Ken to really understand what he had done in his career. Together, they created Ken's "billion-dollar" 160me (in a few characters shy of 160, no less!):

Billion-dollar dealmaker w/major film company win. Comic book geek/Kellogg MBA in Finance. Rock the art of the deal. Looking for next big biz dev film gig.

The Four-Step Pitch Process for Job Seekers

How did Laura write Ken's 160me? She used four straightforward steps adapted from her 15-Second Pitch process. Here's how she explains her method:

Step 1: Who Are You?...in Three Words

Ken uses "comic book geek" to describe himself. This is a fun, standout description. Note, however, that Ken doesn't lead off with those words since he's using this bio for business purposes.

Step 2: What Makes You Truly Unique?

Ken starts his bio with "Billion-dollar dealmaker w/major film company win." This catches people's attention because it's not something you associate with your typical comic book geek. There is power in pairing opposites, and Ken has done that here. Ken also tells us that he has an MBA in finance from Kellogg. This impressive credential helps substantiate his billion-dollar business deal.

"Comic Book Geek" and MBA in Finance are an unlikely pairing, as are "Comic Book Geek" and "Billion-dollar dealmaker." *But* put the three together and Ken now has a differentiated, interest-attracting professional persona.

Imagine if Ken had used only "MBA in Finance from Kellogg" and "Billion-dollar dealmaker." That's impressive, but certainly not unexpected for his background. It's pairing those with his "Comic Book Geek" moniker that infuses a traditional finance persona with something unique and memorable.

Step 3: Bold Equals Gold—Name One of Your Really Big "Wins"!

Laura notes that "Most of the people I meet can't stand the whole notion of self-promotion. I always say that subtlety and poverty go hand in hand. We'd all love to be modest and just get up each day and go to a great job that pays the rent and allows us to save for a few nice vacations during the year. The good news is that if you take the time to learn how to promote yourself in a way that is bold yet authentic, you are going to have a much easier time finding jobs throughout your career."

Ken has already mentioned his billion-dollar deal, yet adds to that with the bold statement, "rock the art of the deal." Laura did a little unscientific test with some of her clients and found that most would be willing to speak to Ken for at least 15 minutes just to hear more. Why? Because he sounds exciting! People want to know all of the juicy details about the players and films he has been involved in.

Step 4: Tell Me What You Want

If you've done a great job on steps 1 through 3, step 4 needs to accomplish only one thing: to tell the reader what you want next. Ken wants a full-time gig as a business-development professional at a major film company. He succeeds in getting this information across very quickly: "Looking for next big biz dev film gig."

The Goal? A Follow, a Click-Through, a Call!

Laura and Ken have done a great job. Ken's 160me is exciting, unique, interesting, and specific about his next steps. It attracts Twitter followers. People who want to learn more about him can click through to his Web site or LinkedIn profile from the link on his Twitter profile. Who knows, one of those people just might have a job opening for a quirky, unconventional, well-educated, billion-dollar dealmaker.

Let's look at Ken's 160me again:

Billion-dollar dealmaker w/major film company win. Comic book geek/Kellogg MBA in Finance. Rock the art of the deal. Looking for next big biz dev film gig.

Ken's 160me can be expanded for use in networking, as an elevator pitch:

> "Hi, my name is Ken. I'm a comic book geek with an MBA in Finance from Kellogg. I love the art of the deal and when I was at New Line Cinema, I helped land a billion-dollar opportunity involving the Lord of the Rings franchise. Right now I'm looking for my next big business-development film gig."

And here's how it might sound when calling a target employer:

> "Hello, my name is Ken. I'm a comic book geek with an MBA in Finance from Kellogg. When I was at New Line Cinema, there was a billion-dollar opportunity on the table involving the Lord of the Rings franchise. Give me a call to learn about the key role I played in making this billion-dollar opportunity into a reality."

Tip: To create an expanded pitch, called an "escalator" pitch (not limited to 160 characters), go to Laura Allen's site (www.15SecondPitch.com), where you'll find her free 15SecondPitch™ Wizard. Visitors to the site have already created more than 20,000 pitches!

More 160me Twitter Bios

Here are a few more 160me Twitter bios. Notice how they follow Laura's four-step process, mix compelling value with personality, and entice hiring managers to say, "Let's talk."

Let's look at this "before and after" example.

Before: PR fab, world traveler, fashion lover, future New York City resident, big dreamer, professional mosh pitter

---

The original has promise, but lacks the value component that attracts employers. It's clever and quirky, but it doesn't tell a hiring manager exactly what he or she would want to know.

After: The Go-To PR Gal to the stars and major corporations. Once sat on PRSSA panel with a football star and got more PR for him than ever before

---

The "After" version tells us who the job seeker is (The Go-To PR Gal), what she wants to do (work for the stars and major corporations), and what makes her truly unique as a candidate (she once sat on a PRSSA panel with a football star and got more PR for him than ever before).

If you were a hiring manager looking for someone who could get PR for your clients, which bio would speak to you?

Let's look at one more example. Remember our friend Pizza Guy? Here are two 160me bios he might use in his job as regional director of the Pie-in-the-Sky Pizza chain. Both are unique, represent his value and personality, and are effective. Depending on his goals, he might use either one. Here's how his 160me might look in his natural, high-energy style (125 characters):

Here's another version that's branded with his enthusiasm, but is a bit more "corporate." This might be more suitable for a job search outside the pizza industry (160 characters).

I deliver double-digit profit increases in a bad economy by infusing contagious energy across the region, engaging teams, and attracting evangelistic customers.

What Will Your 160me Say About You?

Take the time to craft your 160me now following the four-step process. That way, it will be ready to plug into your profile when you get to section 3.

Step 1: Who are you? In three words:

(1)_____ (2)_____ (3)_____

Step 2: What makes you *truly* unique?

_____

_____

_____

Step 3: Bold equals gold—name one of your really big "wins"!

_____

Step 4: Tell me what you want.

_____

_____

_____

_____

Put it all together in draft form:

_____

_____

_____

_____

Now, refine it to your 160me, keeping it to 160 or fewer characters:

_____

_____

_____

_____

SECTION 3

TWITTER BASICS

11. What's in a Name: Choosing Twitter Account Settings to Boost Your Online Presence

12. Branding Your Twitter Account with a Customized Background

13. The Art of Following and Being Followed

14. How to Speak in Tweets: The Language and Style of Twitter

15. The Art and Science of the Retweet

16. Tweeter Beware: Staying Out of Legal Hot Water

CHAPTER 11

WHAT'S IN A NAME: CHOOSING TWITTER ACCOUNT SETTINGS TO BOOST YOUR ONLINE PRESENCE

Featured Contributor: Susan P. Joyce, president of NETability, Inc., and editor/publisher of Job-Hunt.org (@JobHuntOrg)

> *"The new resume is what employers find online about you."*
>
> —*Richard Nelson Bolles, author of* What Color Is Your Parachute?,
> *in a Career Coach Academy interview with Susan Whitcomb*

Employers and recruiters are turning to search engines more and more frequently to find candidates, especially in a down economy. Why? It's free, it's fast, and it's easy.

Finding a candidate via a search of Google, Yahoo!, or Bing can save a recruiter thousands of dollars in fees that would normally be paid to job boards for the privilege of sifting through their database of job seekers. One recruiter we interviewed for this book mentioned dropping his $6,000-per-year subscription to a major job board in favor of using free or low-cost vehicles such as Twitter and LinkedIn.

By leveraging search engine optimization (SEO) techniques in Twitter, you make it easier for employers and recruiters to find you—both on Twitter and in general searches of the Internet. This chapter walks you through setting up your Twitter account settings to make the most of SEO.

Power SEO for Twitter

Susan Joyce, editor/publisher of the award-winning Job-Hunt.org employment portal, who coauthored this chapter as our invited expert, shares her expertise on getting the most out of your Twitter account settings.

The information collected from your Twitter Account Settings page is displayed on your Twitter pages, with most of it visible on your Twitter Profile page. (See figures 11.1 and 11.2, which display the top of Susan Joyce's Profile page and Susan Whitcomb's Profile page.)

Figure 11.1: Susan Joyce's Twitter Profile.

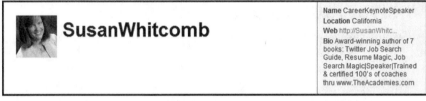

Figure 11.2: Susan Whitcomb's Twitter Profile.

According to social media marketing expert Dan Zarrella, who has done extensive research on Twitter use, 70 percent of Twitter users have no information in their Profiles. The result is fewer followers and also, certainly, fewer opportunities to be found in a search.

Why is an empty Twitter Profile bad for a job seeker? Because:

- Your Twitter Profile provides you with a venue for presenting yourself and controlling, to a certain degree, your image or brand both on Twitter and, very importantly, to the greater online world.

- Recruiters and potential employers do search through sites such as Twitter for possible candidates.

- Search engines index Twitter content, enabling it to be found when recruiters and potential employers use search engines to find candidates for their job openings.

If someone searches on the job title you want, your profession or industry, and/ or your name, as a job seeker, you want a positive view of you to be found. Your Twitter account will be helpful for you even after you've found that next job. This account can become a major long-term asset to your career for these reasons:

- People googling *your keywords* (your job title, profession, industry, common phrases associated with your job, and so on) will find you because your Twitter account will appear in the search results, if you have used those keywords as described in the rest of this chapter.

- People googling *your name* will likely find your Twitter account in the search results if you have used your name as part of your Twitter identity and you have tweeted regularly.

Tip: If you're not sure what Usernames are available, go to Google or Bing and use this query to see what is currently being used:

"[name you are checking]" site:twitter.com

This is not a foolproof method, but it will often tell you whether a name has already been taken on Twitter because a list of the user's tweets will appear, along with the user's Twitter name.

Six Steps to SEO Success with Twitter

"If candidates are on the market, they need to make sure that they are positioning themselves in the best way. Having a clear bio and message that makes it clear what they do, and what kind of job they are looking for, is important.

"It's surprising how many people don't complete the bio sections or use hashtags appropriately. Clarity on the candidate side helps recruiters find potential hires."

—*Jessica Lee, Corporate Recruiter, APCO Worldwide;*
Editor, Fistful of Talent Blog

To implement these steps, you'll need to access the "Account" tab page of your Twitter settings.

If you haven't already created a Twitter account, go to http://twitter.com and click the "Sign up now" button (see figure 11.3).

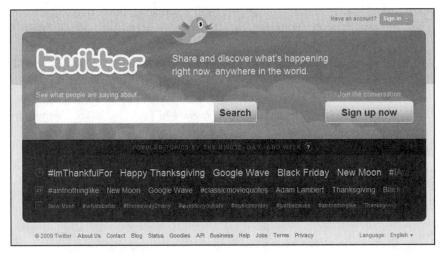

Figure 11.3: Join the conversation.

Next, fill in the boxes for Full name, Password, and Email; however, read the tips in this chapter for selecting your Username before proceeding further with setting up your account (see figure 11.4).

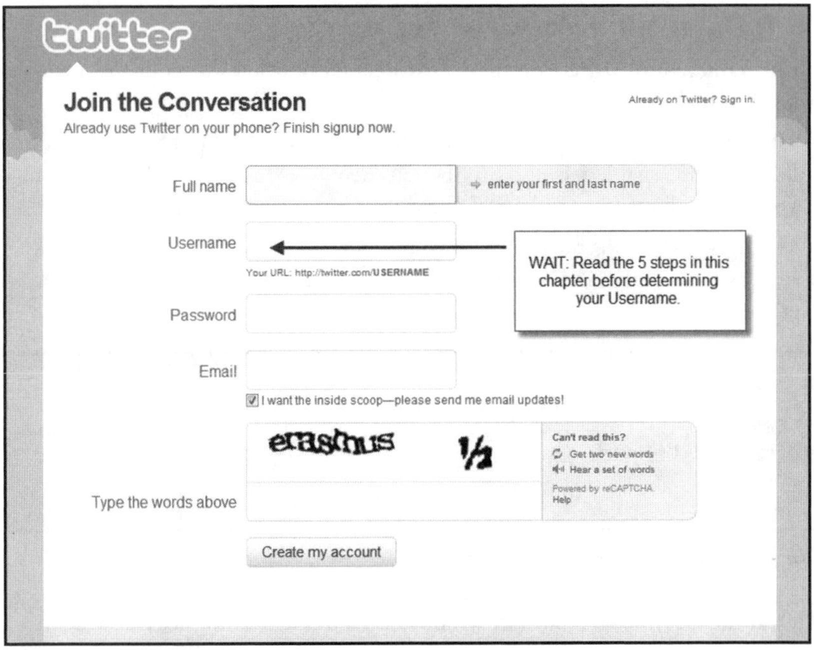

Figure 11.4: Create your account.

If you already have a Twitter account, follow these steps:

- Log in to your Twitter account (http://twitter.com/yourname). Figure 11.5 displays the text-links you will see at the top right of your Twitter page, including Home, Profile, Find People, Settings, Help, and Sign out. Click on Settings.

Figure 11.5 Logging in to your Twitter account settings.

- On the Settings page, click on Account, as shown in figure 11.6. This will take you to the page: http://twitter.com/account/settings.

Figure 11.6 Twitter account settings.

From here, you'll be ready to complete the six steps of choosing your Twitter Username and Twitter Name, listing your Twitter Location and Web address, inserting your Bio, and adding your avatar.

Step 1: Determine Your Twitter Name

Use your name, your profession, and/or other relevant keywords in the Twitter Settings "Name:" field.

The Name field is 20 characters long and will accept spaces and punctuation marks in addition to the usual letters and numbers. When you look at your Twitter home page, you can see how your Twitter Name differs from your Twitter Username.

On Deb Dib's Twitter Profile page, shown in figure 11.7, note how well she connects her Twitter Username ("CEOCoach") with her real name, which is also her Twitter Name.

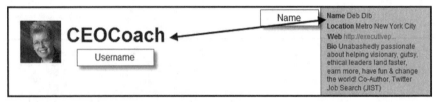

Figure 11.7: Deb Dib name example.

Looking at the very top of a browser window at your Twitter Profile, you will see the strong message Twitter is sending to the search engines: your Twitter Name, followed by your Twitter Username in parentheses, is the HTML page title that the search engines will index (see figure 11.8).

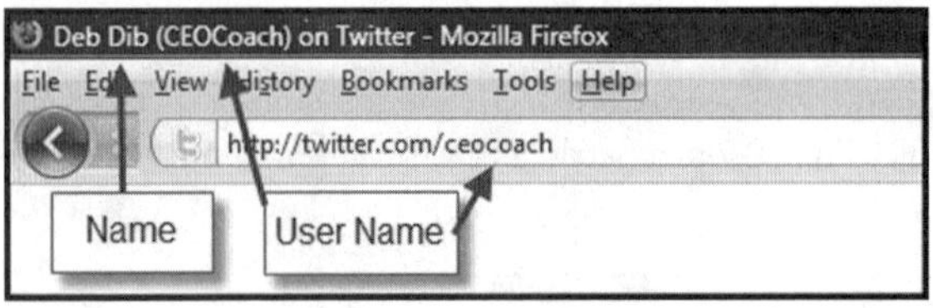

Figure 11.8: Deb Dib search engine page title example.

Your keywords are the words you want to describe you. Keep in mind that, in our example, Deb Dib is building her brand as "CEO Coach." Recall that the preceding chapters on branding helped you think about how to brand yourself and how Twitter can help you do that.

Assuming your name is Mary Jane Smith (guys, work with me here!) and you are a CPA in New York City, here are some options to consider (the Twitter name is listed first and the Twitter Username [@you] follows in parentheses):

- **Mary Jane Smith (@MaryJaneSmith):** name used in both fields, Name and Username

- **Mary Jane Smith (@MJSmithCPA):** name plus name variation with profession

- **Mary Jane Smith (@NYCityCPA):** name plus location with profession
- **Mary Jane Smith CPA (@MJSmithCPA):** name with profession plus name variation with profession repeated
- **New York City CPA (@MaryJSmith):** location and profession plus name
- **New York City CPA (@MJSmithCPA):** location and profession plus name variation with profession repeated

Options you have:

- *If* you've used your real name for your Username (for example, @SusanWhitcomb, @chandlee), the Name field provides you with the opportunity to add some differentiation and marketing. The tagline "New York City CPA" in the last two bulleted examples demonstrates this technique.
- *If* your Username is *not* your name (for example, @JobHuntOrg, @CEOCoach), put your name in this field so that Google and the other search engines as well as Twitter People Search can find your Twitter account if someone uses your name in a search query.

> **Tip:** Twitter allows you to change your Twitter Name at any time, but it's wise to stick to one version of your name for consistent branding and to keep from confusing—and losing—people.

Step 2: Choose Your Twitter Username (@You)

Use your real name, your profession, or your personal brand for your Twitter Username.

Your Twitter Username is your public label in Tweets (for example, @SusanWhitcomb, @chandlee, or @CEOCoach), so focus on maximizing the SEO benefit and the branding of your Username.

Your Twitter Username establishes your Twitter URL, which is sometimes called a vanity URL. When choosing your Username, think long-term and uniquely you. Twitter allots a total of 15 letters and numbers for Usernames. Spaces are not accepted in Usernames, but you can use underscores if necessary (for example, to separate words for clarity).

> **Tip:** Although Twitter allows you to include underscores and numbers in your Username, these characters can make your Username difficult to remember and difficult to spell, so use them with caution.

You have four basic options for your Username:

- **Your name:** Your name is probably the best Username you can have if your profession isn't easily identified in 15 letters or fewer, if you are relatively well known in your field, or if you expect to become relatively well known in your field.

Because she's the published author of seven books, Susan Whitcomb's Username is her real name (@SusanWhitcomb), which should make it easy to find her in a Twitter People Search. (Alternatively, if a search doesn't yield results, try inputting the Twitter Web address, followed by a slash and the person's full name, such as http://twitter.com/SusanWhitcomb.)

- **Your profession:** Your profession may be the best choice for your job search because it loudly broadcasts what you do and provides keywords for the search engines. If you use your profession here, use your real name in the Name field (see Step 1) to help Twitter, Google, and other search engines connect the two.

  Deb Dib's Twitter Username, @CEOCoach, is her profession. These are great keywords for Deb! A CEO looking for a coach will certainly find Deb in a Twitter People search.

- **Your name and your professional designation:** Using both strengthens the connection between the two, particularly when there are inbound links from Web sites outside of Twitter to your Twitter Username. Those links will usually consist of your Twitter Username. Add a relevant and accurate job-related keyword to your Username, such as JohnDoeWriter, JohnDoePMP, JohnDoeRN, or JohnDoeMBA. These name extensions will add a little marketing zing and a place in Twitter People Search results.

  Erin Kennedy is a Certified Professional Resume Writer (CPRW). Her Username is @ErinKennedyCPRW, which is a combination of her first and last names plus her CPRW credential. This makes her status clear and findable in a Twitter People search.

- **Your business name or your blog/Web site name:** If you have a business or blog you want to promote with your Twitter account, you can build brand awareness for it by using its name as your Twitter Username.

  Susan Joyce promotes her job-hunt.org Web site with her tweets, so it's also her Username: @JobHuntOrg.

  By including your name in the "Name" field (see Step 1, previously), you also create some visibility for your name. The disadvantage to using your Web site or blog name as your Twitter Username is that people won't come to identify you as easily with your tweets. This is probably not good long-term personal branding for you as a person, unless you plan never to sell your business.

Finally, when weighing the options for your Username, ask yourself these questions:

- Will it be appropriate for you for at least one year, and hopefully longer?
- Does it include appropriate keywords for you?

- Will it be easy for others to remember and to spell?
- Keeping in mind your 140-character limitation on tweets, is the name so long that it will make it hard for others to manually retweet your great tweets? (Read more about retweets in chapter 15.)

THE PROS AND CONS OF MULTIPLE TWITTER ACCOUNTS

By Katharine Hansen, Ph.D.

The Pros of Multiple Twitter Accounts

- If you have multiple accounts, help potential followers know which account is most relevant to their interests. For example, my personal-account profile says: "Personal tweets here. Story tweets: @AStoriedCareer. Career tweets: @KatCareerGal."
- If you use Facebook for personal socializing and LinkedIn for professional communication, you can choose to synchronize tweets from your personal Twitter account with Facebook by using Facebook's Twitter application. Then you can synchronize your professional tweets to LinkedIn by adjusting your LinkedIn settings and using the hashtag #in.
- From your professional Twitter account, you can tweet things like accomplishments, comments, and retweets that show you are current in your field, and tweet links to your blog entries that demonstrate your thought leadership.
- Having specifically targeted Twitter accounts enables you to focus on the quality of your social-media contacts rather than the quantity.

The Cons of Multiple Twitter Accounts

- Splitting up your Twitter presence does not exempt you from having to watch what you say online. Prospective employers may still have access to your personal tweets, so keep them clean and tasteful.
- The advent of the ability to create specific lists of followers/followees on Twitter may accomplish some of the same advantages as splitting up your Twitter presence.
- Many Twitter client applications aren't set up for managing more than one account, and if you manage your Twitter presence only in a Web browser, you'll have to log off one account before you can log in to another. (See chapter 31 for more on Twitter client applications.)
- Some followers will follow both/all of your accounts, so you'll need to avoid tweeting the same message from multiple accounts.
- Obviously, it's more time-consuming to maintain more than one Twitter account.

(continued)

(continued)

> To illustrate how to differentiate the messages sent from each account, here are examples of tweets from each of my three accounts:
>
> - **@kat_hansen:** Doggy Kaopectate, please work some magic!
>
> - **@KatCareerGal:** Helpful article for discerning whether your cover letter will be read: Cover or Uncovered??? http://ow.ly/zEIS
>
> - **@AStoriedCareer:** Britain names its first storytelling laureate: http://tinyurl.com/ykt5cwh

Step 3: List Your Location

Include where you are living or the location where you want to work.

Location is a *very* important field in your Twitter Settings, particularly for job seekers, because recruiters and employers often search on a job title (or skill) plus location. In the location box, list where you are living or the location where you *want to live* and work.

In her bio, Chandlee Bryan proudly indicates she is in the New York City (NYC) area. If anyone searches through Twitter, Google, or other search engines for people in "New York City" or "NYC," Chandlee will show up.

Step 4: Add Your Twitter Web Address

Use the "More Info URL:" field in your Twitter Settings to connect your Twitter account to one of the following: your LinkedIn Profile, blog, Web site, VisualCV, or other relevant personal Web address.

This will be the *only live, clickable link in your Twitter Profile*, and it will be labeled "Web." The complete URL may not be visible, but it will be clickable.

> **Tip:** Be sure to test your Twitter Web Address link. After saving your changes, go to your Twitter profile page and click on the link to make sure it is live.

Twitter accepts only one URL in this field, so pick the one that shows your most professional face to the online world for your job search. This is where people will go if they want more information about you. Twitter allows you to change this link whenever you need to change it, via the Settings page.

If you don't have a Web site, but you do have other online visibility, use one of those URLs here. Appropriate links include the following:

- www.LinkedIn.com/in/username
- www.VisualCV.com/username
- www.Google.com/profiles/username
- A college alumni resume page or other profile you might have

> **Tip:** If you don't know the exact URL of your LinkedIn, VisualCV, or college alumni profile or resume, go to that Web page. Look at the top of the browser in the long bar that's usually on the same line as the "Back" and "Forward" buttons, and you'll find the URL for the page. Copy and paste that URL into another browser to be sure it's the correct one before you use it.

If you want to share more than one URL (such as LinkedIn, Facebook, and so on) in your Twitter account settings, you may type an additional URL into your Bio. Use the "real" URL, *sans* the http://, not a special shortened version from a URL shortener, unless you are prepared to check it regularly to be sure the shortened link hasn't expired. Because of the 140-character limitation for tweets, people are widely using URL shortener services such as bit.ly and TinyURL to save space in their tweets. But most of those URLs do eventually expire, leaving links that point to dead ends. Bottom line: Don't include a shortened URL in your Twitter "More Info URL" or your Bio if you can avoid it. (For more on URL shorteners, see chapter 31.)

Step 5: Add Your Twitter Bio

Recall the wisdom on writing your 160me bio in chapter 10. In addition, make sure that you weave in keywords relevant to your industry to improve your chances of being found by recruiters.

If you are not conducting a confidential search, it's important to mention in your Bio that you are looking for new opportunities.

> **Tip:** Leaving the Bio space empty is worse than having a blank billboard on a busy highway. It doesn't do you any good, and it could do you some harm. Without some content here, you could look lazy and/or clueless, or like someone who doesn't know what job you want. You may even look like a spammer.

If you haven't done so already, copy and paste those all-important 160 (or fewer) characters that you completed in chapter 10 into the box that says "One Line Bio."

Save your changes at the bottom of the http://twitter.com/account/settings page.

Step 6: Add Your Photo or Avatar

If you want to ensure failure on Twitter, skip this step! Having no picture or avatar on Twitter is the fastest way to look uneducated, disinterested, or even flakey. Forget all the rules you've heard about not showing your photo on resumes and elsewhere in your job search because of fair hiring practices and the like. Those rules do not apply in social media. It's hard to get people to follow you if they can't see what you look like in a photo, or get a sense of who you are through a branded avatar.

> **Need to Know:** In social media, an *avatar* is an electronic image that represents your online persona. An avatar is typically a cartoon, special-effects photo, or other image; however, some people use the term interchangeably to refer to their professional business photo.

To upload your picture or avatar, follow these steps:

- Click on the Picture tab (this tab is under Settings; see figure 11.6).
- Click Browse and select a picture stored on your computer (in the JPG, GIF, or PNG format).
- Click Save.

If you already have a picture on your profile and want to replace it, click Delete Current and then follow the preceding steps.

CREATING A CUSTOM AVATAR

Professional, please! If you're in job search mode, your picture must be professional (or at least project an image consistent with the culture of your target companies). But if you'd like to be creative with your Twitter photo, one of these sites should be able to help:

- **www.BeFunky.com:** Upload your photo and add effects, such as Charcola, Cartoonizer, Inkify, Pop Art, and Oil Painting.
- **www.BigHugeLabs.com:** This site allows you to make customized jigsaw puzzles, mosaics, and magazine covers, among others, from your photograph.
- **www.SouthParkStudios.com:** Create a cartoon avatar, starting with a bald doll in his or her birthday suit. You then choose skin tone, age, facial features, clothing, and accessories.

And if those aren't enough, google "sites for creating social media avatars" and you'll find more!

Although avatars are perfectly acceptable on Twitter, there seems to be a greater sense of connection between followers and followees when each of you can see what the other really looks like.

Other Settings

The Settings tab is also the place to set up a mobile device (such as a BlackBerry, iPhone, or other cell phone) to receive tweets (see the Mobile tab in figure 11.6), as well as set up Notices to receive an e-mail when someone starts following you or sends you a direct message (see the Notices tab in figure 11.6). We recommend receiving e-mails both when you have a new follower and when you receive a direct message. This way, you can respond promptly.

After you have saved your settings, click Profile to see the changes. Review your profile carefully and make any adjustments you might want.

CHAPTER 12

BRANDING YOUR TWITTER ACCOUNT WITH A CUSTOMIZED BACKGROUND

Featured Contributor: Sue Brettell, UK-based personal brand identity designer, of www.id-creativesolutions.com (@SueBrettell)

"A picture is worth a thousand words."

A strong visual identity helps to establish you in people's minds, communicate your personal brand, and show your creativity. It should be applied consistently to all your brand communications: your Web site, blog, bio, resume (for example, in your choice of font or appropriate use of accent colors), and social media strategies, including Twitter.

We asked Sue Brettell, known internationally for her talent in aligning design with personal branding, to coauthor this chapter. She'll guide you through how to customize your Twitter background. (We're also proud to say that she has designed each of our Twitter backgrounds; view them at www.twitter.com/SusanWhitcomb, www.twitter.com/chandlee, and www.twitter.com/CEOcoach.)

Sue shared that one of Twitter's great advantages for promoting your personal brand is the ease with which you can make it your own by using a unique, customized background. It stands head-and-shoulders above other social networking media in this regard.

"Strong personal brands are consistent. At the very least your background and color choices on Twitter should tie up with your branding elsewhere...but you can do so much more.

"A unique Twitter background will

- Communicate who you are at a glance,

- Give you a chance to be creative by telling a visual story about who you are, and

- Enable you to include further information about your contact details or online profiles."

Modifying Twitter's Standard Backgrounds and Colors

Sue shared how easy it is to modify your Twitter background. "The generic blue Twitter background is pleasant enough, but if you want to stand out from the crowd and demonstrate your creativity, the first thing you should do is experiment with changing it. Once you know how to do that, it's a simple step to installing a customized background."

Twitter offers 12 stock backgrounds along with preset colors for the page elements. You can modify the colors of the overall background, text, links, sidebar background, and sidebar border. Sue recommends making a note of the hex values of your brand colors to help you with the settings. Here's how:

Need to Know: In graphic design, a hex (hexadecimal) value is an expression of a color using numbers and letters. For example, black is #000000, navy is #000080, red is #FF0000, purple is #9B30FF, turquoise is #00F5FF, and so on. There are thousands of hex values representing the many subtle shades of color.

1. Select "Settings" from the top navigation bar.
2. Select "Design" from the secondary set of tabs, as seen in figure 12.1.

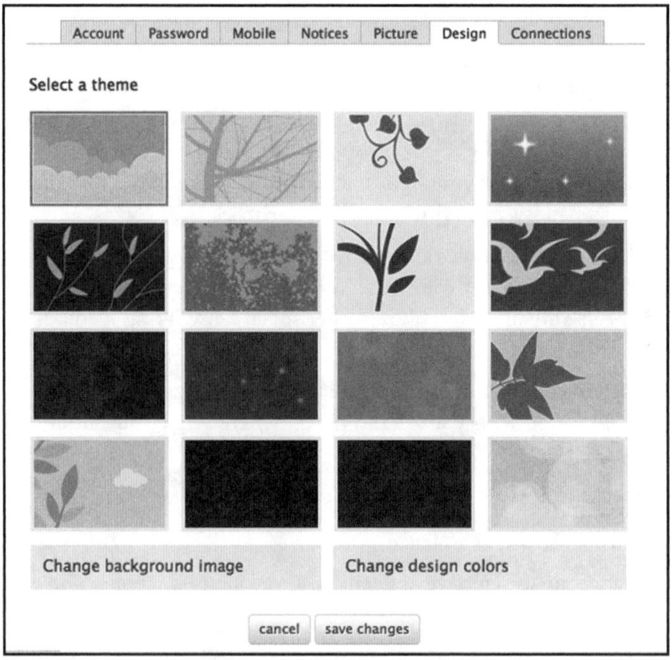

Figure 12.1: Twitter design settings.

3. Click the different designs to preview how they will look. If you like one of them, click "save changes." If you would prefer a plain-colored background, click "Change background image" and then select "Don't use a background image." Remember to click "save changes." This is also where you can upload a custom background, so we will come back to this later.

4. Now click on "Change design colors." A row of boxes showing the current colors will appear at the bottom, as seen in figure 12.2.

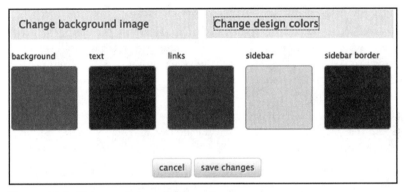

Figure 12.2: How to change design colors.

5. Click on the first color and a color palette will pop up. Select a color by eye, or you can enter the Hex value of a color that conveys your style. If you don't know the Hex value, try to match it up as closely as you can.

6. Repeat this with the other colors to change text, links, sidebar, and sidebar border.

Sue encourages users to experiment. "Nothing will be visible to anyone until you click 'save changes.' And, even if you do save it and then change your mind, you can keep tweaking the design until you're happy with it.

> **Tip:** The color you choose for your text is used everywhere, so bear in mind that if you have a dark sidebar with very light text on it, tweets on the white background will become virtually invisible. Conversely, if you want the text in the sidebar to show up, you will need to keep the sidebar color fairly light or contrasting.

"Ensure your links color stands out from the general text. It can be a complete contrast or a different shade of the text color."

Displaying a Custom Background

Sue explains that uploading and displaying a custom background is extremely simple. To do so, click on "Change background image," browse on your computer to locate the image you want to use, and then upload. Choose whether you want to tile the image (repeat it endlessly) by clicking the check box, and then "save changes."

You have three choices for displaying a background:

1. Find a pattern that will tile (see "Resources," later in this chapter, for links). This is important so that you can't see the joins (the areas where the design comes together and repeats). The original image will be quite small and square. When you select "tile," the pattern repeats endlessly to fit the available page equity, no matter how big the viewer's screen is.

2. Use an image that fades to a solid background color on the bottom and right sides. With this option you will need to choose a plain background color that exactly matches the solid color on the image. This way, it will appear to be part of the overall background. Do not select "tile background" unless your design is intended to repeat.

3. Create a graphic large enough to fill the entire page on large screens. Bear in mind that the file size you can upload is limited to 800K, so there's a limit to the dimensions you can work with.

The third option is the most common choice, but it can take time for the image to load when viewers come to your page, especially on slow Internet connections.

Sue advises that "while the graphic is loading, the background color is visible. This is why it's a good idea to select the right background color, even if you think nobody will see it!" See figure 12.3 for an example.

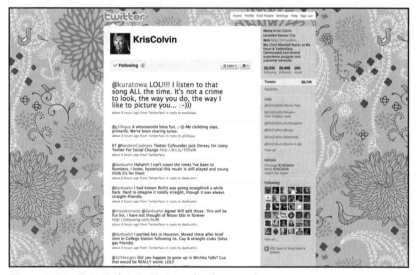

Figure 12.3: Kris Colvin's Twitter background.

Figure 12.3 is a delightful example of a tiled pattern, using quite a large original graphic. The background shown in figure 12.4 uses a single graphic that blends into the background color.

Figure 12.4: Ruben D'oliveira's Twitter background.

The background shown in figure 12.5 is a large graphic that covers the entire visible area.

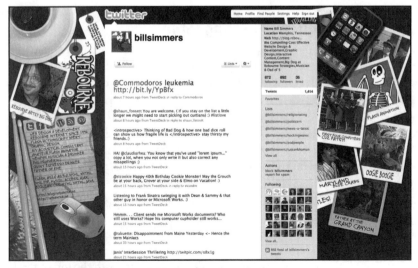

Figure 12.5: Bill Simmers's Twitter background.

A plethora of sites offer free design backgrounds, customizing tools, and other resources. It's a bewildering choice, so Sue has included some recommended resources later in this chapter. Each site offers a huge range of backgrounds, so be prepared to spend some time looking for the perfect one for you.

> **Tip:** Don't be tempted by noisy designs that will fight with your page. Sue recommends choosing something simple and elegant: "Avoid unsuitable designs that make an unfavorable impression."

Creating Your Own Design

If you choose to create your own design, you can include anything you like in it—your logo, photos, URLs, and other links. Bear in mind that a Twitter background is static, so your links won't be clickable. For that reason, make sure you include the full Web address. Avoid shortened URLs because people like to know where a link is going to take them. You can safely include your e-mail address and phone number because they are just part of the graphic and won't be visible to Web robots (also known as crawlers or spiders, the programs that search the Web automatically; search engines use these robots to index Web content, but spammers use them to scan for e-mail addresses).

There are no set rules for Twitter backgrounds; however, you will find a variety of recommendations for spacing. Experiment to see what works for you. Use these dimensions as guidelines: width—1600 pixels; height—1200 pixels.

Designing Around the Floating Page

When it comes to designing a custom background, Sue explains that "the main restriction to consider is the floating page, which obscures everything underneath it. Where it sits on the background depends on the viewer's screen size and/or browser window size.

"Your design should be carefully laid out so that crucial elements are visible to a wide audience, regardless of their screen size. Try altering the size of your browser window so you can observe how it might look to people with smaller screens. If you have a small screen yourself, try to get access to a large screen to see how your background looks.

"The width of the 'sidebar' (the area to the left of the Twitter page) needs to be fairly narrow. For design elements to be visible on the majority of screen sizes, a maximum of 200px is safe, but on small screens this is a mere 120px and on large screens 245px. Allow padding of about 20px from left so your design doesn't look like it's falling off the page. If you want your design to line up with the top of the Twitter logo, allow 10px padding from the top edge. To line up with the top of the white page, allow 63px padding. If you have a long name or logo, you could turn it on its side, placed to the left of the page to ensure it's always visible."

The background in figure 12.6 is of coauthor Deb's Twitter page, one of Sue's designs. It shows how it looks on a wide screen, as with all the other preceding examples.

Figure 12.6: Twitter background of CEOCoach on a wide screen.

Graphics on the Right Side

If your headshot is angled to the left, it will look odd on the left side of the page facing outwards. This is just one of the reasons you may want to add graphics to the right side of your background. Where you place the graphics is a matter of choice. If you want the majority of viewers to see it, create your design for a 1280×720 screen. The center Twitter post page is 765px wide. Figure 12.13 is coauthor Susan's Twitter page, with the design set up for a 1280px-wide screen.

A shout out goes to Web designer Beth Cole of www.thewebservant.com and graphic designer Janelle Reed for the original artwork on the banner at www.susanwhitcomb.com, which Sue worked into the Twitter background. As with Deb's Twitter page and her Web site, this is another example of how your online brand should be consistent across platforms.

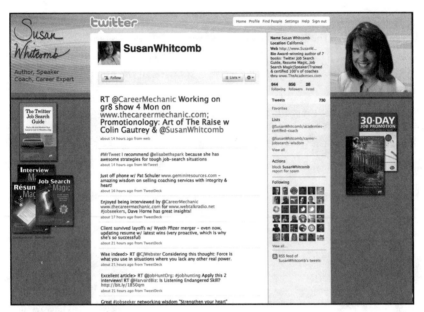

Figure 12.7: Twitter background of Susan Whitcomb, 1280px.

Depth of Graphic

Sue explained that even when a person has a large screen, there may be several toolbars on the browser window that reduce the depth of visible page. She advises, "Keep the important elements of your design above the 600px mark to be on the safe side. You can extend noncritical design elements further down if you wish, to be enjoyed by visitors with large screens."

> **Tip:** When creating your own design, be careful that you don't use images or fonts that are restricted. It is illegal to download images from Web sites without authorization and use them in your designs without permission.

Please note that all information is correct at time of writing, but may become dated as Twitter evolves. For current advice, especially if the Twitter interface has subsequently been modified, please consult some of the expert sites listed in the "Resources" section.

Tailor-Made Designs

The optimal strategy is to hire a designer to create a custom background for you. A designer will incorporate your own images and ideas to create something truly unique. Many charge very reasonable fees for this service, so it's well worth considering. The primary advantages? It saves time (a precious commodity in job search, so you can be out networking) and the end product will be impressive (you need every job search advantage possible with prospective employers).

One of the best ways to find custom designers is to notice whose Twitter backgrounds you like. The designer's name will often be listed somewhere on the background, just as artists include their signatures on paintings. If you already have a favorite Web site designer or graphic artist, engage him or her for your Twitter background. And, if all else fails, use your favorite search engine to search for "Web designers."

Resources

The following resources allow you to download free images and fonts, or purchase them very reasonably. Sue adds, "Always check the terms of use to avoid copyright infringements."

Backgrounds: Tutorials, Tools, Ready-Made, and Tailor-Made

- **DesignReviver:** http://designreviver.com/tutorials/13-tutorials-resources-for-a-perfect-twitter-background
- **Blog.SpoonGraphics:** www.blog.spoongraphics.co.uk/tutorials/twitter-background-design-how-to-and-best-practices—some excellent examples and a detailed tutorial
- **Search for Blogging:** www.searchforblogging.com/microblogging/how-to-create-a-custom-twitter-background.html
- **The Closet Entrepreneur:** http://theclosetentrepreneur.com/create-a-twitter-background-using-powerpoint—create a Twitter background using PowerPoint; downloadable template and instructions
- **twitip:** www.twitip.com/custom-twitter-backgrounds
- **Free Twitter Designer:** www.freetwitterdesigner.com—provides an easy-to-use image editor
- **My Tweet Space:** www.mytweetspace.com—free backgrounds with a tool for creating your own
- **TweetStyle:** http://tweetstyle.com
- **TwitterBackgrounds:** www.twitterbackgrounds.com
- **twitbacks:** www.twitbacks.com

Inspiration

- **Twitter Backgrounds Gallery:** http://twitterbackgroundsgallery.com/2009/03/07/branding-yourself-with-a-twitter-background—a fantastic showcase of Twitter backgrounds for inspiration
- **Twitter Gallery:** http://twitter-gallery.com
- **Smashing Magazine:** www.smashingmagazine.com/2009/09/18/effective-twitter-backgrounds-examples-and-best-practices
- **DesignReviver:** http://designreviver.com/inspiration/25-of-the-best-designed-twitter-homepages
- **Mashable:** http://mashable.com/2009/05/23/twitter-backgrounds—examples and tutorials

Apps

- **peekr:** http://peekr.net—a nifty widget that allows you to see people's Twitter background graphics with one click
- **ClickableNow:** www.clickablenow.com—offers a way to add clickable links to your Twitter background; it's free but it works only for other Tweeters who have installed the add-on to their browser

Useful Design Elements

- **Best Design Options:** http://bestdesignoptions.com/?p=1576—1000+ background patterns you can use for free
- **Twitter Gallery:** http://twittergallery.com/?p=877—40+ follow-me buttons
- **iStock:** www.istockphoto.com—a fantastic resource for reasonably priced photos, vector graphics, and patterns
- **MyFonts:** www.myfonts.com—a huge selection of fonts
- **dafont.com:** www.dafont.com—free fonts; check whether the ones you choose are restricted to personal use

These resources are just a selection. You can find many more excellent sites online with a Google search for "custom Twitter background."

CHAPTER 13

THE ART OF FOLLOWING AND BEING FOLLOWED

"The way of the world is meeting people through other people."

—*Robert Kerrigan*

Twitter is a community in which tweets are posted and read by "followees" and "followers."

If you're using Twitter to actively build your brand, post thought leadership, raise your visibility, and be considered as a potential candidate for posted and hidden opportunities, you need a network of followers. Period. When you post a tweet, your tweet will be carried in Twitter's ongoing stream of live tweets and will also be sent to all of your followers' streams. Twitter is a conduit that connects people, information, and opportunities. To make that happen, you need to actively attract a stream of followers.

"Tweeting" on Twitter without followers reminds us of the classic question: If a tree falls in the forest and there's no one there to hear it, does it really make a sound?

Let's get ready to make some noise!

> **Need to Know:** We went to Twitter's FAQ portal to help us explain the concept of *followers*. Here is what we read, quoted directly from the source:
>
> **What does it mean to follow someone on Twitter?** Following someone simply means receiving their Twitter updates. When you follow someone, every time they post a new message, it will appear on your Twitter home page…in real time. When you log in, you can see what the latest updates are.
>
> **How do I know who I'm following?** After you click the follow button on someone's profile, you're following them…. See a list of people you're following by clicking on the following link on your profile or your home page's sidebar.

> **How do I know who is following me?** Twitter sends you an e-mail when some-one new follows you. Set up your e-mail preferences to notify you when you have a new follower. The followers link on your profile page or home page's sidebar will also tell you how many followers you have.

Creating Connections, One Follower at a Time

We believe that following people on Twitter is an art that requires some diligence and finesse. Sure, you can use automated systems and follow hoards of people in the hopes that many will follow you back. But we don't recommend following people just to build a big list, unless that is part of your job search plan.

The idea of Twitter is to create useful connections. Infusing selectivity into your following process allows you to keep the people you follow within the spectrum of your interests and area of influence, with a smattering of serendipity, for fun.

Choosing Who to Follow

"Strangers are just friends who haven't yet met!"

—*Peter Rosen*

Quality over quantity is your beginning point. Once you're comfortable on Twitter and have created the core group of people you are following, you can expand your horizons if you wish. The bonus? People often follow people who follow them, so if you are following someone you'd like to know, he or she just might follow you back. You now have a potential connection.

When choosing who to follow, consider three scenarios:

- You visit a profile of someone who looks like a potential person to follow. You see she has a brief bio (or perhaps no bio), she has five tweets (done in the past three months), she follows 3,200 people, and 3,100 people are following her. Hint: There is a great deal of auto-following happening here. Why else would that many people be following a "five-tweet wonder"?

- You visit another potentially interesting person. Her profile is fascinating, she has written 25 tweets this week and they are a well-rounded mix of profes-sional and personal information of interest to you, she follows 750 people, and 642 people are following her. Hint: This person is a solidly professional tweeter with "real" followers and good information.

- You visit a third profile of someone you may want to follow. He has an interesting bio, has written only 10 tweets this week (in fact, they are the only tweets he has written), is following 42 people, and is being followed by 18 people. Hint: This tweeter is obviously new to Twitter and is already contrib-uting decent content. He's probably someone to follow.

Whom do you choose to follow? If you are wise, the answer will be tweeters number two and three. (See section 6 for more advice on using lists and searches to determine who to follow.)

> **Tip:** If you're just getting started with Twitter, we recommend tweeting 20 or so tweets before following a number of people. You'll want potential followers to see that you have relevant content, which will encourage them to follow you back.

Attracting Followers

"A good friend is a connection to life—a tie to the past, a road to the future, the key to sanity in a totally insane world."

—*Lois Wyse*

Consider again the "tree falling in the forest." You need followers to be heard, to make reciprocal connections, and to build a synchronous network. Consider, as well, the myriad reasons people follow people on Twitter. They want information, connection, a platform, visibility, job candidates, customers, influence, job leads, and more.

You'll want to make your tweets meet as many of those needs as possible, within the confines of what you think your target audience wants. And yes, if you are in a job search, you have a target audience! That audience includes executives, recruiters, employees, influencers, leaders in your field—anyone who can help you get direct or indirect access to opportunities.

And remember, as in all networking, being on Twitter is a "give-to-get gig." Generosity is the place you begin.

> **Need to Know:** MyTweeple.com (http://mytweeple.com) offers tools for "informed decision-making" on Twitter. These tools include the ability to export a list of your followers into a spreadsheet format, which allows you to see which of your followers are following you, as well as people you follow who aren't following you back.

The Who, What, When, and Where of Attracting Followers

In this section, we share an array of best practices and tips for four areas (the who, what, when, and where) for attracting Twitter followers.

Who: Your Twitter Persona

"The successful networkers I know, the ones receiving tons of
referrals and feeling truly happy about themselves, continually
put the other person's needs ahead of their own."

—*Bob Burg*

- Have a professional headshot (picture) or an exceptional candid photo for your avatar.
- Make sure you're fully clad and not doing anything illegal in your photo.
- Engage with people. Comment on their tweets. Start a dialogue.
- Be giving, not selfish.
- Be fun, approachable, personable. Do not be boring!
- "Salute" other people by retweeting their interesting tweets. Direct traffic outward as much as you do toward yourself.
- Be friendly and positive (not talking about how you hate your job or are depressed about your job search).

What: Your Tweet Content and Ways to Express It

"Position yourself as a center of influence—the one who knows the movers and
shakers. People will respond to that, and you'll soon become what you project."

—*Bob Burg*

- The cardinal rule: Have great content!
- Be interesting.
- Don't be all work or all play. We recommend an approximate ratio of 75–80 percent professional to 20–25 percent personal.
- Add comments to retweets to make them fresh, branded, and not "spam-ish." (We're assuming you are doing it the old-fashioned way and not using the retweet button. See chapter 15 for more on the art of the retweet.)
- Participate on lists. When people see others following you, they often will as well.
- To acknowledge new followers, use both @replies and direct messages (shown in Twitter as DM or D) when someone follows you (more on Twitter lingo in chapter 14).
- Mention relevant hashtags (more on this in the next chapter). That tells people you understand how to participate in the community dialogue on Twitter.
- Get known for something(s). Decide on a focus and make a greater percentage of tweets about that thing. If you are in a job search, your focus will likely be on your area of ability.

When: When to Tweet, How Often to Tweet, and Ratios

"Communication—the human connection—
is the key to personal and career success."

—Paul J. Meyer

- Have tweets already in your stream before you start following people. People won't follow you if you don't have some body of knowledge.

- Be reasonable with the frequency of your tweets—don't muck up people's streams with so many tweets that you become like a spammer.

- Don't take long breaks from Twitter; people expect consistency. An occasional few days or a week is okay. Months away makes you look like a Twitter dilettante.

- Make sure you express interest in others by following people. If you have many followers compared to the number of people you follow, it might appear as though you'd rather talk about yourself than hear what others have to say.

- Have a decent number/quality of tweets in relation to how long you've been on Twitter. Aim for a minimum of 15 tweets a week to maintain your visibility and "Twitter-cred." Active users often tweet multiple times a day. Caution: Be sure to respect your followers' time—do not flood their Twitter stream with an overabundance of tweets (more than 20 a day).

Where: Tying in Social Media Sites and Offline Activity

"Poverty, I realized, wasn't only a lack of financial resources; it was isolation from
the kind of people that could help you make more of yourself."

—Keith Ferrazzi, Never Eat Alone

- Be active on other social networks, such as LinkedIn.

- Have a link on your 160me bio, whether to LinkedIn or a Google profile, so that people can learn more about you.

- Showcase that you're doing other things, such as talking about professional association meetings, conferences, and so on.

Tip: Is someone following you that you're not crazy about—such as a possible spammer? You can block or unfollow anyone at any time. Go to the person's account (www.twitter.com/unwantedperson) and click Unfollow on the "following" drop-down menu (the menu resembles a wheel with spokes) next to their picture. They're gone!

CHAPTER 14

How to Speak in Tweets: The Language and Style of Twitter

Yada, yada, yada. The iconic phrase made popular in the *Seinfeld* series is what you *don't* want associated with your Twitter account. Equivalent to blah, blah, blah, it speaks of mundane details that are of no importance or consequence. As a job seeker casting out messages to engage an employer, your mantra needs to be "content, content, content."

In this chapter, you'll learn how to write tweets worthy of a second mention (otherwise known as a "retweet"). We'll also share the following:

- The five fundamental Twitter terms you need to know
- Tips and tricks for tweeting persuasively and concisely
- Sources to help generate great content

Twitter Terminology and Shorthand

We can recall our first few days on Twitter. At first, we thought @ and # symbols might be typos. Then we saw them everywhere and taught ourselves what they meant. We've created sidebars of Twitter terminology and Twitter shorthand to save you time and frustration. You can also visit http://help.twitter.com/forums/10711/ entries for helpful tips on getting started.

Five Essential Twitter Terms

These are the most common Twitter terms:

- **Tweet (rhymes with "sweet"):** Status update of 140 characters or fewer. Twitter's only mode of communication. Type tweets directly into the status window on your Twitter home page or log in via a third-party host (see chapter 31 on Twitter APIs).

Note: To delete a tweet, highlight the trashcan icon at the bottom of the message footer. You will then be prompted with an "Are You Sure?" message. Click yes.

- **@reply (at reply):** @replies are used to get the attention of a designated recipient, as well as your Twitter community. An @reply is a public message. Sending a user a message preceded by an @ enables the reader—and other users of Twitter—to view contents of the message. Using an @username within the message is the same as a mention and shows up in the @username tab on your home page in Twitter. (You can also find a tab on the menu that connects to your direct messages as well as a tab that connects to retweets—by others, by you, and your tweets that others have retweeted.)

- **Direct Message (DM):** A private message sent from one Twitter user to another. Type D (space) username in your status window to send another user a Direct Message (you can also use drop-down tools and the menu). Many users use DMs to communicate on the go because you can set your Twitter preferences to receive DMs via text message.

- **Retweet (RT):** The sincerest form of flattery on Twitter. A retweet is essentially a forward of someone else's content with a mention of the original author of the message. For tips on how to retweet, see chapter 15.

- **Hashtag (#):** A # (pound or hash) symbol preceding a word in Twitter is referred to as a hashtag. In effect, it's a virtual filing cabinet that groups tweets into searchable categories. For example, #jobs, #work, #resumes, and #jobangels are all hashtags that, when searched for, will bring up tweets containing those hashtags and related to these subjects. Hashtags can occur anywhere in the tweet.

- **Favorite:** Like a browser bookmark. You can save individual tweets as favorites. To mark a favorite, simply click on the star outline at the right of the Twitter message. Favorites are saved in your Twitter account and you can access them through the Favorites section on the right side of your Twitter menu.

For definitions of hundreds of Twitter terms, see www.twittonary.com.

Twitter Shorthand

Because Twitter limits tweets to 140 characters, many users use shorthand to communicate—much of which is similar to the language that evolved earlier for use in text messaging. Social marketing expert Shannon Yelland (www.seedtheweb.com) compiled a list of 50 shorthand tips and allowed us to share them with you.

1. 1—one, won
2. 2—to, too, two
3. 4—for, four
4. 4U—for you
5. fwd—forward
6. ab or abt—about

7. B—be
8. b/c—because
9. b4—before
10. bgd—background
11. BR—best regards
12. BTW—by the way
13. cld—could
14. clk—click
15. deets—details
16. EM/eml—e-mail
17. EMA—e-mail address
18. F2F—face to face
19. fab—fabulous
20. fav/fave—favorite
21. fwd—forward
22. FYI—for your information
23. GR8—great
24. IMHO—in my humble opinion
25. JSYK—just so you know
26. LMK—let me know
27. LOL—laughing out loud
28. mil—million
29. OH—overheard

30. OMG—oh my god/gosh
31. plz—please
32. ppl—people
33. preso—presentation
34. props—proper respect
35. R—are
36. ROFL—rolling on the floor laughing
37. RU?—are you?
38. shld—should
39. thx/tx—thanks
40. TIA—thanks in advance
41. TYT—take your time
42. U—you
43. ur—your
44. V2V—voice to voice
45. w or w/—with
46. w/e—weekend
47. w00t!—an expression of joy/ excitement
48. wld—would
49. yr—your
50. YW—you're welcome

See Shannon Yelland's complete list at http://seedtheweb.com/2008/10/my-twittonary-every-twitter-term-and-tool-i-can-find/.

As fun as Twitter shorthand may seem, you also want to avoid the appearance of being shallow. Delivering meaty and meaningful content will keep your followers hungry for more. The next section shows you how.

TWEETS MAKE YOU REAL

The key to great tweets is delivering tantalizing, powerful content in an engaging manner that makes people—whether industry contacts, potential employers, or hiring managers—want to know you better. Employers like to hire people they know and trust, and Twitter can help that happen. Twitter does for the job search candidate what a nose did for the Velveteen Rabbit: It makes you real.

When you apply online through a job board announcement or company database, employers see you only on paper. Unless you have a connection at the company to which you apply, you're a number—a lifeless application in a pool of applicants. You're flat, and your voice isn't heard. Twitter changes that. With Twitter, people can "hear" your voice.

On the N.O.S.E.: A Four-Point Model for Writing Great Tweets

In keeping with the *Velveteen Rabbit* analogy and the nose that made him real, consider this four-point model for ensuring your tweets are "right on the N.O.S.E.": **N**oteworthy, **O**n-Brand, **S**trategic, **E**ngaging. Let's look at each of these elements in more detail.

Noteworthy

Tweets that are noteworthy are informative, important, and repeatable. Ask yourself, "What do I want my reader to know and remember? Does it pass the 'so what' test? Am I revealing fresh information that people will care about? Does this tweet provide need-to-know, actionable, or relevant content to my target audience? Is it worthy of a retweet?"

Here are a few examples that do *not* qualify as noteworthy:

Just finished breakfast. Love fresh-squeezed oj.

Overslept this morning after late-night speed-dating. Gotta figure out how to explain that one to my boss.

Our examples that follow fit the parameters of informative, important, repeatable, and respectable:

SusanWhitcomb Reading Monster's "Great Recession from Employer Perspective" - 29% report increase in free agent/freelancers http://bit.ly/g1oEL

chandlee Fav. writing tip: "Your language becomes clear and strong not when you can no longer add but when you can no longer take away." Isaac Babel

On-Brand

We mentioned previously that at least 75 percent of your messages posted on Twitter should be professional and on-brand. If you want to attract and retain followers, it's important to tweet about topics that substantiate your brand. If you're off-brand too often, followers won't keep following you. Ask yourself, "Does this tweet substantiate my brand? Does it give my reader positive insights into my personality as a professional?"

Here are some on-brand tweets:

InTheKnowCIO The Convergence of Health Care & Information Technology http://3.ly/n4q

---

ExpatCoachMegan Ask The Expat Career Coach: How Do I Make Sure I get a Fair Relocation Package? http://bit.ly/13bkRe

---

ON-BRAND OR OFF-BASE?

Online identity expert Kirsten Dixson offers these additional insights on staying on-brand:

Beyond demonstrating that you are well-versed in your area of thought leadership by writing about your work and providing insight on industry news, you'll stand out when you express your passions, values, and emotional brand attributes. Share what drives you and makes you an interesting person.

If you were known for your great sense of humor, peppering your tweets with funny items (that would appeal to your target audience) would be on-brand. If one of your top values were family, then it would be on-brand for you to tweet about taking your kids to see *Where the Wild Things Are*. If you were known for being committed to endeavors for the long haul, including endurance sports, then tweeting about your marathon training makes sense.

Have the courage and conviction to be you—even when it won't appeal to everyone. Naturally, you'll want to consider, "Will anyone really care about this?" However, what matters most is that you care. Perhaps you are passionate about your support of a political candidate, your religious views, or your involvement with PETA, and want to tweet about a sensitive or controversial topic. These aren't things that you'd put on your resume or mention in interviews, but they could factor into your job search when you are googled.

Expressing your views could preclude you from getting a job. However, that isn't necessarily a bad thing if you wouldn't be happy working in a culture that didn't align with your beliefs. Be mindful that what you tweet can serve as a filter to help ensure that you are connecting with people and opportunities that are a match for you.

Strategic

Your tweets should strategically position you and move your career or job search forward. Ask yourself, "Is this specific? Does it move my job search agenda forward? Is it salient? Does it showcase my strengths?"

Here are a few less-than-flattering examples of Strategic:

Help! Desperate. Just got laid off. Anyone know of a job?

I just elbowed my competitor out of the way. She's stuck in revolving door. Emergency crew on the way. I'm out of here!

Here are a few positive examples of Strategic:

Just earned my Microsoft Certified Professional (MCP) designation! Long haul, but worth it.

Just registered for the #SXSW conference; great speaker lineup; spaces still available; early-bird ends on the 15th. Hope to see you there.

Engaging

One of Twitter's biggest benefits is its far-reaching ability to create community. Your tweets can help foster those relationships when you ask yourself "Does my material make readers lean forward and want to respond to me or share my message with others? Am I seeing evidence of audience engagement through @responses? Am I being respectful of others in my comments?"

Here are a few less-than-flattering examples of Engaging:

Why are human resource managers so nonresponsive? I've sent out 100s of resumes and haven't gotten one response!

I'm thrilled to have 5,000 new followers on the basis of my new automated bot! You should try it 2!

Here are a few positive examples of Engaging:

Flying from CA to NYC/Manhattan Wed for plastics trade show. Anyone interested in lunch?

Excited about interviewing w/ So Cal Edison tomorrow. Have done my research on co & position. DM me if U have insights on corp culture.

SINGLE-STREAM OR MULTICHANNEL CONTENT?

Some Twitter users choose to have only one content category that they write about. We like to call this a single-stream strategy, where tweets are one-dimensional and focus on a single topic, such as trends in green construction or insurance reform. The disadvantage to this strategy is that employers won't get a feel for your personality.

A multichannel approach—preferred for a job search—means that you blend content, such as news, subject-matter expertise, inspirational quotes, point-of-view comments, and conversational dialogue.

Sources to Create Great Content

If you're in active job search, searching for company and industry news and trends will be one of your priorities. There are several sources you can mine for your Twitter content:

- Sign up for news alerts at www.google.com/alerts to receive e-mail updates of the latest news relevant to your profession.

- Read your target companies' own Twitter streams, Facebook fan pages, or other social media sites to get ideas or material to retweet.

- Subscribe to blogs you find interesting. Save the best to tweet about.

- Reference professional journals online. Visit professional association sites. Talk about your area of expertise.

- Pose a point of view and ask for an opinion.

- Jump into an ongoing Twitter discussion that supports your brand.

- Retweet content that you find compelling.

- Reference your own blog posts.

- Track interesting information from online sources other than blogs.

- Use a search engine to find discussions relevant to your area of interest and job search targets.

- Look at trending topics on Twitter and get involved in those. Get involved in a hot topic related to your brand.

- Review sites with inspirational quotes or insights.

- Choose an article of news interest or trending hashtag topics.

- Drop tips that showcase your hobbies and personal interests—from the husband that insists on attending Blondie concerts in the rain to your secret recipe for Key lime cupcakes.

FINDING RELEVANT BLOGS

To find relevant blogs for tweet content:

- Google "blogs + industry name" or use Google's blog search feature at http://blogsearch.google.com/.

- Ask your friends, colleagues, and Twitter followers what blogs they recommend. (Before tweeting about a blog post, scan your Twitter stream to see whether your followers have already tweeted about it so that your tweet doesn't appear redundant. Or try to be the first to tweet it.)

- Pay attention to tweets that reference blogs of interest to you.

CHAPTER 15

THE ART AND SCIENCE OF THE RETWEET

"Imitation is the sincerest form of flattery."

—*C.C. Colton*

If imitation is the sincerest form of flattery, then retweets are the highest form of praise you can find on Twitter. A retweet provides your virtual stamp of recognition: It says "I think this tweet is important and I recommend that people read it." A retweet of someone else's tweet shows that you are engaged and interested in the subject matter.

When exploring ways to actively use Twitter, the importance of retweeting is a no-brainer. Retweeting showcases your willingness to share the ideas of others, allows you to quickly distribute news or items of interest that engage you, and lets you to do so in 90 seconds or less.

> **Need to Know**: Executing a *retweet* (or RT for short) using Twitter's retweet button is similar to—and as simple as—forwarding a favorite e-mail along to your primary list of contacts.

The Incredible, Flexible Retweet

Since Twitter's launch in 2006, the retweet has been a popular favorite of users—a simple RT in the status update box followed by an @username alerted users to the original source of content and shared tweets worth a second (or hundredth look). In fall 2009, Twitter officially recognized the RT's popularity by adding new functionalities, including the ability to RT with a click of a button and customizable options that let users decide whose retweets they wanted to see in their own Twitter streams.

We are big fans of the retweet, and we applaud Twitter for recognizing the importance of the retweet by giving users these new functionalities. But we also think that the traditional retweet can be an incredibly powerful tool for your job search. In this chapter, we'll show you how mastering the art and science of the retweet can propel your job search forward. Along the way, we'll share with you tips and tricks you can use to retweet efficiently with maximum "bang" for time spent.

Revisiting the RT: Why Traditional RTs Work

"Everything old is new again."

—*Aldous Huxley*

Before the retweet button, users had to compose their own retweets—including introductory content if necessary. This legwork was time intensive, but also offered senders the ability to comment on the retweet itself: You could give a thumbs up to a message's content by starting a retweet with a "Yes!" or other words of approval— or you could disagree or condense the message.

The new retweet button doesn't allow you to do this—it simply forwards the message. It's a timesaver, for sure, and many people like it for that. However, many people complain that it eliminates the sender's input, and with it the ability to share brand-building opinions of the original tweet.

Here's what we mean. Here's a retweet sent using the automated retweet feature button:

Chandlee RT @SusanWhitcomb Will your cover letter content help nail you the interview? Tips here: http://bitly.com/45huxlk

---

Now here's a retweet sent the old-fashioned way:

Chandlee RT @susanwhitcomb shares 10 tips on cover letters [#7-write to the job-is a must-do]: http://bitly.com/45huxlk

---

Do you see any differences? From our perspective, the traditional retweet trumps the new approach: It shows that Chandlee has read Susan's work, likes it, and gives readers a specific tip to engage them further—essential since Chandlee and Susan have many mutual friends who don't need to read the same post twice.

We're happy to report that you can still retweet using the traditional method. Let's look at the how-to's of both methods.

Retweet Basics

Retweeting is simple. As this book went to press, Twitter rolled out a new retweet button, which makes the process nearly automatic.

Here's the new RT process:

- Log in to your home page and view the tweets in your stream.
- Use your mouse to hover over the tweet you want to share, and click on the word Retweet.
- Click "Yes" when the pop-up box appears asking, "Retweet to your followers?"

Here's the traditional Twitter RT method (use this if you'd like to add a comment to your retweet):

- Log in to your home page. Scroll through the tweets in your stream and select a tweet worthy of retweeting. (If you're working from a desktop client, such as TweetDeck or HootSuite, the process will differ a bit.)
- Copy the tweet, including the user's Twitter handle.
- Paste the tweet into the "What's happening?" box at the top of the Twitter. com home page.
- Delete the three or four spaces between the original Twitter user's @handle and the start of the tweet.
- Add RT followed by one space and then the @ sign immediately in front of the user's name on the original tweet. (Don't start the tweet with the @ sign; this will signal people that you're speaking to only one person.)
- If you have a short comment about the tweet, add it in front of the RT, followed by a colon or greater-than sign.
- If a tweet has multiple retweets and there aren't enough characters to easily retweet it all, you can eliminate one of the retweet names (don't delete the original tweeter and the person whom you saw the tweet from), or you can edit the tweet slightly (just don't alter the original intent of the tweet).
- Click "update." That's it!

Tip: You can also shorten tweets for retweeting with Twitter shorthand, substituting "4" for "for" and "U" for "you." If you're removing spaces in the tweet to make room, be sure that @ characters, hashtags (#), and URLs don't touch or they won't be clickable.

THE ART OF THE RETWEET

By Jacqui Barrett-Poindexter (@ValueIntoWords)

Acknowledging people, it seems to me, is the pulse of Twitter. For without acknowledgment, do we really even exist? Retweeting is a vital tool we all can use to recognize our Twitter-mates who add value to our stream, or who we simply like and wish to lift.

I don't propose retweeting at random—without reading what you're retweeting and/or retweeting information that you find no value in or with which you may not agree. However, I do propose stepping out of self-imposed rigid rules of only retweeting what specifically maps to your individual sales pitch or marketing strategy—or even your brand, for that matter.

(continued)

(continued)

Follow intuition and instincts and what sparks an emotional, intellectual, or spiritual reaction. If someone tweets something interesting that you are hesitant to retweet because it may make you feel vulnerable or out of your comfort zone, I encourage you to go ahead and share (as long as retweeting it will not harm your personal or professional reputation or offend others).

If the tweet evoked a positive feeling or a feeling of "a-ha" or somehow left you thinking differently than you thought before (sometimes the feeling may even be one of discomfort), then likely retweeting it will spark a similar feeling and provide similar value to a follower. Twitter is not just about reinforcing others' thoughts and opinions; it also is about personally growing, expanding, and changing, as well as helping others do the same.

Twitter has brought back into vogue small neighborhoods of over-the-fence, honest conversation and chit-chat. As such, acknowledging one another extends beyond the retweet into active engagement and honest, real-time talk.

Be giving, be kind, be gracious, be them-focused. Help perpetuate a friendly, safe, and thought-provoking atmosphere through the respectful art of the retweet.

Tip: Twitter's help section goes into great detail about the many intricacies of retweets, so check out this link for more information: http://help.twitter.com/forums/10711/entries/77606.

The Art and Science of Getting Your Tweets Retweeted

Retweeting is simply good manners, and good manners still count, especially in the realm of social media and job search. Yet retweeting is more than good manners; attracting retweets is part art, part science, and, in our opinion, wholly necessary for a robust Twitter presence.

Social media/viral marketing scientist Dan Zarrella (http://danzarrella.com) spent nine months analyzing roughly five million tweets and 40 million retweets. The results of his research were shared in *Fast Company* magazine and in a guest post he wrote for Mashable (http://tinyurl.com/mashable-twitter-RTs). Let's start with the science, based in part on Zarrella's research:

- **Incorporate links into your tweets—after shortening them with a URL shortener** (such as bit.ly or TinyURL). Tweets with links are three times more likely to be retweeted than tweets without links (57 percent versus 19 percent).

Recommended URL Shorteners: Use Bit.ly (http://bitly.com) to shorten links you'd like to track, and TinyURL (http://tinyurl.com) to condense URLs you want to remain fresh forever. Bit.ly links expire over time but allow you to track your click yield (how many times people have clicked on your bit.ly link). TinyURL doesn't have metrics but lasts forever.

- **Make it novel—the ideas and information should be fresh.** Don't be afraid to express an idea or a different perspective—it can help you get retweeted!

- **Ask for what you want and say please!** When you tweet, consider using one of the following phrases: "Please retweet," "Please RT," or "Please share." Zarrella's research found that "please" and "retweet" were the third and fourth most common words in retweets and precipitated a higher percentage of retweets.

- **Sound intelligent and use punctuation.** Zarrella found that more than 97 percent of retweets contained punctuation. Don't be afraid to use commas, semicolons, question marks, and exclamation points! Sacrificing a bit of your character count to increase readability is good strategy.

- **Retweet when people are on Twitter.** Zarrella found that retweets are highest between approximately 2:30 and 9:30 p.m., peaking between 3:30 and 6:30 p.m. (Eastern Standard Time). Mondays and Fridays are two popular days for retweets. For more tips on timing, see the sidebar on timing your tweets in chapter 31.

- **Retweet other people and thank them when they retweet you.** If people know you participate in retweets, they'll be much more likely to retweet your work. It is that simple.

Tip: Brian Solis in his PR 2.0 blog wrote: "120 is the new 140. Retweeting is one of the most valuable currencies in the Twitter economy. Leave room in your tweets to make it easier for someone to RT and also add a short reaction or endorsement. The magic number seems to hover around 120 characters." (See http://tinyurl.com/briansolis-toptips for the full article.)

Five Ways to Retweet and Boost Your Job Search

Here are five ways that retweeting can help you in your quest for a job:

1. **Retweet industry news**—it shows that you are in touch with developments in your field. (Recall from the preceding chapter the importance of setting up Google News Alerts on keywords; the feed provides you with potential topics for inclusion.)

2. **Retweet experts in your field.** It will help you get on their radar screen, especially if you send a customized retweet (using the traditional retweet method) that showcases your own expertise and knowledge.

3. **Convey passion for what you do.** A retweet that shows emotion—from "No!" to "Love this!" or "Yes!"—shows active engagement with the subject matter.

4. **Be impeccable with your spelling and grammar.** Resist the urge to let customized retweets fly without a review. Networking contacts and employers care about your ability to pay attention to detail.

5. **If you retweet someone you don't know, say hello.** Make a new friend on Twitter and expand the reach of your network by sending an @reply or a DM to the person who generated the content that you liked.

Imagine the appeal to potential employers when they see you as someone who can extend their reach, promote their brand, and represent the company well in the process. That's what well-positioned, strategically timed retweets can do.

> **Tip:** Remember to retweet information that will be flattering to the original tweeters. Your aim is to make them look good and help them extend their reach.

Thanking People for Retweets

It's appropriate to thank people when they retweet you. Typically, that takes the form of a simple @reply tweet:

@tweeter_who_retweeted_you Tx for RT on my blog post about new #project_management tools.

This works fine, but if the retweet involves a lot of users, the number of reciprocal thank-you tweets can clutter up the retweeter's Twitter stream. A recent blog post by Luca Filigheddu offers some excellent advice about how to thank people for retweets and add value at the same time. Here are the highlights:

- **Retweet:** Check the user's timeline and retweet one of his tweets you think could be interesting for your followers.
- **Post a link to the Twitter user's blog:** If the user who retweeted you is a blogger, post a link on Twitter to a blog post relevant to your followers.
- **Recommend:** Recommend the user to your followers. The best way to do that is through Mr. Tweet (learn more at http://mrtweet.com).

Read the entire blog post here: http://tinyurl.com/lucafiligheddu-com-thank-RTs.

Tip: One longstanding method of thanks is Follow Friday (using the #FF hashtag). On Fridays, it is customary (although not required) to tweet usernames of followers you want to share with others. #FF is a good way to create community and widen your circle of contacts by following people recommended by others. It's also a great way to formally recognize respected followers.

Great (and Not So Great) Retweets

Finally, here is a series of retweet examples that capture the essence of community and collaboration. Note that this first example uses "via" rather than "RT" as another form of retweeting.

lydiafernandes Personal Branding: Manage Your Online Brand | WomenWorking.com: http://bit.ly/35gQxO via @addthis by @williamarruda RT @reachbranding

Stylejob RT @TwitJobSearch Horror (and funny) job search stories, Part V from @Keppie_Careers http://bit.ly/4BtoRH

danonofrio RT @RobynGreenspan Be nice to people before you know who they are.

chrisrussell RT @SelenaDehne: Green Jobs That Make $30 an Hour: http://tinyurl.com/yf9gq5c #jobadvice

And here are some examples of what a not-so-brilliant retweet might look like (although inspired by real tweets, these samples are fictitious and edited for PG-13):

RT @cluelessjobseeker - recruiter won't call me back. I've left 6 messages today. Starting to feel like he's avoiding me. Idiot.

RT @cheapjobseeker - Found a cheap resource for resumes - got mine done at www.badresumes.com for only $14.95. Only a couple of typos.

RT @frustratedjobseeker - job search sucks. Can't someone just give me a straight answer. I'm never gonna get outta this place.

RT @britelite - xxxx I hate my job. They take this mess way too serious.

Take a minute to review the tweets of potential employers, networking contacts, or recruiters you're following and identify two or three tweets you'd like to retweet. It will make their day!

CHAPTER 16

TWEETER BEWARE: STAYING OUT OF LEGAL HOT WATER

*"Twitter fans, listen up: Your 'tweets' could land you
or your employer in legal hot water."*

— Tresa Baldas, staff reporter, the National Law Journal *(law.com)*

The use of Twitter and other social media platforms opens a legal Pandora's box for employers, employees, and the general job-seeking public. Questions such as the following arise:

- Can a company sue for slander if you send out a negative tweet about its products or services?
- Can an HR director lose her job for recommending an employee on LinkedIn?
- Can you lose a job offer or your current job if you tweet about it?

The answer to all of these questions is a resounding *yes!*

We know you don't want to lose a job offer or put your current job in jeopardy because of a "tweet gone bad." This chapter will provide you with best practices for keeping yourself—and your reputation—safe from harm through the eyes of an employer.

A New Challenge for the Courts

Social media presents many new wrinkles for the courts to consider—from privacy to self-disclosure. A November 2009 feature story on CNN asks the question, "Can the law keep up with technology?" Legal experts say it's not easy because it's difficult to predict technological innovations—and how the public will react to and use new services. Andrea Matwyshyn, a professor at the University of Pennsylvania's Wharton School of Business, researches issues at the intersection of law and technology and says that the law is generally "at least five years behind technology as it is developing."

As more users flock to Twitter, courts are rapidly reviewing cases of tweets interpreted badly. Celebrity rocker Courtney Love is one of several Twitter users to face legal action in response to her tweets. Others have stayed out of court but have also suffered setbacks due to "tweeting too much" about job offers, confidential issues, or clients.

TO TWEET OR NOT TO TWEET: HOW A TWEET CAN GET YOU OUT OF JAIL—OR INTO IT

In April 2008, University of California–Berkeley student James Buck was detained by Egyptian police after covering an anti-government rally. On his way to the station, he alerted others to his situation with a one-word tweet: "Arrested." The message alerted his friends and network. Within 24 hours, his school had hired an attorney and Buck alerted others to his release with another concise tweet: "Free."

By fall 2009—a year and a half after Buck's arrest—Twitter had become so common that "not tweeting" led to another arrest: Record-company executive James Roppo was arrested after refusing to send out a tweet announcing that teen idol Justin Bieber would not be signing albums at a planned mall appearance in Garden City, New York. The mall had turned into a mob, crowded with thousands of teenage girls, and police felt that sending out a simple status of a "no-show" could help alleviate the situation. When Roppo didn't tweet this, police arrested him on charges of criminal nuisance, endangering the welfare of a minor, and obstructing government administration.

Roppo's case may present the courts with a new issue: the first-ever case of an arrest for not using Twitter.

Your Tweets Are Showing

Unless you protect your tweets, use a pseudonym, and choose not to follow anyone (which essentially defeats the purpose of Twitter, eh?), your tweets are public and will be found in search results of major search engines, including Google, Yahoo!, and Bing.

> *"The most common mistake I see job seekers make on Twitter is not realizing how public Twitter is. Many people tweet about things that would turn employers off. These days, tweets appear in search engines.... So everything you tweet can really tarnish your personal brand."*
>
> —*Dan Schawbel, Author,* Me 2.0

Search engines, retweets (RTs), and your tweet stream will create a digital footprint of your Twitter activity. Because information you write now may be separated later from the situation in which you wrote it, your remarks may be taken out of context. On occasion, you may find yourself saying "that's not what I meant!"

Tip: Chapter 26, which describes tweeting with discretionary authenticity, shares tips on how to compose tweets that allow you to be genuine but professionally polished so that you can keep your search results clean.

From Digital Dirt to Legal Hurt: How to Protect Yourself

Most of us aren't lucky enough to have in-house counsel or a PR team monitoring our online presence, yet it needs to be done. Ignoring it is an option, of course, but as "CEO of Company YOU," you need to manage (and protect) your company's reputation.

Recall from chapter 6 that digital dirt is anything online that can negatively impact your career. Here are three strategies you can use to protect yourself online:

- If you find that a tweet you've written or one that has been written about you isn't true, delete the tweet or request it be deleted.
- Clean up any digital dirt using the strategies in chapter 6.
- Avoid the situation in the first place by reviewing and following best practices for communicating status updates through social media (see the recommendations later in this chapter).
- Follow experts on Twitter who keep up with legal matters. Here are three we can recommend—all of whom spoke on the topic of Twitter and the law at Jeff Pulver's 140 Characters Conference in Los Angeles in October 2009:
  - **Adrian T. Dayton (@adriandayton):** Father, husband, lawyer, published author of *Social Media for Lawyers*, CEO—turning associates into rainmakers with Twitter, blogs, and online strategy.
  - **Brett Trout (@BrettTrout):** Patent lawyer, author of *Cyber Law*, Internet law nerdherder.
  - **Glenn Manishin (@GlennM):** Web pioneer, tech lawyer, double-diamond skier, social media devotee, F1 aficionado, photography buff, bonsai master, iPhone fan. Also tweet as @lexdigerati.

Tip: Twitter gives you the option to delete your own status updates—and deletions won't show up in your stream. You can't delete what others say, but you can ask friends and your Twitter community to remove comments that are inappropriate or misrepresent you. Note that there's a small chance that content you try to remove will be indexed by search engines in the interim; however, it is still good practice to manage your digital footprint as much as possible.

Who Owns Your Tweets?

Under the terms of service, Twitter provides you with ownership of your content but also specifies it has the right to redistribute it in any way it sees fit—in any media that exists or may exist in the future—forever.

The right of people to reproduce your tweets outside of Twitter without permission is—at the time this book went to press—a sticky issue. If you want to specify how others can view and redistribute your tweets, you can state your preferences on Creative Commons (www.creativecommons.org), a nonprofit corporation dedicated to making it easier for people to share and build upon the work of others, consistent with the rules of copyright. The Twitter site for Creative Commons is www. tweetcc.com.

Kodak's Pioneering Social Media Guidelines

As a corporate sponsor of social media conferences, Kodak has made a concerted effort to participate in social media to "strengthen [its corporate] brand, and [its] connection with customers and key influencers." These corporate social media policies were created collaboratively by Kodak's employees from its Marketing, Information Systems, Communications, and Legal departments. Kodak shares these policies in its publicly accessible *Guide to Social Media* (www.kodak.com/go/ followus and click on Social Media Tips), and encourages individuals and businesses to "edit to suit your needs."

Although the guidelines were developed for Kodak employees, they have relevance for job seekers, and all Twitter users in general, and are reprinted here with permission from Kodak. The Kodak company name has been replaced with a generic "[organization]" so as to be relevant to your situation. If you are not currently employed, consider the [organization] as You, Inc. If you are currently employed and your employer has not adopted social media guidelines, encourage it to follow Kodak's advice and "edit to suit your needs."

KODAK'S SOCIAL MEDIA GUIDELINES

1. *Live the [organization's] values.* Always express ideas and opinions in a respectful manner.

   - Make sure your communications are in good taste.

   - Be sensitive about linking to content. Redirecting to another site may imply an endorsement of its content.

   - Do not denigrate or insult others, including competitors.

   In a real-life lesson, a worker in one company made disparaging 'tweets' about a client's headquarters city. Needless to say, some of the client's

(continued)

(continued)

employees followed the individual on Twitter and were offended. Right or wrong, they were upset not just with the individual, but with his company as well.

2. *Be yourself—and be transparent.* The story above illustrates how difficult it is to keep clear lines of demarcation between your personal and professional life in the online world. Even when you are talking as an individual, people may perceive you to be talking on behalf of [your company]. If you blog or discuss photography, printing or other topics related to [your organization's] business, be upfront and explain that you work for [the company]; however, if you aren't an official company spokesperson, add a disclaimer to the effect: "The opinions and positions expressed are my own and don't necessarily reflect those of [organization]."

3. *Protect confidential information and relationships.* Online postings and conversations are not private. Realize that what you post will be around for a long time, and could be shared by others.

   - *Avoid identifying and discussing others—including customers,* suppliers, your friends and co-workers—unless you have their permission.

   - Obtain permission before posting pictures of others, *or before posting copyrighted information.*

   - *Never discuss proprietary [company] information,* including sales data and plans, company finances, strategies, product launch information, unannounced technology or anything considered "confidential."

   To better understand what is—and is not—acceptable in any type of communication, review [your organization's] Conduct Guide.

4. *Speak the truth.* If you are in a discussion that relates to *[your organization]* or its products, don't make unsubstantiated claims about features, performance or pricing. If you need to respond or make a comment on something specific, verify details through *company-published information....* Also, because situations change, make sure references or sources of information are current.

5. *Keep your cool.* One of the aims of social media is to create dialogue, and people won't always agree on an issue. When confronted with a difference of opinion, stay cool. Express your points in a clear, logical way. Don't pick fights, and correct mistakes when needed. Sometimes, it's best to ignore a comment and not give it credibility by acknowledging it with a response.

6. *Stay timely.* Part of the appeal in social media is that the conversation occurs in real time, or close to real time. So, if you are going to participate in an active way, make sure you are willing to take the time to refresh content, respond to questions, regularly update information, and correct information when appropriate.

   Protecting your, and [your organization's], privacy and resources

7. *Be careful with personal information.* This may seem odd, since many sites are created to help promote sharing of personal information. Still, astute

criminals can piece together information you provide on different sites and then use it to impersonate you or someone you know—or even reset your passwords. Similarly, "tweeting" real-time about your travels may confirm you aren't at home—letting someone target your house. So, be careful when sharing information about yourself or others.

8. ***Don't be fooled.*** If you do post personal information on a site like Facebook or Twitter, criminals can use it to send you e-mails that appear to come from a friend or other trusted source—even the site itself. This is called "phishing." The lesson is: Don't click links or attachments unless you trust the source. For example, be wary of e-mails that say there is a problem with your account, then ask you to click on a link and input your username and password. The link may connect to a site that looks exactly like Facebook, Twitter, your bank's Web site, but is really a fake site used to get even more personal information. This ploy can also be used to infect your computer with a virus or keystroke logger.

9. ***Disable dangerous privileges.*** If a site allows others to embed code—like HTML postings, links, and file attachments—on your page or account, criminals can use them to install malicious software on your computer. If possible, disable the ability of others to post HTML comments on your home page.

10. ***Heed security warnings and pop-ups.*** There's a reason your security software provides warnings like

   • "A process is attempting to invoke xyz.exe. Do you wish to allow this?"

   • "The process 'IEXPLORE.EXE' is attempting to modify a document 'X.' Do you wish to allow this?"

   Never allow or say "yes" to such actions, unless you know that they are safe.

A final note from Kodak to its employees:

Social media is growing at an amazing rate—and Kodak is a leader in this area. The ability to engage online with our customers, prospects and industry influencers is an important part of our marketing and our brand strategy. Following these procedures will help ensure we stay on course as a company, and at the same time safeguard your personal privacy.

Legalese and Parting Advice

And, of course, this chapter wouldn't be complete without our own "legalese," so here it is:

Legal disclaimer: This chapter with all the materials and links it presents are for informational purposes only and are not intended to serve as or substitute for individualized legal advice.

Although it's more likely the exception to the rule that you'd find yourself in legal hot water from participating on social media sites such as Twitter, we want you to be safe. So here's our parting advice for covering your assets, gleaned from the collective wisdom of our wisest counselors (our mothers Marlene, Mary Lowndes, Donna, and Emily): "If you can't say anything nice, don't say anything at all."

SECTION 4

JOB SEARCH, TWITTER STYLE

17. Job Search Advice from the Trenches

18. Recruiters Reveal Job Search Secrets

19. Turbocharge Your Resume with Tweets

20. Cover Letters Are Just 10 Tweets

21. Using Twitter to Help Ace the Interview

CHAPTER 17

JOB SEARCH ADVICE FROM THE TRENCHES

*"Insight, I believe, refers to the depth of understanding that
comes by setting experiences, yours and mine, familiar and exotic,
new and old, side by side, learning by letting them speak to one another."*

—*Mary Catherine Bateson*

Now that you've mastered Twitter's essentials, it's time to turn your attention to job search, Twitter style. Recall the PB&J metaphor from chapter 7 and how personal branding, job search, and social media go together. If you've got your personal branding and social media/Twitter strategies in place but don't pair them with solid job search strategies, you'll be missing a key ingredient!

Our job search clients have taught us what works, and what doesn't, especially during tough times. They, and the successful job seekers you met in chapter 5, played by rules dictated in the current economy.

> **Tip:** We realize that the depth and breadth of information in this book may be intimidating or overwhelming. We don't want you stalled in inaction because it all seems like "just too much." For this reason, we've given you an array of simple "jump-start" strategies in this chapter to keep you focused during your search.

Ten New Rules for a New-Economy Search

The following job search rules will help you achieve career success. Make them the foundation of your search, and they'll complement your Twitter strategies. You'll likely recognize a few items based on the work you did in section 2. As you review these 10 rules, rate yourself on a scale of 1 to 10 (10 is highest) on how well you are implementing each rule in your job search.

1. Assess Your Assets, Interests, and Priorities

Start with knowing who you are and figuring out the Master F.I.T.™ (we're assuming you've already done so in chapter 7). Know what strengths you bring to the table, what industries or companies interest you, and what will be a deal-breaker if it's not present in the job (for example, salary, commute, advancement opportunity, health benefits, boss, and so on).

Consider sending a tweet with the question:

"How would you describe me in one word?"

This is a playful way to get feedback on how others view you. Oftentimes, you'll hear important adjectives or nouns that reflect your key assets and strengths.

Your rating: 1 2 3 4 5 6 7 8 9 10

2. Align Your Assets with Market Needs

Several industries were decimated when the economy took a hit, and technology has made other jobs redundant or obsolete. One of your strengths may be underwater photography. If there's no need for that in the marketplace, you're (pardon the pun) dead in the water. You must know the market, including how employers are hurting or in need and where they need to be more productive and profitable.

> **Tip:** Mark Hovind, whom you met in chapter 9, releases a free "trends and hotspots" jobs report every month at www.jobbait.com. You can see state, region, county, and major city trends for what's slowing and growing.

Intersecting your assets with the bottom line will give you confidence and create demand for your services; you become the hunted and not the hunter. This can happen only when you do preliminary field research and talk to hiring managers to understand the trends, opportunities, problems, and projects they are facing. Then synthesize that information to determine a clear job search target that pinpoints the following: position; industry sector; company profile (size, corporate culture, public or private); geographic area; salary range; and type of gig (full-time, temporary, free-lance).

> **Tip:** Consider alternative forms of employment, including a freelance or inde-pendent contractor arrangement. A CareerBuilder.com/Harris Interactive poll indicated that 28 percent of employers would utilize freelance or contract workers to cut costs.

Observe how others with similar interests present themselves on Twitter or other social media sites, such as LinkedIn.com. This can give you ideas on how to position yourself.

Your rating: 1 2 3 4 5 6 7 8 9 10

3. Articulate Your Assets into a Compelling Brand

Once you understand how your assets intersect with market needs, you'll be able to articulate that into concise personal marketing materials (160me Twitter bio, resume, inquiry letters, and so on). This value prop must be woven throughout your resume, networking sound bites, and behavioral interviewing response stories. (Recall from section 2 the wisdom of the pithy and punchy BVP and 160me. And watch for groundbreaking wisdom on incorporating a Twitter-esque style into your resume and cover letter in the following chapters.)

Your rating: 1 2 3 4 5 6 7 8 9 10

> **Tip:** Practice weaving the "short form"—the less-is-more, abbreviated style of Twitter—into all of your writing and speaking. Employers love candidates who can convey the essence of information clearly and concisely. (Refer to chapter 14 for more on how to do this.)

4. Target Specific Companies (Before They Publish Job Openings)—This Is the Hidden Job Market!

This is crucial. If you don't target specific companies that are a good fit with your background and BVP, you will be distracted and will indiscriminately chase positions you hear about or find online. Like a pinball, you'll get knocked around.

Depending on the size of your industry, consider starting with a list of 25 to 50 companies; if there are few players in your industry, three to five companies might be plenty. Of course, it's helpful if you know that the companies are hiring, but it's not essential. Most hiring managers are always looking for great talent and often find a place for them even if there isn't an immediate opening.

To get recommendations of companies to include, pose a question on Twitter, such as this:

Considering new career oppty; what tech companies would you recommend in Boston area?

You can also search for companies that are using Twitter and follow them (more on this in section 6).

Your rating: 1 2 3 4 5 6 7 8 9 10

> **Tip:** Use a "CIO" approach to job search. CIO typically stands for Chief Information Officer or Chief Innovation Officer. In this case, you will innovate by targeting not just job openings, but **C**ompanies, **I**nfluencers, and **O**pportunities.

5. Develop "ROI Relationships" with Hiring Managers and Influencers, Both Online and in Person (aka Networking!)

ROI relationships mean you provide a return-on-investment, or value, to the people you meet (even if they can't immediately help you). Craft a strong social media campaign to convey this value, and leverage your online activities to support face-to-face encounters.

If you're not talking to or meeting with hiring managers, people who have influence with hiring managers, or other people who can give you insider information about your target companies—*en vivo,* **several times a week or preferably daily**—you're not conducting an effective campaign. These interactions build trust and credibility with your network.

Follow hiring managers, company employees, and other influencers on Twitter. Engage in conversations with these people. Help them, without expecting anything in return. It will eventually come back to you. (See chapter 13 for more on following people.)

Your rating: 1 2 3 4 5 6 7 8 9 10

6. Research T.O.P. Issues

T.O.P. is a helpful model for structuring your research on each of your target companies:

- **T** stands for *trends*: What are trends, whether positive or troubling, for the company or industry. How is the company responding?

- **O** represents *organizational culture*. People hire people, not automatons. If a hiring manager has to choose between you and another candidate of equal qualifications, and the other candidate is a better fit personality-wise and culture-wise, you'll lose.

- **P** has several meanings, including position, projects, problems, and people. Research the *position* you're targeting: Is it old or new? Who was in the position previous to you? How does the role interact with other functions and impact the bottom line for the company? And what are the key deliverables expected in that position in the next 30, 60, 90 days?

  What *projects* are either on the table now or slated for the future; how can you contribute to them? What *problems* are standing in the way of success; how can you be part of the solution? And finally, who are the *players*—to whom would you report; who influences the hiring manager's decision; who would your coworkers be; who are your customers/end-users and what's important to them?

You can pose many of your questions on Twitter and other social media sites to expand your research. Type the phrase "I need help with…" in Twitter's search box to find people who might need your skills.

Your rating: 1 2 3 4 5 6 7 8 9 10

7. Gain an Advantage with Endorsements

Endorsements are recommendations from people, or influencers, whom a hiring manager likes, respects, and trusts. Influencers might be bosses or supervisors of the hiring manager, coworkers, subordinates, advisors, customers, clients, vendors, strategic partners, or industry thought leaders. They might even be the hiring manager's next-door neighbors or friends from the gym.

Your network tacitly recommends you when it retweets your thought leadership. They will be more likely to do so if you've also retweeted and recommended them.

Your rating: 1 2 3 4 5 6 7 8 9 10

8. Cover Your Bases by Applying to Published Jobs

In step 4, we urged you to target companies instead of job openings, since the competition is fierce and odds are against you online. Nonetheless, you *should* apply online—just don't waste hours each day doing so.

First, post your resume to your target companies' Web sites. Then search Indeed.com or SimplyHired.com, which aggregate jobs from all job boards, or www.LinkUp.com, which searches the job postings on more than 20,000 company Web sites. In addition, choose a couple of niche sites and a regional job board from the AIRS Job Board & Recruiting Technology Directory (available free at www.airsdirectory.com/mc/rpo_forms_jobboard.guid). Check postings at craigslist.org as well, since the aggregators don't pick up jobs from this site.

Your rating: 1 2 3 4 5 6 7 8 9 10

> **Tip:** Check out www.TwitterJobSearch.com and www.TweetMyJobs.com, which have job postings and enable you to communicate with recruiters.

9. Embrace Job Search as Marketing: Use Radar-Screen Activities to Link Up, Pop Up, and Follow Up

Job search is marketing, with you as the product and the employer as the consumer. Link up regularly with your key influencers through phone calls, e-mails, and face-to-face meetings (shoot for daily meetings with your various contacts). Pop up unexpectedly on Twitter and other social media sites. Out-of-site means out-of-mind in the online world. And follow up relentlessly on commitments you've made.

Your rating: 1 2 3 4 5 6 7 8 9 10

> **Tip:** Tweet during the hours when your target company networking contacts are most likely to be on Twitter. See chapter 31 to learn more about Tweet O'Clock (http://tweetoclock.com/), which tells you the best time of day to tweet to improve your chances of specific Twitter users (for example, potential employers or networking contacts) seeing your tweets.

10. Interview as an S.O.S. Consultant

The Morse Code signal "Save Our Ship" in this case means Solve Or Support. Walk into interviews with your consultant hat on, ready to learn about how you can help solve the employer's problems or be of support in the process. Consultants ask a lot of questions before providing solutions. Make inquiries, such as "What are the key deliverables you need accomplished in this position in the next 30, 60, and 90 days?" and "What strategies have you used thus far?"

After gathering key information, offer examples of how you've solved similar problems and how you might approach the solution in the role. The more the employer can envision you in the role, the better.

Your rating: 1 2 3 4 5 6 7 8 9 10

> **Tip:** Use a tool such as www.Monitter.com to gather intelligence before your interview. (More on this in chapter 21.)

Are You New Economy or Old School?

How did you fare on the rating scale we suggested at the beginning of the 10 rules? If you scored yourself a seven or higher on each item, you're going to be ahead of most of your competition. If your scores are below sevens on any of the items, and your job search is more "old school" than "new economy," develop an action plan to correct any shortfalls.

The Psychology of the Search

Although this book focuses on "can-do" strategies for the job search using Twitter, we're taking a brief timeout to acknowledge the psychological side of the job hunt: It's not always easy. We turned to our colleague Donna Sweidan (@careerfolk), a career coach and licensed mental health counselor in New York state, to share strategies for managing what she calls "the inner struggle" of job search.

"For some, job loss can invite a host of unwanted feelings and beliefs—from shame and embarrassment, to denial and self-sabotage, to an exaggerated sense of anger and futility," notes Donna. "Self-defeating self-talk ensues: 'I'll never find a job… I'm not good enough… Networking events are a waste of time… What's the point of Twitter, anyway?'"

Giving in to the inner struggle can make job seekers feel isolated, insecure, and immobilized, but Donna offers some helpful truths and tips for taking control.

Winning the Inner Struggle

The inner struggle can throw you (and your job search) off balance. However, notes Donna, "Job seekers who regularly remind themselves of these two truths have greater success than those who don't":

- You have a unique thumbprint that will bring value to employers. (Recall the importance of section 2, on branding and identifying your branded value proposition.)
- You have more control in the process than you think.

In fact, you might be pleasantly surprised by what you can accomplish with a little effort. Here are Donna's five tips to use Twitter to manage the psychology of the search:

- **Connect with others who can empathize and help.** Search http://search. twitter.com for the phrase "looking for a job" or follow @jobangels (they can connect you with volunteers who are willing to help).
- **Find perspective and hope.** Identify and follow positive sources of encouragement, such as http://listorious.com/HNatarajan/inspirational-gurus. For more choices, visit www.wefollow.com, click "just browsing," and plug in keywords such as motivation, humor, or inspiration.
- **Expand your network and web of support.** Type in "jobseekers" at WeFollow.com and Twellow.com to find events and people to expand your web of support. And don't overlook following your professional association on Twitter to stay connected with people, trends, and continuing education opportunities.
- **Take a break from your job search.** Find lists or people to follow with common hobbies. One job seeker who loved to knit followed @knittydotcom on Twitter—the diversion added some life balance and buoyancy to her day. (But be sure to put limits on your activities so you don't lose track of time!)
- **Convert Twitter conversations to face-time connections.** Consider offline events, such as Meetup.com groups for job seekers (@careerfolk and @chandlee host programs near New York City, and other career coaches offer this service nationwide).

  Don't limit yourself to organized events; many use Twitter's advanced search function to find people in their area and have in-person, impromptu "Tweetups" (see chapter 30 to learn how to find people).

Job seekers should remember that the choice of when, how, and with whom to connect, both online and off, remains a personal decision. "Take steps to protect your safety throughout the process," advises Donna.

> **Tip:** Be careful about sharing your insecurities, doubts, and fears on Twitter. Employers can access your entire Twitter timeline if they know the right place to look. If you feel compelled to express negative feelings on Twitter, create a separate, anonymous account (such as @frustrated) that doesn't point to your true identity in any way.

Donna sums up nicely the battle of the inner struggle: "I've found that, in the end, the cure is this: If you persevere and work hard, you *will* find a job." Our heartfelt hope for each of you is that you will tap into that best part of you—your ideal "future" self—and step out with courage, confidence, and conviction.

CHAPTER 18

RECRUITERS REVEAL JOB SEARCH SECRETS

"You're only as good as the people you hire."

—*Ray Kroc*

Where can I find lists of recruiters? How do I work with recruiters? Who can connect me with recruiters? Why won't recruiters call me back? Why do recruiters want to talk with me only when I'm employed? Why didn't the recruiter answer my e-mail?

These are some of the most common questions we hear, on Twitter and in our practices. For job seekers, the world of the recruiter (sometimes called a headhunter, and not to be confused with an employment agency) is shrouded in mystery and frustrating to job seekers. And recruiters are sometimes just as frustrated when job seekers don't "get" how they work—their first priority is the company that hired them to find the proverbial needle in the haystack, not the job seeker.

You'll find an insider's list of recruiters on Twitter in chapter 28, but that doesn't mean we think you should start off by sending a direct message or an @reply and ask for a job. Quite the contrary: In the Twitterverse, as in life, relationships take time. So we asked for their advice to job seekers on the search process and Twitter.

Not surprisingly, we turned to some recruiters who are leveraging the power of Twitter. In alphabetical order by Twitter username, we're sharing nuggets from our conversations with them—in tweet-style, of course.

Recruiter Tweets
@Absolutely_Abby, Abby Kohut
www.absolutelyabby.com

President of staffing consulting company with 15 yrs of HR & recruiting experience provides daily absolute truths for job seekers

Absolutely_Abby Don't just sit on the sidelines; join in on the fun. If you don't tweet, no one will know who you are. Twitter helps you get known.

Absolutely_Abby Make sure you put keywords in your bios. (If you are a turtle caretaker, put it in--it's searchable and recruiters will find you.)

Absolutely_Abby When cold calling a prospective employer, you are asking them to buy something…and the something is YOU!

Absolutely_Abby Finding the right boss is nearly as important to your happiness as finding the right mate.

Absolutely_Abby When you are searching for a job, anything & everything you do is being evaluated, including your e-mail & voice mail.

Absolutely_Abby Being asked back for 6 interviews at one company is not a hurdle - it's an opportunity.

Absolutely_Abby Even if your old boss resembled Attila the Hun, you need to find their redeeming qualities to discuss in an interview.

@Animal, Recruiting Animal
www.recruitinganimal.com

Host of the 1st online call-in radio show about recruiting in world history. ----------------
---------------------- IF YOU'RE sensitive DON'T FOLLOW ME

Animal To be found easily by recruiters list your job title 1st & don't clutter your bio with extraneous info. Use a LinkedIn link for the Web URL.

Animal There is no reason for you to have a dark, fuzzy picture or one in which you have a tiny face that no one can see.

Animal List your Twitter account @Username on your business card, resume, LinkedIn profile, so people can easily find and follow you.

Animal Use hashtags (#) with industry-specific terms in your tweets, because recruiters often search for hashtags when looking for candidates.

Animal If recruiters contact you with job leads that aren't right for you, ask if they'd like you to retweet the lead to your network.

@BillVick, Bill Vick
www.billvick.com

Helping and advising boomers, recruiters and job seekers to be all they can be. Author, vlogger, social media leader. USMC 2nd Force Recon alumni.

BillVick Jobseekers need to understand they are a "product"-they must position, package, and promote themselves throughout the search.

BillVick Understand the 80-20 rule: give before you get. As important as it is to plug into centers of influence, give value first.

BillVick Intelligently tweet 5-6 times/day. For every 5 tweets, 4 should "give" & 1 could point to an accomplishment, online white paper, etc.

BillVick If I was beating the bushes for a job today, I'd be on the phone rather than keyboard. You can get tangled in emails and tweets.

BillVick In the end, hiring is a "belly to belly" situation, a contact sport-not somethig done with technology & tools. There must be relationship.

BillVick People don't understand how inundated recruiters are-their inbox is full every day. You must find a way to raise your head above the noise.

BillVick Savvy recruiters have their lists of candidates they follow closely; find a way to get on that targeted recruiter's hot list.

@eExecutives, Harry Urschel
www.eexecutives.net/select

Professional Technology Recruiter; Job Hunting Coach; and Online Networker I Very blessed Husband and Dad to four I Always seeking Truth and Wisdom!

eExecutives Search #splits, a tag recruiters use to source candidates & share commissions w/ other recruiters. If hired, recr. keeps 100%-you both win.

eExecutives If you're an open networker, tweet "are we connected on LinkedIn yet?" and include your LinkedIn URL to build connections.

eExecutives Every conversation, every email, every tweet is part of job-interview process. Be professional every step of the way. Don't get too casual.

eExecutives Many recruiters go straight from meeting you on Twitter to checking your LinkedIn profile. Make sure your LinkedIn profile is professional.

eExecutives See job leads posted by a recruiter but you don't fit? Refer a colleague who does. That's a great way to build relationship with recruiters.

eExecutives If you only tweet 1-2 times a day, it won't be enough for anyone to get to know you. Manage your time carefully, but do spend time to build relationships.

@Jessica_Lee and @APCOjobs, Jessica Lee
www.fistfuloftalent.com

DC gal + corporate recruiter/HR pro for APCO Worldwide + editor for FistfulofTalent. com. Tweeting about all of the aforementioned. Thanks for following!

Jessica_Lee Using Twitter to look for job? Complete your bio and use hashtags accurately. Clarity on candidate side helps hiring managers scout you out.

Jessica_Lee The biggest mistake candidates make is looking at job search as if it is a transaction and not an organic process that develops over time.

Jessica_Lee Job seekers: Flattery never hurts. Show you've done your homework about me or our company. That's a good way to grow conversations.

Jessica_Lee Should you DM a recruiter that you've applied for their job? It's ok. But don't ask for help. Just say, "Hey, I've applied."

@JLipschultz, Jeff Lipschultz
http://jefflipschultz.wordpress.com

IT and Exec Recruiter • Co-Founder of staffing firm A-List Solutions • interview/resume coach • blogger • avid road cyclist and bike whisperer • Cubs fan

JLipschultz Facebook is your personal side, LinkedIn is your professional side, Twitter is your everything.

JLipschultz Your core Twitter group are your research assistants; pick them well. They funnel info to you. It just comes to you. You can act upon it.

JLipschultz Know what your aim is. What you are about. What you can do. Telling a recruiter you can do anything is like telling him you can do nothing.

JLipschultz Get to know people. Do favors. Be a source - suggest people to a recruiter. A little interaction can go a long way with recruiters.

JLipschultz I use Google. If someone writes a tweet that I'm interested in it might just show up if it's got good SEO. That could get us connected.

JLipschultz Research. Get to know me. I'm more likely to contact you if you read my latest post or ask about blog/Twitter/cycling. Build connection.

JLipschultz Bloggers have passion and expertise. Recruiters, employers, media like/follow good bloggers. Twitter is the billboard for your blog.

@Karla_Porter, Karla Porter
www.karlaporter.com

All things workforce, employment, recruiting and new media... maybe more.

Karla_Porter Follow recruiters and check out their Twitter Lists. In 15-20 minutes, you can build yourself a captive audience as a job seeker.

Karla_Porter Create a dashboard using iGoogle or other tool to receive industry news alerts, news on your name & RSS feeds of key people you follow.

Karla_Porter Make it clear on your Twitter bio that you are open to new opportunities, and include keywords in your bio. It helps recruiters find you.

Karla_Porter College student soon to graduate? Say so in your Twitter bio so recruiters know your status.

Karla_Porter Test your "findability." Can you find yourself using http://search.twitter.com/advanced search function? If not, add keywords to your bio.

A Recruiter Sounds Off on Resumes

JLipschultz I hire humans; I don't hire resumes. I know exactly the personality that will fit with my clients. You can't understate the human side.

We believe in fit, too. And we believe you can begin to build the chemistry and fit that lead to great hires before anyone ever meets you. Where? On Twitter, on LinkedIn, on Facebook, and in your resume and other career documents.

CHAPTER 19

TURBOCHARGE YOUR RESUME WITH TWEETS

"The terrifying reality regarding your resume is that
for all the many hours you put into fine-tuning, you've got 30
seconds to make an impression on me. Maybe less."

—*RandsinRepose Blog (www.randsinrepose.com)*

In job search, a resume will get a grand total of 10 to 30 seconds of attention (on a good day). We believe that by using the same techniques you use to write effective tweets, you can develop a resume with career-building precision and power that maximizes those 30 seconds, entices a second read, and compels a call to interview—and do it in 20 to 30 tweets. Deb has titled this the Twit-Fit CareerCom Concept™, reminiscent of how companies extend their brand and capture customers through marketing communications (marcom).

> **Need to Know:** The Twit-Fit™ resume is today's new Twitter-inspired resume. It looks like a resume, but it's a resume on speed—a turbocharged one- to two-page document powered by value-packed, 140-character sentences, bullets, or phrases focused on impact.

Let's be clear. A Twit-Fit resume is not a tweet. When people on Twitter ask for your resume, follow their directions for how they'd like to receive it. Typically, they will ask you to e-mail it and will likely provide their e-mail address via a direct message (DM). Alternatively, if you keep your resume online somewhere (for instance, at your own Web site or at a service such as VisualCV.com), you could also share the link to it in a tweet.

In this chapter we'll show Deb's 10-step strategy to develop a Twit-Fit resume. We'll also use our friend Pizza Guy to show you how to write a six-tweet resume profile and a 10-tweet job description.

What Is a Twit-Fit Resume? Why Use One?

*"Strong brands are usually known for one thing.
They are not all things to all people."*

— *William Arruda*

Imagine tweeting your way to a resume. Imagine a resume with *one* employer-attracting sentence in the middle of the page (your bio from chapter 10). That power-packed value message is the core around which you build a Twit-Fit resume.

Imagine creating a cluster of tweets that defines that value, a cluster that defines your career impact, a cluster that describes your most recent positions, and clusters of tweets that describe your impact and best accomplishments.

> **Need to Know:** A *Twit-Fit* resume's core content is composed of clusters of succinct "tweets" focused on your essential message of value and connected by traditional resume components (employer, dates of employment, education, and so on).

Your job is to make it as simple as possible for an employer to read your resume, understand your value, and contact you. A Twit-Fit resume looks like a resume, but its content is so well-defined, so targeted, and so easy to read that a traditional "job graveyard" resume just can't match its impact. It's today's answer to employers' limited time, limited attention, and limited opportunities.

Through precision and clarity it stands out and commands attention. It says you're a clear thinker of high value. It says you are willing to step outside the box. It says you are different and desirable. We understand that creating a precision personal marketing document focused on *one* goal (as opposed to one-size-fits-all) may feel radically different and radically risky in an economy where the stakes are high. It takes real courage to step away from the norm. But we also believe that with great risk comes great reward.

Ten Steps to a Twit-Fit Resume

*"Writing is easy. All you do is sit staring at a blank sheet
of paper until drops of blood form on your forehead."*

— *Gene Fowler*

Although a Twit-Fit resume is less wordy than a traditional resume, it takes more time to write and requires deep preparation on a brand and value level. Use Deb's 10 steps to help you understand and streamline the process:

1. **Develop a branded value proposition (BVP).** What's your sweet spot? What's the most critically important thing that you do with your brand at work?

Tip: Before writing a Twit-Fit resume, be sure that you've read through chapters 7 through 10 and have done the work to understand your particular value, build your branded value proposition, and compose your 160me (Twitter bio).

2. **Research your best fit.** Determine the industry and employers you like and for whom you have the most value.

Tip: Planning a strategy to get you where you want to go is critical. Know your value proposition. Know your target industry and employers. Know how your value proposition relates to their needs. Decide how you will convey that on your resume. What will be your main focus? What will be value-added detail? How will you build your case for hire? In a Twit-Fit resume, success requires Steven Covey's wisdom: "Begin with the end in mind."

3. **Brand to NOW.** Determine how your branded value fits current market need. Why should employers salivate to hire you?

Tip: Employers want to know—need to know—what you have done in your career that made a difference. Susan Whitcomb, in *Résumé Magic* (JIST), calls these things "buying motivators." Did you save money, make money, or enable others to do that? What did you do that would cause the employer to want to invest in you?

4. **Think impact.** Prove the past and potential impact of what you have done so that an employer *will* salivate to hire you!

Tip: As Steven Covey says, "Priority is a function of context." Ask yourself "So what?" every time you write a phrase on your resume. If your phrase doesn't answer that question, it probably won't entice an employer to invest time in speaking with you, let alone hire you. You need to know not only that it *is* important, but also *why* it is important. You need context to create impact and priorities to choose only the impact statements that speak to the employer.

5. **Strategize content and format.** Establish your resume's overall design and "above-the-fold" profile structure. The "real estate" that is the top one-third to one-half of your resume is where you capture attention and build the reader's interest.

Tip: A Twit-Fit resume, by nature, is about two pages. Your concise tweets and connectors will naturally keep your page count down. But the objective isn't more or fewer pages. The objective is attraction. The goal is a resume that is interesting, informative, and clearly formatted, and gets the reader in and out fast, yet invites a second, more in-depth read.

6. **Power your profile.** Will you use a tagline in your profile? A personal or career brand statement? What else will be in your profile that proves your value, suggests potential, and maximizes that key "above-the-fold" position?

7. **Strategize company and position placement.** Decide how many companies and positions you'll feature and how you'll feature them. How many companies and positions will you showcase? What will you feature in Education and Activities sections? Do you have gaps or underemployment to hide? Are there other issues to be strategized?

8. **Create tweet clusters.** These will be succinct, 140-character (or so) phrases that describe the preceding qualifications with a power punch of precision. They should fit into your strategic resume format. They must answer the employer's assumed questions: "So what?" and "Why should I care?"

Tip: Use your 140 to 160 characters wisely. Write your tweets with strategy, precision, and impact in mind. Front-load the impact into the beginning of the tweet and edit, edit, edit!

9. **Nest.** Place these tweet clusters within traditional resume components, including heading, company name/position/dates, education, professional activities, and so on.

10. **Review, revise, repeat.** Don't rest until your document is a defined, powerful, and irresistible call to action.

Tip: "The main thing is to keep the main thing the main thing," says Steven Covey. Digging through a job history to find the essence of what needs to be said isn't easy, but it's essential to develop a precise, undeniable value message. Keep "the main thing the main thing"; don't hide it in mountains of detail. And if something is the best accomplishment of your career but isn't relevant to your target, fearlessly delete it; don't tweet it!

We Twit-Fit Pizza Guy's Resume

Our friend Pizza Guy has worked for 15 years for Pie-in-the-Sky Pizza—from the time he was a kid in high school. He's now director of the Northeast region and is thinking about looking for a job. Let's see how the Twit-Fit resume process can work for him.

A 6-Tweet Resume Profile

Pizza Guy needs to build a profile for his resume—it will lead off the resume "above the fold," meaning that it sits upon the top third or so of page one. The profile anchors the resume, summarizes a career in just a few inches of space, and invites the reader to dive in. It should *not* be boring, long, rambling, or vague. It must be so strong that if the rest of the resume dropped away, the profile could get enough interest to generate an interview.

Pizza Guy can do that in six tweets of 140 (or up to 160) characters or less. Here's how:

Tweet 1: Heading

The first tweet—the heading—is typically a tagline, brand statement, or on-brand action item. It's the intersection of personal brand and career brand. It is the "title" of the Twit-Fit resume and should be compelling or intriguing.

Tweet 2: Brand/Value Proposition

The second tweet is the intersection of brand and value—it's what anchors the resume and captures the reader's interest.

Tweets 3 and 4: Impact/Proof of Performance

The third and fourth tweets are accomplishments—the magnets that hold the reader to the resume. They define and support the value proposition (Tweet 2) with proof of performance. If they are what the employer wants, they make the resume "sticky" and propel further reading.

Tweet 5: Career Snapshot and/or Differentiators

The fifth tweet is the "where I've been, why I'm different, and why you should care" tweet. It's a differentiation from others in the field.

Tweet 6: Personal Brand "Soft Skills" and Process

The sixth tweet is a "chemistry and fit" message. Use this tweet to demonstrate the "how" of work—process, passions, team skills, and so on.

Figure 19.1 shows what his 6-tweet resume profile could look like.

The 10-Tweet Job Description

Pizza Guy needs to create descriptions for each of the jobs he has held at Pie-in-the-Sky Pizza. He'll start with his most recent position, director of the Northeast region, and move backward through his earlier positions.

In our example we'll help him work on his director position. We'll start with the usual: title, company, location, dates of employment, and company description. Then we'll create his job description in just 10 powerful tweets that briefly focus on his areas of accountability and then quickly move on to the heart of the Twit-Fit

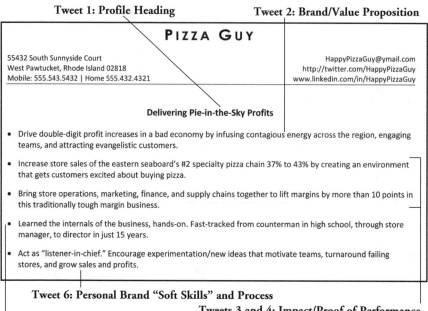

Figure 19.1: 6-tweet resume profile.

resume: his impact and accomplishments (written in tweet-style as paragraphs or bullets). Here's the process for the 10 tweets:

Tweet 1: Position Description

Tweet 1 focuses on the scope of the position, not responsibilities.

Tweet 2: The Mission

Tweet 2 is all about the challenge of the job. Why does it exist?

Tweet 3: No More "Responsible for…"

Tweet 3 replaces the bland "responsible for." Instead, use a "stats snapshot" of reports, goals, budgets, P&L, and duties.

Tweet 4: Impact

Tweet 4 is an impact statement—the *one* best thing that made the biggest difference in revenue, market share, and productivity.

Tweets 5 to 10: Accomplishments/Strategies

Tweets 5 to 10 are accomplishments or strategies that can be directly tied to any or all of the following: impact, market need, brand strength, and soft skills.

Tip: Use this "tweet your job" description process for every job on your resume. As the jobs get older, the number of tweets will shrink. Your earliest jobs (typically, your resume should go back about 15 years) will have the fewest tweets—usually tweets 1 through 4, 5, or 6.

Let's see how that looks (figure 19.2).

Tweet 1: Position Description—focuses on scope of position, not responsibilities.

Director, Northeast Region 2007 to present
Pie-in-the-Sky Pizza, Providence, RI
Pie-in-the-Sky Pizza is the #2 specialty pizza restaurant chain in the Eastern US with locations in 12 states. Sales: $50 million.

Oversee 15 restaurants in Northeast region: staffing, supply chain, finance, menus, marketing, customer care, store design, and store "personality."

Tweet 2: The Mission—is all about the challenge of the job. Why does it exist?

Promoted from manager of best-performing location to help Northeast region survive the ripple effects of the economic meltdown.

Tweet 3: No More "Responsible for…"—replaces the bland "responsible for" with a "stats snapshot" of reports, goals, budgets, P&L, duties.

P&L accountability: $18 million. Direct Reports: 15 store managers.

Impact

Within 1 year, stabilized falling sales across the region. Within 3 years, delivered triple-digit sales growth and double-digit margin increases.

Tweet 4: Impact Statement—the one best thing that made the biggest difference in revenue, market share, and productivity.

Strategies & Accomplishments

- **Cost Savings:** Delivered $450,000 in annual cost savings by strategizing and introducing formal store-by-store budgeting program.

- **Staff Retention:** Saved an estimated $150,000 in hiring costs. Developed fun in-store incentives to keep traditionally high-turnover staff engaged.

- **Store Environment:** Drove sales up 10% (as per surveys) by instituting 12 months of seasonal decor, creating a welcoming, fun atmosphere that customers loved.

- **Revved-up Morale:** Created a rollicking rhythm to staff and customer interactions. Bright stores and fun banter drove business.

- **Social Media:** Connected to customers—using very little budget—on Facebook, Twitter, and permission-based e-mail for coupons, and incentive, birthday, and school reading programs.

- **Best Practices:** Instituted weekly staff meetings to keep the highest standards at the forefront of operations, with zero tolerance for critical transgressions.

Tweets 5–10: Accomplishments/Strategies—accomplishments or strategies that can be directly tied to any or all of the following: impact, market need, brand strength, and soft skills.

Figure 19.2: 10-tweet job description.

How does your resume measure up? Compare your existing resume to the suggestions in this chapter and make revisions accordingly.

CHAPTER 20

Cover Letters Are Just 10 Tweets

"Good things, when short, are twice as good."

—*Baltasar Gracián*

Who likes cover letters?

We know very few people who like to write cover letters. And we know very few employers and recruiters who like to read cover letters. Yet a great cover letter is a golden opportunity to create connection between you, the employer or recruiter, and your resume.

Many job seekers would rather go to the dentist for a root canal than write a cover letter. At the very least, they'd rather procrastinate and watch some TV, clean out a closet, or hit Starbucks for a caffeine pick-me-up. They've done the hard work of writing their resume; the cover letter seems like an avoidable burden.

Take heart, cover-letter-averse job seekers (and cover-letter readers!). We think the process can be infinitely better.

In this chapter, Deb provides you with a new "Twitter-based" model for writing cover letters. We can't promise it's easy, but we can promise that it's a way to communicate with brevity and power. And it has got a *big* bonus: If you do it right, you're already prepped for the heart of the interview and ready to answer the "Why should I hire you?" question.

Before we begin, we must credit Mark Hovind, of JobBait.com, with encouraging us to adopt a brief, bold, value-infused cover letter—long before Twitter took flight. We tried it, we use it, we love it. It works. Thanks, Mark!

Does Your Cover Letter Pass the Yawn-Meter Test?

"If any man will draw up his case, and put his name at the foot of the first page, I will give him an immediate reply. Where he compels me to turn over the sheet, he must wait my leisure."

—*4th Earl of Sandwich*

In our experience, many traditional cover letters don't get read for simple reasons. These are a few frequent mistakes that frequently result in a yawning loss of effectiveness:

- If e-mailed, they extend beyond the screen.
- They read like a nomination letter for an award or who's who.
- They are densely packed with far too much information.
- They have too much text.
- They tell too much about what you did before.
- They don't mention your understanding of current market conditions or the job itself.
- Every sentence starts with "I."

In short, if your cover letter is too long, too rambling, too "me" centered, too vague, or too boring, it just might not get read.

And you worked so hard on it, didn't you? It just doesn't seem fair. We agree; you should be heard! But you'll need to sharpen your editing skills and bravely go forth to cut all but the most critical information.

For Cover Letters, as for Twitter, Brevity Rules

"It is with words as with sunbeams. The more they are condensed, the deeper they burn."

—*Robert Southey*

We encourage you to make this your cover letter mantra: "Be brave and brief to get belief!"

Can brevity attract and persuade? We believe it can, if you succinctly communicate value that is irresistible to your target employer. Why? Because in an employers' multitasking, 24/7 workday, you'd better make your case fast, or don't bother making it at all. In job search, quickly conveyed "precision value" gets a hearing. Save rambling for a relaxing walk, not for job search.

The Case for the 10-Tweet Cover Letter Technique™

"If you can't write your idea on the back of my calling card, you don't have a clear idea."

—*David Belasco*

In the remainder of this chapter, Deb shares her 10-Tweet Cover Letter Technique. It's bold, it's brief, and it gets belief.

We've said if you don't have two lines you can put in the middle of a blank piece of paper and get an employer interested in speaking to you, you are not ready to go to a networking event, write a resume, or interview. The same holds true for your cover letter.

Your cover letter is the magnet that draws the employer to read your resume. It's your 160me bio expanded to a 30-second value-based message that tells an employer that *you* have the potential to be exactly the right fit—you have the skills, accomplishments, and chemistry he wants.

If you don't yet have a carefully constructed 160me bio, review chapter 10 and get that done. You'll need to know the essence of your value and how that relates to the employer to whom you are writing before you can compose a 10-tweet cover letter.

Ten Tips for a 10-Tweet Cover Letter

A brief, magnetic, call-to-action cover letter requires precision and strategy to convey exactly the right value message. You'll need to be brave: Every word counts and ruthless editing is needed to write within a lean and powerful structure. We'll talk more about that later. For now, think about how you might use these tips to develop your content in just 10 tweets:

- Tweet 1: The state of the employer or industry.
- Tweet 2: Tie the solution to you.
- Tweet 3: Tell them you've "been there."
- Tweet 4: What did you face?
- Tweet 5: Give some context.
- Tweet 6: Prove you made (or supported making) money.
- Tweet 7: Tie it to your brand.
- Tweet 8: Tell them something that worked really well.
- Tweet 9: Tell them another thing that worked really well.
- Tweet 10: Tie your brand to your value for the close.

Short Writing Isn't Fast Writing; It's Winning Writing

"If I am to speak 10 minutes, I need a week for preparation; if 15 minutes, three days; if half an hour, two days; if an hour, I am ready now."

— *Woodrow Wilson*

We wish we could tell you to click your heels three times, whisper, "There's no cover letter like a short cover letter," and have the process be done. We can't. Even with a strong 160me bio in place, great cover letters can actually take more time at the outset because each word you use speaks volumes. You can't short-circuit the writing process.

Yet once you know the formula, you will have the ability to create a magnetic cover letter in an astonishingly brief, yet powerful, 150 to 300 words.

Pizza Guy Looks for a New Job

We met Pizza Guy in chapter 7 and he has been pretty steady since then. The Pie-in-the-Sky Pizza chain has been his home since he was in high school. He has done well and has risen through the ranks from counterman, to manager, to Director of the Northeast region.

He has made some big contributions but is wondering if, after more than 10 years, this may be the time to make a move. He's sending letters to a few select targets and tying his brand and accomplishments to what they need in the current economic environment.

Pizza Guy's Tweet Preparation

Before our pizza guy writes his letter, he researches his target company and industry, he reviews his brand, and he decides how his value proposition fits the needs of his target. He knows that he

- Enthusiastically tackles every job as though it's the most important job in the world.
- Loves people and gets customers and teams engaged and excited.

He is confident that his 160me clearly expresses his brand and value:

I'm a Happy Pizza Guy. Happy customers buy more pies...37% more! The devotion in every slice, helps to lift the NASDAQ price!

Pizza Guy's research tells him his branded value should be useful and compelling to his target companies: large fast-food chains that are struggling to stay profitable and competitive in a bad economy.

Because he is writing an executive-level job search letter, he converts the essence of his 160me to his more traditional branded value proposition (BVP): "I deliver double-digit profit increases in a bad economy by infusing contagious energy across the region, engaging teams, and attracting evangelistic customers." His BVP is the foundation of his letter.

Pizza Guy's 10-Tweet Cover Letter

With his value and targets connected, he's ready to begin his 10-tweet cover letter. Here's what Pizza Guy wrote, and what each tweet aims to present:

Tweet #1: The state of the employer or industry.

Times are tough for the $170 billion fast-food industry. One *Wall Street* analyst recently called the current environment a "vicious, competitive, zero-sum game."

Tweet #2: Tie the solution to you.

If that's where you are, and you need an infusion of executive talent, I can help.

Tweet #3: Tell them you've "been there."

At Pie-in-the-Sky Pizza, the nation's #2 pizza chain, we faced those same challenges.

Tweet #4: What did you face?

Our sales and profits were in free-fall, and I was called in to stop the bleeding in the Northeast region.

Tweet #5: Give some context.

In the past 12 months, while our competitors lagged in year-on-year and same-store sales, I have:

Tweet #6: Prove you made (or supported making) money.

* Reversed our losses, grown sales by 22%, and delivered double-digit profit.

Tweet #7: Tie it to your brand.

* Infused contagious energy across our teams and the region.

Tweet #8: Tie it to something that worked really well.

* Developed exciting customer-appreciation programs that created an evangelistic following.

Tweet #9: Tie it to another thing that worked really well.

* Used social media like Facebook and Twitter to promote our brand, spread the fun, and build excitement around our products and promotions.

Tweet #10: Wrap your brand and value together for the close.

My passion is making the work of "making money" fun. I'll keep your teams charged up, growing profits, and obliterating sales goals.

Putting It All Together

Here's how it looks in final format.

PIZZA GUY

55432 South Sunnyside Court	HappyPizzaGuy@ymail.com
West Pawtucket, Rhode Island 02818	http://twitter.com/HappyPizzaGuy
Mobile: 555.543.5432 | Home 555.432.4321	www.linkedin.com/in/HappyPizzaGuy

[date]

Chris Stone
Big Box Pizza King
1234 Easy Street
Warwick, RI 02819

Dear Chris:

For the $170 billion fast-food industry, times are tough. One Wall Street analyst recently called the current environment a "vicious, competitive, zero-sum game." If that's where you are, and you need an infusion of executive talent, I can help.

At Pie-in-the-Sky Pizza, the nation's #2 pizza chain, we faced those same challenges. Our sales and profits were in free-fall, and I was called in to stop the bleeding in the Northeast region. In the past 12 months, while our competitors lagged in year-on-year and same-store sales, I have:

* Reversed our losses, grown sales by 22%, and delivered double-digit profit.

* Infused contagious energy across our teams and the region.

* Developed exciting customer appreciation programs that created an evangelistic following.

* Used social media like Facebook and Twitter to promote our brand, spread the fun, and build excitement around our products and promotions.

My passion is making the work of "making money" fun. I'll keep your teams charged up, growing profits, and obliterating sales goals. Can we meet to discuss how I might contribute?

Sincerely,

Pizza Guy

Figure 20.1: Pizza Guy's 10-Tweet cover letter.

How does this 10-tweet letter fare on the yawn-meter? Does it

- Fit on one screen when e-mailed?
- Stay away from a laundry list of self-praise?
- Appear enticingly readable, with plenty of white space?
- Tell just enough of what he did to strongly suggest that he may be a solution?
- Mention his understanding of current market conditions or the job itself?
- Avoid beginning paragraphs with "I"?

Yes! It passed! It's yawn-free on all counts.

Mr. Pizza Guy has written a 10-tweet, no-fluff, power letter: 178 words, 1,085 characters (and spaces)—all value-driven, all branded. A winner.

> *"I notice that you use plain, simple language, short words, and*
> *brief sentences. That is the way to write English—it is the modern way*
> *and the best way. Stick to it; don't let fluff and flowers and verbosity creep in.*
> *When you catch an adjective, kill it. No, I don't mean utterly, but kill most of*
> *them—then the rest will be valuable. They weaken when they are close together.*
> *They give strength when they are wide apart."*
>
> *—Mark Twain*

Measure your cover letters against the yawn-meter test. If needed, deconstruct and reconstruct. You'll prove your value and emphasize how your experience aligns with the job you seek. In 10 or so tweets (or 1,400 or so characters) you can make a winning case.

CHAPTER 21

Using Twitter to Help Ace the Interview

Featured expert: Jan Melnik, author of seven career/business books, including Executive's Pocket Guide to ROI Resumes and Job Search (@JanMelnik)

"Sorry, is this rude?"

—Stephen Colbert to Twitter founder Biz Stone during an interview Colbert was conducting while simultaneously tweeting (April 2009)

Can tweeting help you land a job? Yes, in millions of ways, as this book carefully details. But can using Twitter really help you to prepare to interview more effectively? Absolutely.

It is also possible that you might actually be interviewed *via Twitter* (called a "Twitterview"). But remember that anyone in the Twitterverse could be watching and might even chime in. Confidentiality? Out the window.

We asked our colleague Jan Melnik, an expert in interviewing with a dual perspective of both former human resources executive and career coach, about her favorite Twitter tips for interview preparation. Jan shared the following strategies for using Twitter in pre-interview research, the live interview, and interview follow-up.

Pre-interview Research

Your current employment status will largely dictate how you use Twitter for interviewing. Jan advises, "If you are currently employed and conducting a confidential search, you'll probably keep your interview-preparation tweeting to a minimum for a low profile. But let's suppose you are

- An out-of-work job seeker
- Employed, but about to be laid off
- Working for a company that's going to close or move to another part of the country

- A new graduate or about to graduate
- Seeking an internship/externship

"If you fall into one of these categories, the more people that know you are job seeking, the better, so use Twitter with free abandon to network and collect ideas and tips. Of course, you've already refined your 160me Twitter bio, but make sure to adapt it for job search. You'll want it to clearly show you're job seeking and to identify your targets and your brand."

Review the tips for researching from chapter 30. Augment your research efforts by searching for information about the company with which you'll be interviewing. For confidentiality, you should avoid tweeting any direct questions about a particular company.

Researching a specific company or interview? Jan suggests, "Look for the company's corporate Twitter name or a relevant hashtag. For example, if interviewing with Accenture, you'd follow @accenture and search for the hashtag #Accenture."

> **Tip:** To search for hashtags, put a "#" character before the one-word phrase you are searching for. You'll find more on this, plus a directory of job search–related hashtags, in chapter 28. You cannot follow a hashtag on Twitter, but you can do so on a number of third-party applications. You can find these apps listed in chapter 31.

Another of Jan's favorite resources for real-time research is monitter. Go to www.monitter.com and put in a set of three search terms. These terms should be

- Company name
- People you might be interviewing with (either their Twitter handle or their real name)
- Products or other terms relevant to the position you'll be interviewing for

Jan explains that monitter will immediately give you a feed of all the references to those terms, allowing you to glean insider information on the company, influencers, products/services, or other important subjects.

Interview Advice

"Tweet to ask for everyone's best interview prep advice…stagger these similar-sounding questions over the span of several days," suggests Jan. "Your tweets should not be one way—offer your best techniques, too. Here are some suggested tweets:

"What's your favorite strategy for preparing to interview effectively?

"What are some of your favorite responses to difficult interview questions?

"What are some job-specific questions being asked these days for a [fill in the blank with your profession]?

"If you could give one suggestion for someone preparing to interview, what would it be?

"What's your favorite question to ask at the end of an interview?"

Tip: For a comprehensive look at interviewing, check out coauthor Susan's book, *Interview Magic,* also from JIST.

Following due diligence, you've likely brought to the surface information about the company's newest product launch…or consolidation…or other activity/program about which you know little. Jan suggests that you consider tweeting before the interview to get on the inside track—for example:

I'm interested in learning more about GE's joint venture with Aviation Industry Corp. (China) to supply avionics. Opinions?

Would love to explore working at United Way, Salvation Army, or AmeriCorps. Any ideas to get started?

New mechanical engineering graduate hoping to make connections within industry. Any suggestions? Thanks!

Twitter can help you during the interview as well. One insightful job seeker printed a copy of his tweet stream and brought it to the interview to help document his subject-matter expertise. His strategy worked—he got the job!

FOUR QUESTIONS FOR INTERVIEW SUCCESS

Nick Corcodilos, author of *Ask The Headhunter: Reinventing the Interview to Get the Job,* says, "You can judge every opportunity by applying the Four Questions. The Four Questions will reveal your knowledge, attitude, and ability regarding a specific job. These are the true sources of success in any interview because they are the things an employer needs to know:

1. Do you understand what needs to be done?

2. Can you do the job?

3. Can you do the job the way the employer wants it done?

4. Can you do the job profitably for the company?

"If you can answer yes to The Four Questions for a particular job, you will… be powerful, you will be relaxed, and you will be one of the best candidates the employer will meet because you will know there is a match between you and the job."

Follow Up

Of course, you'll likely want to follow the majority of people who connect with you on Twitter. And, just as in F2F (face-to-face) networking, we agree with Jan's assertion that "a thank-you is required for every bit of assistance you receive:

- D via Twitter is appropriate for a quick, helpful tweet (recall that D or DM is a private, direct message that goes to just the person you are addressing).
- A lengthier thank-you letter via e-mail or traditional mail is more in line for those offering significant advice or help."

One of Jan's favorite strategies is regularly blogging on topics about which you have expertise, and then including a shortened link to these blog posts in your tweets. This will help you to gain traction within a discipline as you build followers.

Jan advises that job seekers "keep the visibility by regularly tweeting regarding your job search and interview. Focus on sharing questions and suggestions that could prove useful to others. If you uncover a job lead you can't use or if you coin a particularly masterful end-of-interview question, share it with the job-search Twitterverse." Some examples might be

---

VH1Mobile-MTV Networks New York is hiring a production assistant. Check out @mtvnetworksjobs.

Great interview language for #jobseeker: "If hired, what would be my first priority and who would I work with to get it done?"

Interview tip: "I understand your priorities are 'xyz' for 1st 90 days. What would hitting a home run look like in terms of deliverables?"

Always try to create value and contribution in your tweets. Don't just look for help and advice. As you ask for referrals, offer to make introductions and referrals for others.

> **Tip:** Don't post interview results during the process—nor provide an update to your status until your offer has been confirmed *and accepted* in writing.

We are excited about the growing power of Twitter to support job search efforts. Jan's final advice? "Leveraging the capabilities of Twitter for effective job interviewing is taking advantage of one more tool to help expand—possibly exponentially—the connections you can make and the job you might take."

SECTION 5

THE NEW NETWORKING

22. Jump into Twitter to Jump-Start Your Network

23. Leveraging Twitter Throughout Your Job
    Search and Networking

24. Twitter Networking: A Safe Space for
    Introverts; a Party for Extroverts

25. Niche Market Networking on Twitter

26. Discretionary Authenticity: How to Share, How
    Much, and with Whom

CHAPTER 22

JUMP INTO TWITTER TO
JUMP-START YOUR NETWORK

Featured Contributors: Lindsey Pollak (@LindseyPollak); Marshall Sponder (@WebMetricsGuru); Wendy Terwelp (@WendyTerwelp); and Brian Simpson, Director of Social Hospitality at the Roger Smith Hotel (@bsimi)

"You can get everything in life you want if you will just help enough other people get what they want."

—Zig Ziglar, author and motivational speaker

You know networking works. You know everyone says networking is the best way to get a job. Maybe you even got a job from a lead a contact gave you. But you've been too busy doing your job to keep your network alive and vibrant, or maybe you've never networked. And now your network is nowhere. You keep meaning to get out there and get started or reengaged in networking. When you have time. When you need to. When it feels right.

Now you're afraid you waited too long. You're afraid that your job may be in jeopardy, or that you are being passed up for a promotion, or that you are stagnating where you are, or that you need more professional visibility. Or maybe the worst has happened: You've lost your job and you need a network *now*.

Building a vibrant network of professional and personal contacts doesn't have to take years. You can jump into Twitter to jump-start your network—even if you've not networked for many, many months. Even if you have *never* networked. And if you're already an active networker, you can bring another dimension to your networking by connecting on Twitter, frequently, in real time.

In announcing new tools to integrate Twitter with LinkedIn, Twitter cofounder Biz Stone said the two platforms were a natural fit "like peanut butter and chocolate." We think Twitter and networking go hand-in-hand in a similar fashion: Used well, Twitter takes networking from awkward to awesome.

Twitter and Networking = Career Momentum

Using the tips our invited experts will share with you in this chapter, you can create a Twitter networking plan (see chapter 27 on using Twitter in just 15 minutes a day for ideas) that will get you out there, get you known, get you traction, and get you set for a lifetime of powerful and satisfying networking. We're talking career momentum!

Lindsey Pollak, an author, speaker, and consultant specializing in career and workplace issues, is passionate when she "talks Twitter." "Get it out of your head that Twitter is about what's for lunch!" is her frustrated reply to skeptics. "The comments I get from people who don't want to use Twitter is the same push-back that I get from people who don't see the value of networking.

"Twitter is a tool that you can use to engage with others in professional, authentic, and mutually beneficial ways—and it can help further your career. In many professions, using Twitter is essential for career management. I try to network in a mutually beneficial, authentic, and meaningful way. That's exactly how I engage people on Twitter."

Eight Best Practices for Networking on Twitter

We asked Lindsey to share her top tips for authentic, engaging networking on Twitter, which you'll find here:

1. **Show that you are worth knowing.** Part of networking is being interesting and having something to say. Writing interesting tweets that showcase what you know helps you become a valued resource—the "go-to" person.

2. **Help others get known.** When I meet people, I always ask them "What's your Twitter handle?" Then I follow them—even if they are new to Twitter. When you follow people on Twitter, it shows you care—that you have a vested interest in their success. It helps you build and reinforce relationships, especially when you retweet their content.

3. **Reinforce real-world relationships.** Networking is not just about building new relationships and meeting new people; it's about maintaining the relationships that you have. Twitter is a fantastic tool to tend those relationships—by retweeting other people, by sending shout-outs, by saying thank you. By simply following and listening to others.

4. **Listen.** "Listening" to what other people tweet is a form of networking—a sign of what's important to them. Lindsey's grandpa used to say, "There's a reason you have two ears and one mouth. Listen twice as much as you talk."

5. **Learn.** You can use Twitter to educate yourself about topics you don't know enough about. Lindsey has a friend who is working to raise startup funding for her company. Her friend follows a lot of venture capitalists and other investors. Through the Twitter stream, she learns as she watches them share

expertise, tips on what they look for as they decide what to fund, and trends in investing.

You can also use Twitter to follow people you know or admire to see how they are using Twitter. Whom do they admire? Whom do they quote?

6. **Throw people an icebreaker.** The best way to build relationships on Twitter is to behave as you do in real-life networking. If you are searching for a job, the fastest way to kill a new networking contact is to begin with the "ask statement": "I need a job." It's the same on Twitter.

An icebreaker can help you find common ground or a place to start. Lindsey talks about cupcakes every so often on Twitter. Her followers know she loves to bake them and loves to eat them. For her, cupcakes are a good entry point for conversation. She has even received direct messages (DMs) from other Twitter users who want to meet up for a cupcake.

7. **Be humble; be real; give back.** Be sure you show yourself as someone who can do more than just talk about what you want to do. The biggest mistake you can make on Twitter is the same as the one you can make in real life—being oblivious to those around you. Talking about yourself all the time, not saying thank you or acknowledging the role that others have played in your success, not showing that you are interested in what others have to say…all of this can be fatal to your Twitter presence and to your career momentum. So make sure that at least 30 percent of your tweets are ones that give back to others.

8. **Do one thing every day.** Lindsey shared her final advice in a tweet: "Do one thing every day to advance your career—including tweeting."

Professional Association Networking on Twitter

Professional associations and nonprofits in your field and industry can be a wonderful source of community and connection—and many have Twitter accounts. (These can generally be found through Twitter's directory—often under an acronym—or on the organization's home page.)

We tapped Wendy Terwelp, founder of the Rock Your Network® system, to talk with us about "working the room" in real-world professional associations. Wendy's all about teaching "networking without begging" and says, "Know that the more you give, the more you get. It's not all about you."

Like Lindsey, Wendy believes in icebreakers. Offline or on Twitter, Wendy advises that you should know "how to start a conversation. Develop at least three open-ended questions you can ask a person in your new networking group. And it's not, 'Hey, know anyone who's hiring?'"

Wendy stresses the importance of knowing when a group is a great fit for your career or business—and when it is not. For example, if you're active in the group and meeting the right people, it may be a good fit and conducive to building relationships that grow with you and your career. You can take that same concept to Twitter.

To make the most of a group, you've got to take an active role. Wendy is adamant that networking "is more than just showing up. Joining a networking group is a commitment." On Twitter it's essential to engage in dialogue, share information, and serve as a resource to your followers.

Wendy's advice to the networking-averse? "Know that networking is simply having a conversation with friends. Following good networking practices takes away the pain for your career gain." Twitter surely helps with that!

One of the fastest ways to get a job in your field is to spend time "in the sandbox" with other people who do the work you do. When you look at your peers as collaborators instead of as competition, you open up room for connections to happen organically and create a wider space for other people to help you. It is easier to create a space for yourself if you share resources, tips, and expertise before asking for a job. It also increases your chances.

One of the best ways to connect with colleagues is by following a professional association on Twitter. Doing so can be the equivalent of going to a professional conference 24/7, with 24/7 shop talk: You can connect with people who share your interests, find people who speak your language, and exchange ideas with those with different perspectives. A majority of the people who show up and engage in conversation are open to getting to know you.

Reach out and connect as you would at a physical conference or professional-development seminar and imagine the professional connections you could make. Some association Twitter accounts have thousands of followers, so find and follow your group now.

Many conferences now use Twitter hashtags to publicize the content of sessions and invite others to participate in the dialogue. If you can't go to a conference, you can still follow the hashtag, weigh in on conversation, and make connections. Now that's virtual reality!

IF YOU BUILD IT, THEY WILL COME

An Expert in Web Analytics and SEO Shares an Old-Fashioned Perspective on Networking

"Networking tools work best when you don't try to use them to network.... Instead, use them to connect and share. At the end of the day, the job seeker needs to understand the community and what they need. You should be building relationships all the time. Job search never works well when you are hunting down things, because people can feel it. You have to build up credibility before you ask for anything."

—Marshall Sponder (@WebMetricsGuru, former Monster.com SEO expert)

It's All About the People

We close this chapter with a visit to the Big Apple's Roger Smith Hotel. Using a hotel as a model for transforming online connections and making lasting relationships may seem like a stretch, but once you learn more you'll understand why we chose this destination.

According to the *Wall Street Journal*, New York hotels have slashed room rates by up to 50 percent since 2007 due to declining tourist demand. In spite of the down market, the Roger Smith Hotel (RSH) has flourished by taking a unique approach with marketing and social media. It has quickly become known not just as a hotel, but also as a go-to destination for conversation and connection—much like the artist-in-residence communities that famously existed at Manhattan's Algonquin and Chelsea hotels in the past. From tweetups and social media breakfasts to conferences and fund-raisers, the Roger Smith is a networking mecca.

Chandlee sat down with Brian Simpson (@bsimi), the hotel's Director of Social Hospitality, and walked away with five tips for networking that have put the Roger Smith Hotel on the map. You can repurpose these tips for your own job search and career:

- **Put relationships before the bottom line.** The feeling at the Roger Smith Hotel is that it is driven by people. Brian's insight is that "the bottom line will follow. If you focus only on the bottom line, you will miss it."

- **Partner with others to grow your own success.** By partnering with clients to market their events as if the hotel were a cosponsor, the Roger Smith invests in the success of its clients. In doing so, it has created its own niche. (Don't miss chapter 25 on creating your career niche.)

- **Give to get.** The Roger Smith shares event news and successes of its visitors via Twitter, blogs, and YouTube. The result? Viral marketing, increased attendance, and a win-win.

- **Use Twitter to learn what others need, as well as to connect and engage others.** Brian and his colleagues use Twitter to listen to client comments, engage in conversation, and help customers make serendipitous connections: They even invite people to stop by for a drink with out-of-town guests.

- **It's all about the people and their stories.** Imagine all the great people you've met briefly and wished you could stay in touch with. Twitter can make that happen, and that's how Brian and his colleagues use it: to stay in touch and help friends make connections.

Brian's parting advice for potential visitors to the Roger Smith, in tweet style:

Welcome to a community built with people, their stories, and the willingness to share with strangers in an open forum. Pull up a chair.

The Roger Smith Hotel's staff has used social media to create a dynamic global community and put their hotel on the map as an international hub of social networking. They've used Twitter to initiate and cultivate strong online connections that then become solid, even life-changing, offline relationships.

Use the advice in this chapter and *you* can become a virtual destination hub for *your* Twitter community, initiate offline connections, and perhaps welcome some employers as they stop by!

CHAPTER 23

LEVERAGING TWITTER THROUGHOUT YOUR JOB SEARCH AND NETWORKING

Featured contributors: Jason Alba (@JasonAlba) of JibberJobber.com, and William Arruda (@WilliamArruda) and Kirsten Dixson (@KirstenDixson) of Reach Branding Club

> *"No man is an Island, entire of itself; every man is a piece of the Continent, a part of the main..."*
>
> —*John Donne*

We believe in the power of Twitter.

We believe that Twitter has the power to help move you from hunter to hunted, from reactive to active, from job seeker to career manager, from chaos to control. We also believe that Twitter is not, nor should it be, a singular job search resource. In other words, don't put all your eggs in one basket.

One of the advantages of Twitter is that it connects and propels the power of so many other traditional and social media platforms. It may help to think of Twitter as a project manager, internist, or editor—a force that brings together and maximizes the strength of many related activities, resources, and professionals.

We asked Jason Alba, William Arruda, and Kirsten Dixson—all experts in social media, branding, and online identity—to guide us through the integration of Twitter with online and offline resources that best support job search and career visibility.

> **Need to Know:** *Social media* includes the various online technology tools that enable people to communicate easily via the Internet to share information and resources. Social media can include text, audio, video, images, podcasts, and other multimedia communications (http://tinyurl.com/alison-doyle-social-media).

Connecting the Real with the Virtual

"The best way to use Twitter is to connect the real with the virtual." That's what William Arruda, personal branding guru and coauthor of *Career Distinction* (Wiley, 2007), told us when we asked him about Twitter and job search.

He continued, "With all the talk about Web 2.0 and social media, people seem to have forgotten about real-world communications. Of course, you need to be visible on the Web to succeed in the new world of work, but you can't look at Twitter and other social media in isolation. You need ways to leverage what you are doing in the real world to build community with those who could help you find a job."

People don't live or work in the virtual world, so it makes sense to use offline activities to connect and expand your brand with your target audience. William suggests thinking about the traditional real-world communications you use to express your thought-leadership and brainstorm ways you can use Twitter to maximize those brand-building activities.

Continuing with that concept, William took us through how a training and development (T&D) executive could use Twitter to integrate on- and offline strategies to propel thought leadership that supports her brand.

Let's say she's known for expertise in how mentoring plays a role in employee satisfaction and retention. That's what makes her stand out from her colleagues and what should be made visible to her target audience—to the people who could help her get her next position. Her audience includes hiring managers, HR executives and recruiters who work with human resources professionals, and other influencers.

William suggests that our T&D executive do two things:

1. Identify a few ways to increase her visibility with her target audience, including writing an article for HR.com, speaking at a SHRM conference, and volunteering at her local HRNY chapter.

2. Take components of those offline activities online to deepen their quality and expand her reach. The next section shows 10 ways she can do that.

Ten Ways to Use Twitter to Integrate the Real and the Virtual

"Social media isn't the end-all-be-all, but it offers…unparalleled opportunity to participate in relevant ways. It also provides a launchpad for other marketing tactics. Social media is not an island. It's a high-power engine on the larger marketing ship."

—*Matt Dickman, Techno//Marketer (technomarketer.typepad.com)*

Pretend you are our training and development executive and you have a conference presentation to prepare and deliver. Here are 10 ideas from William for using

Twitter to help your offline event go virtual and vastly extend the content and dispersal of just one speaking engagement:

1. **Tweet for presentation content.** Use Twitter to engage your community to come up with the content for your presentation. Tell your followers you are speaking about mentoring at SHRM and would like to know what they would like to learn. This will start a conversation with your brand community and help you create content for your presentation. Be sure you are using hashtags such as #mentoring so you can reach people who may not be following you but are interested in your topic.

2. **Tweet your press release.** Create a press release indicating you are speaking at the conference. Post it to free press release search engines, such as prleap.com, and then tweet with a link to the press release.

3. **Tweet an event reminder.** Before leaving for the event, tweet to remind your followers that you are going to be at the conference. Mention that you would love to meet anyone who is going to be there. Encourage those who are interested to come to your session.

4. **Tweet a video.** Get your presentation filmed so you will have video clips you can use later. You can often arrange this with conference organizers. It's a great way to get quality video at no/low cost. Take the video clips from the conference, post them to sites such as YouTube, blip.tv, and Vimeo and tweet out the links. Video is a great way to deliver a complete communication.

5. **Tweet real-time data.** During the presentation, encourage audience participation and get data related to your thought-leadership by polling the audience—either during your presentation or with a survey they can fill out. For example, you can ask, "How many of you have official mentoring programs in your company?"

6. **Tweet real-time PR.** While presenting, encourage audience members to tweet about the presentation real-time. This is a powerful way to engage others in building your personal brand. And remember to include your Twitter name in your contact details so you can grow your following. If you bring business cards or other takeaways, include your Twitter name on these communication tools as well.

7. **Tweet your slides.** When you return from the conference, you can post your slides to sites such as sliderocket.com and tweet the link so people who were not there can access your words of wisdom.

8. **Tweet new stats.** Take the data you got from your audience and post the stats to your Web site or blog and share these via Twitter. For example, you could tweet this:

Only 25% of the people who attended my presentation work for a company that has an official mentoring program.

---

9. **Tweet new learnings.** You can tweet about your experiences and what you learned from the audience. One speaking event can have many relevant and compelling tweets!

10. **Tweet your thanks.** Send a thank-you tweet to all those who contributed to the conversation and to your presentation content, remembering to use @ before their Twitter names. It's important to acknowledge your followers!

You can take these same strategies and adapt them to other offline activities. Think about some of the things you do at work, and for work, and how you might use these tactics to better them, promote them, and leverage them.

> **Tip:** Read in appendix C how successful job seekers Desiree Kane, Shannon Yelland, and others leveraged Twitter across platforms during their job searches.

Go Virtual to Get Visible

"Blogging, podcasting, and staying up-to-date on Twitter, Facebook, and more is real work. It's this kind of real work that affords me the luxury to acquire new clients, build interesting digital marketing and communications initiatives, speak all over the world, and think ever more deeply about this space."

—*Mitch Joel, TwistImage.com*

Our colleagues, Jason Alba, author of *I'm on LinkedIn, Now What?* and *I'm on Facebook, Now What?* and Kirsten Dixson, coauthor of *Career Distinction* (Wiley, 2007), also volunteered their best strategies for building your visibility across online platforms. We hit pay dirt, with a treasure trove of advice for integrating Twitter with two of the most popular online social media sites—LinkedIn and Facebook—as well as e-mail, blogs, and more:

- If you don't have another Web site, put your LinkedIn URL as your Web site in your Twitter bio.

- When you make relevant changes to your LinkedIn profile, let your Twitter followers know about it with a tweet.

- Tweet the link to any questions you put up in the Answers section of LinkedIn, or any questions that are relevant to your industry or profession.

- Tweet LinkedIn Group URLs you recommend or join; if they are relevant to your industry or profession, you might be seen as a filter of good recommendations.

- When you find professional, interesting things in Facebook (such as Groups, Pages, or Events), share them with your Twitter network.

- Ask your Twitter network to join your Groups, Pages, or your Facebook and LinkedIn networks.

- Use the Facebook/Twitter application to update your Facebook status with your Twitter tweets.

- Make sure the contents of your tweets are consistent with the content of your Facebook and LinkedIn profiles and activities.

- In LinkedIn and Facebook, share your Twitter URL on your profile so others can follow you there, if that is their preferred networking tool.

- Consider rewriting some of your tweets to become your LinkedIn status. (Don't do this for all tweets, just tweets that are relevant to your LinkedIn network. The LinkedIn status seems to have a longer shelf life—in other words, it doesn't need to be updated frequently.) Use the #li or #in hashtags on tweets you want to share with your LinkedIn network.

- Have your recent tweets display in the sidebar of your blog (if you blog).

- Use your Twitter handle in the signature of a blog comment.

- Put the "Follow Me on Twitter" call-to-action with a link to your Twitter page in your e-mail signature.

- Tweet about a blog post that you wrote.

- Tweet when you've been quoted in an article (if the journalist has a Twitter account, be sure to promote and/or retweet him or her).

- Tweet to remind your followers of an upcoming chapter meeting, teleclass, or other offline or virtual event.

In closing, Kirsten explained why linking off- and online activity is so important: "Since only 20 percent of executives have taken proactive steps to increase the positive information found about them online (according to ExecuNet), you have a huge opportunity to stand out. And certainly using Twitter will put you ahead of the game and result in rewarding opportunities."

> *"How can you squander even one more day not taking advantage of the greatest shifts of our generation? How dare you settle for less when the world has made it so easy for you to be remarkable?"*
>
> *—Seth Godin, Seth Godin's Blog*

We challenge you to start with just one idea and see how it works. We predict you'll be hooked by the power of Twitter.

CHAPTER 24

TWITTER NETWORKING: A SAFE SPACE FOR INTROVERTS; A PARTY FOR EXTROVERTS

Featured contributors: Kim Batson (@CIO_Coach), August Cohen (@Resume_ Writer), and Wendy Gelberg (@WendyGelberg)

> *"You can't stay in your corner of the Forest waiting for others to come to you. You have to go to them sometimes."*
>
> — *Winnie the Pooh*

We like Twitter because it is the great equalizer: satisfying and effective for introverts, extroverts, and ambiverts. In simple terms, introverts get their energy from within and extroverts get their energy from people. Ambiverts enjoy social interaction but also relish some time alone. Statistics say that the latter describes most of us.

If you're an introvert, says Wendy Gelberg, author of *The Successful Introvert: How to Enhance Your Job Search and Advance Your Career,* "there's a good chance you prefer to have a small number of close friendships in your life rather than a larger number of more casual relationships. Too much social interaction is draining, and you need quiet time to recharge your batteries. Twitter can provide that."

"On the other hand," declares August Cohen, our extrovert expert, "extroverts can more easily demonstrate many of the talents employers value, and Twitter is the perfect platform to showcase these skills."

For both introverts and extroverts, the challenge in job search is to become known and trusted by those in a position to hire you or recommend you to others, and do so in a way that is both authentic—true to your personality—and manageable in terms of energy.

As we asserted in chapter 1, "Twitter is what you want it to be." We might also have said that Twitter is what you *need* it to be! If you are an introvert, Twitter is the quiet, controllable, "safe" space you need to build relationships that are so critical to job search. If you are an extrovert, Twitter unites you with a universe of people who can provide the energy and stimulation you need to stay upbeat and connected in your job search.

Top 10 Twitter Tips for Introverts

We tapped Wendy Gelberg and Kim Batson—a coach and personal brand strategist for CIOs and other technology executives (60 percent of her clients are introverts)— for their best advice on using Twitter for an introvert's job search. Here are their recommendations:

1. **Network.** By definition, people who use Twitter are open to building new relationships and interested in attracting followers. You can search for people that you'd like to get to know and initiate a conversation with them; most people will be quite receptive to your overtures. And if you connect LinkedIn (another introvert "safe place") to your Twitter account, you'll have even better results.

2. **Target.** Look for people in your industry, occupation, or target companies; use Twitter's "Find People" feature to identify them. You can use the Direct Message (DM) feature for a private reply. Suggest a phone or e-mail follow-up for a more in-depth exchange.

3. **Break the ice.** Introverts frequently prefer to dispense with superficial chat, but even face-to-face conversations begin with some kind of superficial ice-breaker comment, which then leads to a more in-depth conversation. On Twitter, you can initiate a conversation privately in a DM. Once you establish an initial connection, you can continue the conversation through e-mail, by phone, or in person.

4. **Build relationships.** One key to relationships is demonstrating an interest in others, and introverts often have a desire for deeper understanding. Draw on this strength and read, comment on, and retweet people's links, blogs, Web sites, and tweets. When you read what others have written and show a genuine interest in them, you build relationships.

5. **Deepen relationships.** You can further a relationship with networking contacts by spending a week or two retweeting their tweets or responding to their conversations. Then send them a public message when the time is right. For example:

@YourContactsName Enjoyed hearing your thoughts on [fill in the blank]. Would love to have a deeper conversation if you're available. Please DM me to exchange email/phone info.

---

6. **Give to others.** Many introverts love Twitter for its treasure trove of information. Expand your own professional knowledge and, in turn, become a resource for others by passing along information. They will appreciate your passing it along, and so will those who originated it. It's a win-win.

7. **Focus on what you know.** Many introverts are subject matter experts (SMEs) who can find and garner Twitter followers around that expertise. People often follow other tweeters based on topic. This is a terrific way for introverts to build a network, connect with recruiters and companies who seek that type of expertise, find opportunities, and even stay confident in a job search.

8. **Get on the radar.** It can be difficult, even exhausting, for introverts to keep up with a lot of relationships. By frequently tweeting about your professional activities and sharing links to other resources that are helpful to others, you can almost effortlessly connect with your followers. When opportunities or projects come up that match your background, you're top-of-mind.

9. **Feel free to think.** Many introverts like to think first and act later. Twitter allows them to do just that. Unlike face-to-face conversations that require an immediate response, you can read a message, think on it, and then reply.

10. **Feel free to listen.** Twitter allows introverts to listen intently to the views, comments, and questions of others and to look and listen for clues on industry, company, products, and service challenges. Introverts pay attention to what is going on around them. This observing trait may allow you to find opportunities that others may miss!

Top 10 Twitter Tips for Extroverts

"It has been said that Twitter is a virtual cocktail party," August Cohen told us when we asked her about Twitter's fit for extroverts. "It provides immediate engagement, a continuous stream of small talk, and connection with the external world. In short, it is a perfect fit for extroverts' need for constant connection and stimulation as well as a conduit for the relationship building necessary for effective job search."

We asked August to share her best practices for extroverts' job search on Twitter. Here are her recommendations:

1. **Go from bored to busy.** Turn your tendency to be easily bored into motivation to use Twitter. Twitter provides variety and immediate gratification. You can review the activity of your favorite people, create a new industry-specific list, review your @ mentions, or thank people who retweeted your posts. Every time you log on, there will be something new for you to explore.

2. **Optimize without overwhelming.** While it is tempting for extroverts to rapidly build a large network of followers, focus on finding people in the industries or companies where you want to work. This will allow you time to develop meaningful online relationships that could lead to opportunities.

3. **Start conversations.** After finding people you want to follow, review their timelines to learn more about them. Go back several pages. Through updates you will learn more about their personas, the companies they work for, and

issues they may be struggling with. Extroverts enjoy small talk, so use this skill to start some casual conversations and build rapport.

4. **Balance your brand.** Review your tweets on occasion to ensure there is a nice balance among information, discussion, and advice, while being brand consistent every time you post. Extroverts are enthusiastic and positive in their approach to life, and these characteristics, supported by your unique value proposition, will draw potential employers your way.

5. **Be generous.** Extroverts love being the center of attention, and without real-world verbal cues that can keep that behavior in check, you risk having it be all about you. Retweeting a post or helping someone solve a work-related problem can capture his or her attention—and gratitude—which can pay off.

6. **Organize.** Combine your expertise with your enjoyment in participating in and conducting group events. Demonstrate your leadership skills by organizing a virtual mini-conference or think-tank using a hashtag (#). Make sure you invite followers from companies where you would like to work. If you are attending an offline conference, be sure to tweet it for your followers who can't be there in person.

7. **Be patient.** Receptive and tuned into their environment, extroverts are quick to respond. Just as in the workplace, Twitter is a diverse community of personalities, so don't take offense if someone is not as responsive as you are; he or she may be busy or could have missed your comment.

8. **Think before you tweet.** Extroverts tend to think as they speak. This can backfire online where comments have a long shelf life. Don't get caught up in the moment and become involved in a controversial or heated topic. You don't want a prospective boss or coworker to have something harsh or negative be their first impression of you. Quickly delete anything inappropriate.

9. **Feed your energy.** Extroverts are energized by people and fade when they are alone. Twitter offers 24/7 companionship and can be a great antidote. And by using your mobile device, you can even manage your search activity while away from your PC. A job search can be a lonely process; Twitter will help keep you engaged. Just be aware that Twitter can be so much fun that it is easy to lose track of time. Stay focused!

10. **Take it offline.** Extroverts are great at marketing themselves, and love being in social situations. Organizing a local event will increase your chances of meeting company decision makers that may know of hidden job openings. Arrange a local tweetup, or DM a follower you may be able to help. Or invite a connection to have lunch or coffee with you. The odds are good he or she will say yes, especially if he or she is an extrovert like you.

Notice that many of the tips for introverts and extroverts are similar—best practices that have the same intent, but can be applied in ways that meet introverts' and extroverts' particular needs.

CHAPTER 25

NICHE MARKET NETWORKING ON TWITTER

Featured Expert: Cindy Kraft of CFO-Coach.com and networking and niche marketing expert for the Career Thought Leaders Consortium (@CFOCoach)

"Mass markets are irrelevant; it's all about niches: identifying what you do really well and doing it supremely well."

—Deborah Gallant in her newsletter summarizing points from the new book, What Would Google Do?

One of the frequent challenges that job seekers encounter in the employment market is standing out from the crowd. Consider this: Googling "operational CFO Biotech" yields almost two million hits.

Here's where having a niche can help. We tapped Cindy Kraft, one of the career industry's leading experts on career niching, to help us understand how to whittle down those two million hits. "Narrowing that search string to 'operational CFO Biotech Startup' generates under 10,000 hits," advised Cindy. "For even fewer hits, apply that keyword search at sites like Twitter or LinkedIn, which are much smaller in scope than Google, and you'll see the importance of targeting a niche market."

"You have to know what your aim is—what you are all about and what you can do. You have to have a short summary. Telling a recruiter you can do anything is like telling them you can do nothing."

—Jeff Lipshultz

Mind Your *Ps* and *Qs* (Positions, Quality, and Quantity)

In job search, the most effective seekers often take a contrarian approach: They apply to a dozen positions as opposed to a hundred and yet still have a very high rate of interviews to applications because they understand the value of niche marketing. It's all about quality over quantity.

The show tune from *Little Orphan Annie*, "I'll Do Anything for You," may work well for Annie and Daddy Warbucks, but it doesn't work in job search. As we've discussed, it's important to know your strengths and how you fit an employer's needs. The ability to market yourself in this way is essential to your success.

In this chapter, Cindy shares tips and tricks to find your niche—to position yourself as an expert in a particular field, job function, or both. According to Cindy, "Hiring managers frequently look first for specialists with deep expertise in one particular area—typically a function, an industry, or a specialty—then evaluate finalists based on the candidates' ability to also understand how their role fits into and contributes to the larger organization."

We agree with Cindy that niche marketing can help you do this. Branding and niche marketing are related. While branding is about you, a niche is about where or with whom you'll apply your "you."

> **Need to Know:** According to BusinessDictionary.com, a *niche* is "a focused, targetable part of a market," while *niche marketing* is "concentrating all marketing efforts on a small but specific and well-defined segment of the population. Niches do not 'exist' but are 'created' by identifying needs, wants, and requirements.... As a strategy, niche marketing is aimed at being a big fish in a small pond instead of being a small fish in a big pond."

We asked Cindy why Twitter works so well for niching. She told us that, "Through Twitter, you have multiple opportunities to define your niche—from your bio 'Twitpitch' and Twitter background to the content of your tweets. You also have multiple options to niche market and build your community—from lists to the people whom you decide to follow and engage in conversation."

Five Strategies for Niche Marketing on Twitter

Throughout this book, we share strategies you can use to advertise your niche on Twitter. You'll want to choose wisely your Twitter handle (the name you use on Twitter), create a compelling 160me (your 160-character Twitter bio), upload an avatar (an on-brand photo or graphic), and consider a special background that gives readers an immediate impression of your brand and niche. (Review chapters 10, 11, and 12 for more details.)

Cindy suggests using these five strategies to advance your niche marketing:

1. **Find and follow people in your niche market.** Use the Twitter search feature to find and follow people within your niche. Most people will follow you back, particularly if you have interesting tweets and are engaging others through dialogue and RTs. However, Cindy cautions, if you have a long list of people you follow, with few followers and no tweets, this will quickly undermine your credibility, as well as your niche-market expertise.

   Think "third-party" affiliations when building your stream of followers. Who are your targets following and how might they also be valuable for you to follow? These are your third-party affiliations. You can cast your net wide as long as you also cast it strategically.

2. **Build lists of people within your niche market and follow their lists of potential contacts.** Cindy says that visibility—branded visibility—must be your continuing focus. The greater your visibility among your target market, the greater your opportunity for being known as an authority within your niche market.

3. **Create Google alerts to provide a consistent stream of information and resources to share with others.** Set up multiple alerts using industry-specific keywords that will come directly to your e-mail inbox. Cindy advises, "Rather than tweeting just the title of the article and the link, provide your perspective and the link. That small act can move you from being perceived as merely a peddler of information to reinforcing your credibility as a subject-matter expert possessing a true understanding of the situation."

4. **Track the success of your tweet links.** Use bit.ly to shorten those long URLs and track clicks to the links you are providing to your niche market. Tracking those clicks can serve as a guide to being more strategic and targeted in the information you provide, and confirm the direction you should take to reinforce your area of expertise.

5. **Use Twitter Lists to create a networking list of experts in your field to follow on Twitter.** Cindy says Twitter's list feature is one of the best ways to demonstrate your knowledge of your niche market. Mark the list as public; then register with Listology (http://listology.com). Listology allows you to share the public URL with your Twitter community and showcase your expertise as an information "curator" (see chapter 29).

Make Your Network Aware of Your Niche with Twitter

There is no point in being an authority within a niche market if no one in that market knows about you! Cindy's take on today's niching? "The old definition of networking used to be 'who do I know?' Today, the definition is 'who knows about me?' Enter Twitter, a great mechanism for expanding the reach of people who know you and also know about you."

Once you have your Twitter identity cemented (as described in sections 2 and 3), it's time to expand your network by tweeting. Doing so will simultaneously build your credibility and raise your visibility as an authority in your niche. "While you have a wealth of information to share with your followers," Cindy cautions, "remember that Twitter is about engaging readers—it's not a one-sided conversation. Just as in face-to-face networking, merely showing up doesn't build trust. You must talk *with* your followers, not *to* them."

Who You Are Is as Important as What You Do

Cindy is adamant that good niching is good branding: "One of the most overlooked parts of niching is the 'power of the personal.' Nobody is truly one-dimensional and most employers don't want an employee who is. Being authentically branded within a niche market allows your true personality, passions, and interests to be visible to employers who are seeking well-rounded clients."

> **Tip:** Make your tweets multidimensional. Having a niche doesn't mean you can tweet only on your area of expertise. Just remember the 75/25 rule: For job seekers, approximately 75 percent of tweets should be on-brand and professional, whereas 25 percent of tweets can convey conversational and personal, yet appropriate, content.

Cindy continues, "Since culture fit is the most difficult part of hiring, wrapping your niche in your brand can position you as unique, interesting, and intriguing while attracting exactly the right opportunities."

Our expert suggests "creating lists of followers who also share your passion and interests. These lists make it easy for a recruiter or company decision maker to scroll your posts and understand who you are from a 360-degree perspective.

"Finally, integrate your Twitter and LinkedIn accounts to allow those niche-specific posts to also appear on your LinkedIn profile and update status. If you are using your Facebook account as a professional rather than personal vehicle, you can also send your niched tweets to that account, adding even more depth to your online visibility."

This integrated strategy is the first step in creating a credible online presence that positions you as *the* authority within a niche market. And, as with all niches, the tighter and more narrow your niche, the deeper and more expert you become.

Niche Market Networking Checklist

To determine (and pump up) your niche's bench strength, Cindy offers these 12 questions to consider:

- Have you identified your sweet spot? (What is it?)
- Do you know the keywords employers use to find you?
- Are you clear on what market you serve?
- Do you know who else is operating in that space?
- Do you know where the gaps are between you and your competition?
- If the market is saturated, have you niched yourself more narrowly?
- Are you executing a strategic communication plan that broadcasts a tight and focused message?

- Do your Twitter bio and LinkedIn tagline scream "niche"?
- Are you building strong relationships among your target market?
- When you google yourself, do the results convey a clear, consistent, and compelling message around your niche?
- Are you raising visibility among your target market by writing articles, posting on industry blogs, and participating in forums or online communities?
- When people hear your name, do they immediately finish the sentence with your niche of expertise?

You should be able to answer a resounding "yes" to all!

Niching and Networking: A Career-Long Strategy

Carving out a niched presence on Twitter isn't a short-term job search technique. The real strength of this communication strategy is in developing a longer-term career management plan that keeps you visible to your target audience throughout the remainder of your career.

We asked Cindy for the most important thing to remember when niching using Twitter. She replied, "Before you tweet, ask yourself: Does this post positively portray my overall personality, strengths, passion, and interests? Does it further my positioning as a well-rounded subject-matter expert? If the answer is yes, then tweet it!"

CHAPTER 26

DISCRETIONARY AUTHENTICITY: HOW TO SHARE, HOW MUCH, AND WITH WHOM

Sharing information on Twitter is a balancing act between the personal and professional. Frequently, users follow others based on profile, interests, and field of expertise, only to sign off later if the content is too dry. Even the most agile leader loses crowd appeal if cues and overtures from others are ignored. The ideal content blend on Twitter is a dance that showcases both personal engagement and professional expertise.

Although being authentic—sharing hints of your personality and individual preferences—is an important part of Twitter, it is equally important to use discretion in what you show to your audience. Very few audience members attending a ballet would be equally interested in viewing all the practice hours that go into a performance. Fewer still are interested in viewing the calluses, blisters, and malformations frequently found on a dancer's feet. The performance is a part of the magic—only a glimpse of what's going on backstage is necessary. We call this ability to know what (and what not) to share *discretionary authenticity*.

> **Need to Know:** *Discretionary authenticity* is the art of presenting your genuine voice in an accessible, positive, and professional light.

If "sharing but not baring" constitutes Twitter success, how do you determine what is—and isn't—appropriate to share? What elements should be incorporated into your dance? We've talked about "on the nose" content in chapter 14. Now let's examine what not to share.

What Not to Share: The Blacklist

Sex. Politics. Religion. Jokes or disparaging remarks about race, ethnicity, or geographic location. Trash talking about your coworkers, boss, or former colleagues. These are hot buttons that you should handle with extreme care when tweeting—

unless you plan to use a pseudonym, have sworn off running for public office, or have chosen a career path that makes a Google search of your name unlikely.

The Twitterverse and popular press frequently cover off-the-cuff remarks that have created career catastrophes for users. You may have heard about the PR consultant who, headed to a training session he was leading at FedEx headquarters in Memphis, badmouthed the city after a late-night flight. Ironically, he encouraged the entire marketing staff to follow him on Twitter. When they did, they discovered his tweet—and his comments almost cost him his position. A recent graduate was not so fortunate: She questioned whether she should accept a job at Cisco with a "fatty salary and work she hated" or not have a job. She didn't get to make the decision herself; Cisco made it for her after an alert employee shared her public decision-making process.

Although controversial content can increase followers, you could pay a professional price for the attention. Use common sense in deciding what to write about and how. If in doubt over whether you should say something, sleep on it. As an example, this "before" example reeks of frustration, pessimism, and self-focus:

Blew another interview yesterday; having to prep for another one tomorrow. I'm so frustrated. I'll never get a job.

The after version conveys energy, curiosity, and community/engagement:

Preparing for interview. Friend was recently stumped by this question: What is your second biggest weakness? How would you answer?

How to Share

As discussed in chapter 27, you do not need to tune into Twitter 18 hours a day to be an active community participant. In fact, many community members feel that less is more and quickly choose to unfollow those who tweet too much. If you send out an average of five tweets an hour throughout the day, you stand a fair chance of losing your readers instead of engaging them.

Here are a few best practices for sharing information.

Keep It Bite-Sized

Write for the "goldfish" attention span of seven to nine seconds, and limit yourself to one tweet at a time. While it may seem simple to continue one lengthy thought over three tweets released almost simultaneously, you may annoy your readers. Further, they may not see your "chain of thought" in natural sequence, since it may be interrupted midstream by tweets from others.

Let Your Audience in on the Joke

Avoid using an @reply to someone for inside jokes or comments that cannot be understood independently; send direct messages (DMs) instead.

Who likes to feel left out? No one we know. If you have the option to respond to a message with a Direct Message, use this feature. Likewise, use a Direct Message if an @reply is unlikely to engage other members of your audience or encourage others to view your Twitter stream.

Be careful sharing information about yourself—or others—that has the potential to create a negative impact. There are very few tweets worth losing a friend or a job offer over.

How Much to Share

> *"The secret of being tiresome is in telling everything."*
>
> *—Voltaire*

If you are in an active job search or currently employed in a visible role, decisions on "how much to share" may be determined for you. For example, if you are applying for any position that requires a security clearance, your best Twitter strategy may be not to tweet at all. You may also be bound by confidentiality agreements and social media bans that keep you from tweeting about work.

With the exception of the "hot topics" mentioned above, there are no hard-and-fast rules on how much sharing is too much for the Twitter community. That being said, our general recommendation is to tweet in moderation—and to observe the strategies used by your most professional peers in doing so.

As we mentioned in chapter 13, shoot for a minimum of 15 tweets a week and no more than 20 tweets per day. Recall the "on the N.O.S.E." advice from chapter 14, and the information on the art of retweeting in chapter 15, for insights on what to share in those tweets.

With Whom to Share

> *"Your audience gives you everything you need. They tell you.*
> *There is no director who can direct you like an audience."*
>
> *—Fanny Brice, actress and inspiration for* Funny Girl

One of the nicest aspects of Twitter is the opportunity to receive automatic feedback: Through monitoring your @replies and direct messages, you can get a sense of which types of messages are well received by your audience. If you choose to have an open network on Twitter (in other words, you're not restricting potential followers from viewing content), you can also gauge your relative success by the number of followers you have whose interests are similar to, or compatible with, your own.

(For additional tools to measure your reputation, reach, and readability, see chapter 31 on Twitter APIs.)

As we've discussed, knowing your audience—and potential readership—is essential for determining your messaging strategy and sharing appropriately.

A Three-Point AIM Model for Appropriate Sharing

The following three-point process will help you determine how and when to share information on Twitter.

- **A = Audience:** Ask yourself, "Who is my target audience? Will this message appeal to my followers? Is this message appropriate for my viewers?"

- **I = Intended Impact:** Consider these questions: "Does this message share information that I feel comfortable disclosing with others? Will the message result in engaging my followers? Can this tweet help me build community and facilitate conversation?"

- **M = Messaging:** Check yourself: "If I had my own PR expert, would he or she advise me to send this message? If not, and the message is important, how can I reframe my 140 characters?"

Here's how the three-point process could look given the following scenario: You've lost your job or been downsized.

Some people might be tempted to tweet their gut response:

I lost my job, need a new one fast. I am sooooo angry. After all I've done for them! How dare they! Anybody got any job leads?

The AIM model prevents the job seeker from tweeting unflattering content:

- **A = Audience:** "I interact with a diverse community on Twitter, many of whom work outside my field and industry. I don't want the Twitterverse to know that I feel anger toward my most recent employer. I can reserve sharing my feelings for close friends and family."

- **I = Intended Impact:** "I want to receive job leads and suggested resources for my job search, but I also want to preserve my reputation. I want to play offense, not defense. My goal is to scout out opportunities that align with my skills and areas of expertise."

- **M = Messaging:** "I will use language that doesn't reflect anger, bitterness, or discouragement. I will make this an opportunity to make people aware I am available."

After filtering through the AIM model, the tweet now reads like this:

Exploring new options on the career front. Esp. interested in working in videography. Suggestions on co.s doing cool things in this area?

We're not suggesting that you look at the Audience-Intended Impact-Message points before each and every tweet. However, do remember them when you might feel an urge to respond in anger or share personal information.

Twitter Tips for Discretionary Authenticity

Finally, remember these tips to find the right tone for your tweets:

- **Share your status, but don't lead with a need.** If you're not conducting a confidential search, let people know about your availability. In addition to occasionally tweeting about your availability, also mention it at the end of your 160me Twitter bio (for example, "open to new opps" or "on the market" or simply "job seeker"; see chapter 10 for more info on the 160me Twitter bio).

- **Use good judgment.** When tweeting, consider potential negative impacts. Think twice before you tweet.

- **Stick to the facts.** Avoid language that describes negative feelings.

- **Reframe problems as questions.** Avoid sharing information that could be taken out of context or misinterpreted.

- **Beware the overshare (aka OS).** If you're using Twitter to advance your career, avoid tweets about your love life ("I broke up with Chris today"), financial status ("Running out of money; gotta find a job fast"), physical condition ("I'm sick to my stomach…been in the bathroom all morning"), everyday comments about your kids ("Susie was so cute today finger-painting"), and the like. None of these tweets is likely to advance your career or fast-forward your search!

For a humorous list of what not to say on Twitter, see ResumeBear.com's compilation of "30 Ways to Lose a Job on Twitter," a few of which are included here:

I used a new Auto-send email feature last night on my boss. Completely fooled him! He called me this a.m. to thank me for working so late!

Anyone know ANYONE who is hiring? I'm officially quitting my job asap. I'll do whatever people!

I hate the fact they have Twitter blocked at my job… I can't twitt like I want to. Gotta do it from my phone.

Find the entire list here: http://tinyurl.com/resumebear-lose-job-on-Twitter.

SECTION 6

CONDUCTING YOUR TWITTER JOB SEARCH IN 15 MINUTES A DAY

27. Maximize Twitter in Just 15 Minutes a Day

28. Using Twitter for Job Leads, Feeds, and Advice Needs

29. Twitter Lists: Streamlining Tweets and Optimizing Your Experience

30. Research on Twitter: Finding People, Positions, Places to Work, and Other Puzzle Pieces

31. Twitter APIs: There's an App for That!

32. Parting Tweets of Wisdom from Savvy Job Seekers

CHAPTER 27

MAXIMIZE TWITTER IN JUST 15 MINUTES A DAY

"Live in day-tight compartments."

— *William Osler*

At the turn of the 20th century, renowned physician William Osler became a master of time management, astounding his colleagues with his seamless ability to combine patient care, student mentoring, writing textbooks, and humorous fiction. He was a strong advocate of what he referred to as "managing your time in day-tight compartments"—essentially budgeting your time so that one task does not interfere with another.

If you love people and information (even gossip!), Twitter can be addictive. And when in job search mode, online activity can be like a Siren's call, seductively holding you to that computer screen or smart phone. But it's important to break free and stay focused on all of your job search activities, not just Twitter. Twitter requires discipline—a "day-tight compartment." We're here to help.

> **Tip:** Be in it for the long haul—learning the nooks and crannies and nuances of Twitter takes time. When it comes to Twitter, those who persevere prosper.

Strategies for Optimizing Your Time on Twitter

You can integrate Twitter into your job search activities and you *can* do it in 15 minutes a day (after some learning-curve time for setting up your account and reviewing the basics).

It's disturbingly easy to spend hours watching and responding to your Twitter stream—it's as easy as spending hours applying to positions online, or as easy as spending far too much time Web surfing. We like the concept of spending 15 well-planned, solidly productive minutes a day on Twitter, at least initially, because it imposes a strategy and discipline that keeps you focused on the big picture—your job search—rather than the procrastinator's playground of the Web.

"Take charge of your Twitter time so it doesn't leak into other activities. Schedule it just as you would a meeting: Take a few minutes to prepare; be alert and fully engaged during the 'meeting'; and after it's over, quickly evaluate your effectiveness, note key insights, and jot down strategies for the next meeting. Avoid lingering after the 'meeting' so you're not late for your next job search activity!"

—*Nancy Branton, Director of Leadership Coach Academy*

Your 15-Minute-a-Day Schedule

As the subtitle of this book states, we promised you strategies to make Twitter work for you in just 15 minutes a day. Here's how.

Ten Steps to 15 Minutes

We have found these 10 simple steps will make your 15-minute-a-day Twitter approach simple, swift, and strong:

1. **Know what you want to accomplish and track your progress.** Monitor your momentum and value. Twitter provides instant feedback: You can tell if you are reaching your intended audience by the number of @replies, DMs, and retweets you receive. Who needs Nielsen research?

2. **Know your limits.** What's your attention span? Should you be tweeting at work? Do you get lost Web surfing? Are you easily distracted? Don't let yourself get sidetracked dreaming of tweets while you are taking care of other things. Bookmark or star favorites online, and keep a notebook or file of topics and themes that you would like to tweet about later.

3. **What's your best time to tweet and how often?** When are most of your targets online? (See chapter 31 for information on discovering the ideal tweeting times to engage your target audience.) Are you going to break up your tweet times during the day? Are you going to tweet once a day? Of course, you'll have a better chance of having your tweets seen if you tweet several times throughout the day or schedule tweets to be sent later. (If you are in an active job search, your Twitter time may be fundamentally different than using it for your job or for fun.)

4. **How will you schedule your tweets?** You don't need to be online to tweet. You can do so from your mobile device, or jot down what you want to share and tweet later. (See chapter 31 for information on APIs and tools to schedule tweets for later delivery.)

Tip: Although much of the power (and fun) of Twitter is in its spontaneous conversation, there will also be times you'll want to schedule tweets to go out later. www.SocialOomph.com (formerly TweetLater) allows you to do just that. Set up an account (it's free); then schedule a few tweets of an informative nature to go out throughout the day.

5. **Find and create content.** Tongue tied? You're not alone. That's often what halts people in their tracks as they begin to use Twitter. If you find yourself on the verge of tweeting about what you had for lunch, take the advice of Heidi Richards Mooney of SpeakingWithSpirit.com, who recommends getting up from your desk and getting a breath of fresh air. Recall the tips at the end of chapter 14 for content ideas.

6. **Find and follow people.** Be selective about whom you follow. If you have too much information in your stream, you'll miss much of it and risk being overwhelmed. Use Twitter Lists (chapter 29) or Twitter APIs (chapter 31) to organize and review your stream by follower, topic, and more.

7. **Find and pursue leads and opportunities.** See chapter 28 for tips on finding job leads and more on Twitter.

8. **Share the glory.** Maximize your time—and develop your community—by making it more about them and less about you. Don't spend all your time creating your own tweets; participate in the community dialogue and disseminate ideas and news from others by retweeting (refer to chapter 15 for more details).

9. **Don't share too much!** Don't populate your entire Twitter stream with retweets or @replies. With too many retweets, people will think you don't have anything to say, whereas too many conversational @replies will make people feel left out—neither of which are great impressions for a prospective hire.

10. **Give of yourself.** Join @jobangels and other philanthropic groups and give back when you can. Watch for opportunities to offer a tip, insight, job lead, or helping hand.

FIVE FACTS THAT WILL INCREASE YOUR INFLUENCE ON TWITTER

Marshall Sponder (@WebMetricsGuru), former Monster.com SEO Expert

To increase your influence and impact on Twitter, remember to

1. Tweet more, using targeted keywords and hashtags.

2. Gain followers. Use Google HotTrends to find hot topics, look for a match on Twitter, and then find, follow, and engage with those participating in conversation.

3. Follow influential people. Use http://twitter.mailana.com/ to find local thought leaders and influencers by keyword. Follow, engage, and help people with their needs.

4. Offer free information for your followers, which will help you with retweets.

5. Attend tweetups to meet new Twitter peeps and deepen relationships.

Plan Your Work and Work Your Plan

You may find making (and keeping) a 15-minute schedule challenging at the beginning of your new Twitter experience. However, as the weeks progress, you'll find favorite people and tools, and you'll develop a rhythm to your engagement.

Keep your goals in mind and decide where to best use your time. Your schedule does not have to be the same each day. Perhaps one day you share research, one day you share thought leadership, one day you engage in conversations, and one day you retweet. The idea is to be multidimensional. Most people do an array of activities on Twitter, and your "Twitter for Job Search" days might consist of a bit of research, a bit of conversation, a quick look at job listings and related hashtags, and a check-in with employers and recruiters you follow.

Although you can find value quickly on Twitter, it does take some time to gain momentum. We recommend phasing into your plan.

CHANDLEE BRYAN'S DAY-TIGHT TWITTER JOB SEARCH BLUEPRINT

Go from NOOB (Newbie) to "Nailed It!" in Just Four Weeks

This four-week blueprint will ease you into the Twitterverse.

Week One: Twitter Boot Camp

- Allow yourself time for a learning curve.

- Create your account, claim your username, and design your background.

- Set goals for job search—how do you want to use Twitter: as a source of job leads, for company research, to expand your network...?

- Read chapter 10 and write your 160me Twitter bio.

- Read chapter 14 on content and write 10 to 12 tweets offline. Tweet one or two of them each time you log in.

- Follow 15 people you know who won't be judging your account (start with your authors—we're rooting for you!).

(continued)

(continued)

Week Two: Lurking and Cultural Immersion
- Search for hashtags and industries of interest to you.
- Actively begin following people you don't know in your field.
- Observe posts of others and how they use hashtags.
- Subscribe to job feeds (see chapter 28).
- Subscribe to Twitter Lists (see chapter 29).

Week Three: Full Throttle
- Ask engaging questions that start conversations.
- Retweet others.
- Tweet blog posts and other items of interest that align with your brand or career goals (save space by shortening URLs in your links).
- Don't forget the 75/25 rule: approximately 75 percent of content should be professional and 25 percent can be personal.

Week Four and Beyond: Onward, in 15 Minutes a Day!
- Expand your reputation, including creating Lists.
- Revise retweets to include your own opinion.
- Incorporate both online and offline content for tweeting (from attending association meetings and workshops to sharing Google News Alerts or blog comments).

We predict that if you use Chandlee's blueprint for the "Day-Tight Job Search" to plan your work and work your plan for 15 minutes a day, you'll find that your network will grow, your relationships will deepen, your job search will become more productive, and you'll just have more fun!

CHAPTER 28

USING TWITTER FOR JOB LEADS, FEEDS, AND ADVICE NEEDS

"Finding my job on Twitter was pure serendipity. At the time I was working two contract jobs, both of which could have possibly turned into something full time, so I wasn't really looking for a new job. My now-colleague Greg Swan tweeted about an opening for a junior Web developer at the PR agency where he worked. I asked for more information about the position, but wasn't seriously considering it. A few weeks later, some circumstances changed, and I immediately thought of Greg's tweet. I sent my resume, and now I work with a great team at Weber Shandwick."

—*Doug Hamlin (@doughamlin)*

Expanding your network, discussing news and trends in your industry, and showcasing your interests and expertise are all indirect—and effective—approaches to the job search. This chapter, however, focuses on a more traditional—and direct—approach to the job search: the position opening. We'll share how you can find and follow loads of leads for job listings through Twitter.

In some ways, looking for a job on Twitter is not unlike looking on major job search boards: When you start looking, you will quickly find that there are hundreds of places to search, and that screening out the best places to find qualified leads can be a job in itself. But take a closer look and you'll see what many recruiters, hiring managers, and job seekers have already discovered: Twitter is a revolutionary forum to post and share job leads. With no charge to tweet positions, employers have a free source for advertising—and a faster way to communicate real-time openings. Twitter is, as a June 2009 article in *BusinessWeek* proclaimed, "enough to make a Monster [.com] tremble."

A caution: If you choose to find listings exclusively by following other Twitter users who post jobs, you may be flooded with information in your Twitterstream. You can filter out the "noise" of openings and focus on the positions that are most relevant to your skills using Twitter lists, RSS feeds, and job search engines.

Need to Know: A *feed*, sometimes referred to as a syndicated feed or an RSS feed, is Web content from a source such as a blog or Twitter that can be delivered to your cell phone, e-mail, or a designated Web page you set up. You can subscribe to a feed with services like Feedreader.com or Google.com/reader to receive updates for viewing when and where it's convenient for you.

Feeds enable you to actively review new content on a relevant topic without having to search for it on your own; once you've established a feed, the information will be delivered to you automatically. Feeds can help you optimize your time in conducting employer research, monitoring trends in your field, and subscribing to job openings.

Sources of Job Leads: Search Engines for Job Listings

Job leads abound on Twitter. Here are our favorite Twitter destinations for finding job leads and insider information on how to apply:

- **TweetMyJobs.com:** With some half-million job tweets per month (and growing), you're likely to hit pay dirt here. TweetMyJobs.com obtains job listings directly from 4,000+ employers and then tweets those announcements out through its 6,300 job channels. At the site, specify that you're interested in receiving tweets, for example, for management jobs in Fresno, CA, or programming jobs in Atlanta, GA. Since job tweets originate here, and you can receive job tweet text messages on your cell phone, you can get first crack at the freshest openings (a big advantage), avoid spam, and eliminate the noise factor on Twitter when it comes to job hunting.

  Some of the 6,300 job channels include @tmj_bos_sales (sales jobs in the Boston area), @tmj_atl_it (IT jobs in the Atlanta area), @tmj_sfo_health (healthcare jobs in the San Francisco area), and so on.

- **TwitterJobSearch.com:** Similar to the Web aggregators Indeed.com and SimplyHired.com, TwitterJobSearch.com is an aggregator of job postings on Twitter. It takes the fire-hose feed of all Twitter tweets, identifies which tweets are job announcements, and aggregates them into its database. Search by job title, career field, and location. If you want to look for Twitter-posted jobs in just one place, look here.

You can also search for job postings via Twitter's general search engine:

- **http://search.twitter.com:** Search for jobs by common hashtags: #jobs, #jobpostings. To find jobs by location, search for city name and #jobs. For example, #chicago and #jobs finds jobs in Chicago, Illinois. (Learn more about hashtags in the next section; we'll discuss the search feature further in chapter 30.)

THE DEATH OF JOB BOARDS?

The demise of the resume has long been predicted. Is it time to ask the same question about job boards? When sites like TweetMyJobs offer companies the ability to tweet their job openings at a fraction of what it costs to advertise openings on sites like Monster and CareerBuilder, there is cause to wonder. On top of that, employers are optimizing the employment sections of their own Web sites so that their results can show ahead of the general job boards in search engine results.

What's the draw? In the *2009 Jobvite Social Recruitment Survey,* recruiters explained their rationale for using social media networks: "77 percent use the networks to reach passive job seekers; 74 percent because of the lower cost; and 72 percent to find candidates with hard-to-find skills or experience."

Hashtags: Organizing Information, People, and Leads

As discussed in chapter 14, hashtags (#) can be described as Twitter's answer to the file system. When you search for a hashtag using Twitter's search tools, all related postings will appear. Look for hashtags in your field. For example, if you are looking for project manager positions, search for hashtags such as #project management, #project_management, or #projectmanager. A hashtag search will generate all of the tweets that contain these "tagged" words.

If you want to find tips from resume writers, search for #resumes; new job postings, #jobs; and so on.

JOB SEARCH–RELATED HASHTAGS

Susan Ireland (@SusanIreland), author of *The Complete Idiot's Guide to the Perfect Resume,* Fifth Edition (Alpha, 2010), provided a compilation of job search hashtags on her blog (http://joblounge.blogspot.com/). Using any of these job search–related hashtags in Twitter should generate leads:

#____jobs (fill in the blank with your city or state)	#employment	#job
	#followhr	#jobadvice
#career	#greenjobs	#jobangels
#careercoach	#hire	#jobhunt
#careerconsultant	#hireme	#jobhunting
#careermanagement	#hiring	#jobinterview
#careers	#hr	#jobpostings

(continued)

(continued)

#jobs	#negotiate	#resumewriting
#jobsearch	#recession	#salary
#jobsearchtweet	#recruiters	#success
#jobseeker	#recruiting	#tweetmyjobs
#jobseekers	#resume	#unemployment
#jobtips	#resumes	#work
#laidoff	#resumeservices	
#needajob	#resumewriter	

You can also use the following sites to scout for hashtags specific to your field and area of interest:

- **What the Hashtag?!** (http://wthashtag.com): A searchable, user-edited encyclopedia of hashtags.

- **Twemes** (http://twemes.com): Discover and track hashtags, and subscribe to RSS feeds for tags of particular interest.

Q&A WITH JOBANGELS FOUNDER MARK STELZNER (@JOBANGELS)

One of the most well-known hashtags for job seekers on Twitter is #jobangels. On January 29, 2009, HR veteran and management consultant Mark Stelzner (@stelzner) asked a question: "Was wondering what would happen if each of us committed to finding one person a job? You game?"

This spark ignited a movement. As Stelzner recalls, "This one tweet encouraging others to pay it forward was retweeted 150 times. People got fired up. Within 90 minutes, we had a name, "JobAngels," and a hashtag on Twitter (#jobangels). Within two hours, we had three networks on LinkedIn, Facebook, and Twitter. Within seven days, we were in the *LA Times*. We had the right message at the right time."

Through JobAngels (@jobangels), job seekers communicate their needs and receive help from other members—from job leads to resume assistance.

Fast-forward less than 10 months, and JobAngels set off a media firestorm with more than 250 stories on TV alone. There are 30,000 people in JobAngels helping through different networks—LinkedIn, Twitter, and Facebook—as well as JobAngels groups and chapters around the globe. In this Q&A with Chandlee, Stelzner reflects on the evolution and success of @jobangels.

How many people has JobAngels helped?

It's hard to estimate. I know we've helped about 1,000 people find jobs, but I believe we've helped more than that. It has encouraged people to reach out to help a coworker, a friend, or a relative with any number of needs.

What's the ratio of job seekers to volunteers?

Fifty percent of our members are job seekers who ask for help. There's a stigma in our society about asking for help. We live in a country with values that say, "Pull yourself up by your bootstraps." There's truth in that statement, but it's equally true that we should let other people know how they can help us when we need it.

The amazing thing about the JobAngels is that these people were 30,000 complete strangers before the program started. Now, they are connecting, putting themselves out there, and helping one another.

Why does JobAngels work?

JobAngels is not about asking. It's about helping anyone you can, opening up your professional network, and doing something.

How can job seekers learn more about JobAngels?

Search for our hashtag (#jobangels) on Twitter. You can also follow the JobAngels network on Twitter (go to www.twitter.com/jobangels and click Follow), where you can communicate your own needs and share leads with others.

Sources of Feeds: General Directories of Employers and Job Postings on Twitter

For jobs specific to your field and location, check the Web sites of your target companies and organizations; many actively advertise their Twitter accounts. Here are several aggregate lists of employers with a presence on Twitter (see chapter 29 for instructions on following):

- **Employers Recruiting on Twitter**
  http://tinyurl.com/job-hunt-org-recruiting
  Curated by Susan Joyce (@JobHuntOrg) of Job-Hunt.org.

- **Companies Recruiting on Twitter**
  http://tinyurl.com/strayer-recruiting-list
  Curated by Susan Strayer (@dailycareertips).

- **Where to Find Your Job on Twitter** (Directory)
  http://tinyurl.com/career-rocketeer
  Employers, job sites, and resources; curated by Chris Perry (@careerrocketeer).

- **Phil Rosenburg's Jobtweets Twitter List**
  http://tinyurl.com/listjobtweets
  Observe job listings in the Twitterstream en masse.

- **International Directory of 400+ Twitter Job Feeds**
  http://tinyurl.com/400twitjobfeeds
  Got wanderlust? Check out this list. Curated by Jacob Share of JobMob, the directory includes local and field-specific resources around the world.

Advice and Trends from Job Search Experts and Recruiters

Savvy advice from career coaches, resume writers, and job search strategists around the globe can be found at some of these lists:

- **Twitter Job Search Guide**
  http://tweepml.org/Twitter-Job-Search-Guide/
  Like what you've read here? Find and follow the official stream of contributors to this book, or subscribe to follow individual experts.

- **Career Collective**
  http://tweepml.org/Career-Collective-Professionals/
  A collaborative network helping job seekers, curated by Miriam Salpeter (@keppie_careers) and Jacqui Barrett-Poindexter (@ValueIntoWords).

- **Career Hub**
  http://tweepml.org/Career-Hub/
  Free advice from career experts, curated by Louise Fletcher (@louisefletcher).

- **Career Thought Leaders**
  http://tweepml.org/Career-Thought-Leaders/
  Free advice from a consortium of career experts, curated by Wendy Enelow (@wendyenelow).

- **Certified Career Management Coaches & Certified Job Search Strategists from TheAcademies.com**
  http://tweepml.org/Certified-Career-Coaches/
  A listing of certified coaches and job search strategists from coauthor Susan's training organizations, Career Coach Academy and Job Search Academy.

In addition to advice from job search experts, it's important to listen to the voices on the other side of the table: the recruiters, hiring managers, and human resources professionals who, in a sense, hold your future in their hands. (Recall the tweet tips from chapter 18.) The three recruiter lists here are just the tip of the iceberg:

- http://twitter.com/animal/recruiters
- http://twitter.com/JLipschultz/recruiters
- http://twitter.com/teenarose/recruiters

CHAPTER 29

TWITTER LISTS: STREAMLINING TWEETS AND OPTIMIZING YOUR EXPERIENCE

*"Invention, it must be humbly admitted, does not consist
of creating out of void, but out of chaos."*

—*Mary Wollstonecraft Shelley*

Every so often, a previously used product gets a facelift with an innovation so profound that it is hard to imagine life without it: Think of the personal computer before the mouse became mainstream in 1984, or without the graphical user interface (GUI) we commonly refer to as Windows.

Twitter lists are the equivalent of the "point-and-click" revolution that occurred in the mid-1980s: Lists make Twitter radically easier to navigate. They are also key to decluttering your Twitter stream and staying focused on priority people in your job search (employers, networking contacts, and career/job search experts).

Prior to the rollout of lists, Twitterholics and critics shared a common frustration: If you followed a number of people, your Twitter stream could become cluttered, noisy, and fast moving. Keeping up with specific users or conversations required special efforts to look up users by hand, searching for common hashtags, or conducting keyword searches on Twitter's search engine (http://search.twitter.com). While some users migrated to APIs (including Seesmic and TweetDeck) to create their own lists with customized user "columns," managing the stream of tweets within Twitter was akin to navigating a class-5 river rapid in a canoe: in a word, tricky.

LISTS LAUDED

Many have celebrated Twitter's recent innovation of lists. Clayton Morris, anchor and host of *Gadgets and Games* on FoxNews.com, describes it well:

"Twitter's list feature gives members the power to group those they follow into simple lists based on certain qualifications.

(continued)

(continued)

"...Before lists, logging into Twitter around 10 a.m. meant I missed a quality tweet at 8 a.m. from a journalist I regularly read and respect. Now I can log in whenever I want, click on my "journalists" list, and voilà! Quality tidbits of useful data lying before me in a tidy list of informative goodness."

As Dolly Parton and Kenny Rogers crooned in their 1983 hit, "Islands in the Stream," lists are the equivalent of an island—or a solid oasis—in the midst of your Twitter stream. Lists enable you to cluster content that can be viewed separately from your primary Twitter feed. This makes it radically easier to organize, filter, and view related content on Twitter in a finite amount of time.

Need to Know: *Lists* enable you to organize users into groups. Through lists, you can view tweets from users you don't follow. If you don't want updates from hundreds of users in your stream, creating or subscribing to lists by subject area is a great way to optimize your time on Twitter. (We also recommend that you follow any user with whom you wish to initiate or cultivate a personal connection.)

Use Lists to Save Time and Boost Job Search Efficiency

Use lists to create your own islands of information and view them separately from your general Twitter stream. Here are five ways the list feature can save you time and help boost your job search efficiency:

- Follow streams of career experts and job listings in your field of interest. See our lists of job leads and feeds in chapter 28.

- Keep tabs on hiring managers, influencers, and networking contacts. Monitoring feeds of individuals you'd like to work with will give you a unique perspective on their needs and interests; it may also tip you off on their vacation plans so you're not fretting over an unreturned message.

- Develop and manage private lists to keep tabs on hiring managers, network contacts, and target companies. If you don't want others to know that you subscribe to lists for job seekers, you can make your own private lists of leads and experts for advice that are accessible only by you.

- Obtain new perspectives and insights by following lists created by others in your field. An added benefit: You can subscribe to a list someone else set up without having to follow every user on the list. This allows you to connect with many other people without increasing the number of people that you are following.

- Showcase your interest, knowledge, and expertise of your intended field or industry by creating and sharing public lists with other people. Just as Twitter allows you to have followers and a following, you can be "listed" on other user lists and create lists of your own. When you list others, they will see that they have been listed and may list you back! Creating lists can help you get known—and share your goodwill with others.

Bottom line: Twitter lists allow you to organize what can be an overwhelming amount of information and customize how you'll review your Twitter stream. It's the equivalent of tackling an overflowing wardrobe: The process is much easier when you have storage receptacles to group similar items.

On CNN.com, Mashable founder and CEO Pete Cashmore hailed the arrival of Twitter lists as the "long-overdue cure to information overload" and the "birth of a new editor: the real-time Web curator."

> **Need to Know:** As you dive into lists, you'll find additional references to *information curators*. Many Web sites, including Listorious (http://listorious.com), use the "curator" metaphor to describe the work of users who create lists. Much like a museum curator who selects, summarizes, and prepares objects for display in exhibits, list curators filter and disseminate content for others.

Getting Started: Using and Maintaining Lists

Now we'll show you how to select lists that align with your needs and preferences, and then provide you with tips on how to curate your own. Either way, Lists make Twitter easier to navigate in 15 minutes a day!

> **Tip:** You can find step-by-step instructions for creating a list, checking out your list stats, subscribing to and following lists, and more at Twitter's definitive guide to lists: http://tinyurl.com/twitter-lists-help.

Finding Lists to Follow

The easiest way to start using Twitter lists is to subscribe to lists that others have already created. Here are three separate ways to find these lists.

1. Search for Lists Through Individual Twitter Accounts

Go to individual user accounts of people you follow (click on "following" or go to http://twitter.com/username, in which *username* is the name of the person you are following).

Using the example of http://twitter.com/CEOCoach, as seen in figure 29.1, note the text link "listed" immediately below Deb's bio and to the right of "following" and "followers." This "listed" link shows the number of lists that @CEOCoach appears on. Clicking on the "listed" link will bring you to a new page to view "Lists following CEOCoach" and "Lists CEOCoach follows," as seen in figure 29.2.

Figure 29.1: Twitter account showing "listed" text link.

Figure 29.2: Lists following CEOCoach and Lists CEOCoach follows.

Click on either tab (Lists following [username] or Lists [username] follows) to view the lists. Review the lists; clicking on one of interest will bring up a stream of tweets from people in that list. To follow the list, click the "Follow this list" button beneath the name of the list near the top of the page.

2. Follow the Employer and Career Lists in Chapter 28

Many of the lists you'll find under "Sources of Feeds" and "Advice and Trends from Job Search Experts and Recruiters" can be followed with just one click. You will need to share your Twitter login information with Listorious.com (a directory of lists on Twitter) or TweepML.com (a helpful list-sharing program) to follow some of the lists.

3. Search Directories by Keywords to Find Lists Tailored to Your Industry or Profession

Visit Listorious.com to find and subscribe to industry- or profession-specific lists that will help you in your job search. Create an account and search for lists by keyword. For example, if you want to follow lists for architects, search by keyword "architect" or "architecture."

To join a list, click on "follow this list."

How to Be a Curator of Your Own Lists

> *"New media does not mean getting rid of editors. From the moment we launched* The Huffington Post, *I insisted that we needed to have editors. New media allows citizen journalists to go global, but we still need editors."*
>
> —*Arianna Huffington, #140Conference*

You can create your own Twitter list manually, or you can use tools from a third-party application (otherwise known as an API). Here we provide two approaches to creating your own list: one manually and one with the aid of two APIs, MyTweeple (http://mytweeple.com) and TweepML (http://tweepml.com).

THE BENEFITS OF CREATING YOUR OWN LISTS

These are just a few reasons you may want to create and curate your own lists:

- **Privacy:** When you subscribe to a list, it shows up in the directory of "lists you follow." But when you create a list through Twitter, you have the option to mark it as private. Creating your own Twitter lists of job leads, career advice, and target companies—and marking it "private"—keeps your job search confidential.

- **Visibility:** If you want to showcase the depth of your knowledge of your industry or field, creating and sharing public lists is a great way to increase your visibility, especially if you list in public directories such as Listorious (http://listorious.com).

  Adding others to lists can also boost your popularity on Twitter since users may add you to their own lists as well.

- **Customization:** When you create your own lists, you become your own editor. You can self-select the information that you want to receive. Do you want to follow 15 industry experts for your field, 9 of your peers at competitor companies, and 10 career coaches? If yes, are you interested in reading them at the same time? Probably not.

By creating your own lists, you can organize content into separate categories and streams—enabling you to optimize the time you spend on Twitter.

Create Your List Manually Through Twitter

For this process, you'll need a list of Twitter usernames you want to add to your list.

1. To begin, log in to your account (www.twitter.com/your_username). Position your cursor over the "Lists" icon and a popup balloon appears that says, "Manage lists in which [yourname] appears." Click the "Lists" button and choose "New list."

2. Follow the prompts to name your list (use self-explanatory keywords) and provide a brief description. Save your settings and close.

3. Visit the individual Twitter URLs for each of the users you want to add. At this page, click the drop-down arrow on the Lists button. It will now display your newly created list(s). Add the person to the appropriate list(s). You're done!

Create Your List with the Help of an API

For this process, you will need to gather a list of the Twitter accounts that you want to include in your list (for example, if you want to add Susan Whitcomb to your list, you would need her Twitter account name, @SusanWhitcomb).

This method will save you time if you have more than 10 users to enter in your list (Twitter allows lists of up to 500), but also requires that you create accounts with two third-party API providers.

> **Tip:** You can skip steps 1 and 2 if you simply want to make modifications to an existing list. If you want to use an existing list, you will need the list's URL (which you can copy from your browser when viewing the list).

1. **Visit MyTweeple.com,** a tool to manage your friends and followers (http:// mytweeple.com). After creating an account, follow the directions under the Import/Export tab to import a list of your Twitter community (people you follow and those who follow you) into an Excel spreadsheet or other list that you can copy and paste by columns.

2. **Save the spreadsheet of your followers/following** on your desktop with a new file name using Microsoft Excel or another spreadsheet application such as the free Open Office (www.openoffice.org). Create a list of individuals you want on your list with a column of Twitter usernames without the @ sign (for example, @CEOCoach is ceocoach; @chandlee is chandlee; @SusanWhitcomb is susanwhitcomb, and so on).

3. **Go to Tweepml.org** (http://tweepml.com), a third-party application that allows you to share groups of Twitter users. Create an account, and then select Create a List. Follow the directions to add users. Copy and paste Twitter usernames into the list in the order that you would like to see them displayed.

4. **Give your list a short name with keywords** that can be found online. Enter tags, or keywords that the list can be found with (for example, if you are creating a list of photography, include *photography* and *photographers* as keywords). Provide a brief one-sentence description for other users to view—and make it catchy. Save the list.

5. **You will then be prompted for permission to access your Twitter account.** After logging in, your list will be added to your Twitter lists. TweepML will provide you with a URL, buttons, and widgets to promote your Twitter list. (You can also list the URL on Listology.com, on your e-mail signature, and other places to promote it.)

A Final Word on Lists

We hope that you'll find Twitter lists to be as accessible, user-friendly, and efficient as we do, especially because monitoring and following Twitter lists should be an integral component of your strategy to optimize your job search on Twitter in 15 minutes a day.

Because the lists feature is relatively new, be sure to check the support section on the Twitter Web site for updates. You can also find news of innovations through the Twitter section on Mashable (http://mashable.com) and oneforty (http://oneforty. com), a site that reviews popular APIs (more on that in chapter 31).

CHAPTER 30

RESEARCH ON TWITTER: FINDING PEOPLE, POSITIONS, PLACES TO WORK, AND OTHER PUZZLE PIECES

"There is nothing like looking, if you want to find something. You certainly usually find something, if you look, but it is not always quite the something you were after."

—*J.R.R. Tolkien*

With Twitter users averaging 27.3 million tweets per day and 10 billion tweets per year (according to pingdom.com), it's an understatement to say that there is a lot of information on Twitter; try tons of terabytes' worth!

Sorting through it all can feel a bit like someone dumped all the pages from all the books in the Library of Congress into one gigantic, chaotic pile. Buried in those mountains of data are companies, job leads, and people to help you uncover the hidden (and not-so-hidden) job market. To echo the line from the old Western movies, "there's gold in them thar hills." Yes, for the adventurous and perseverant, there's treasure to be mined.

In this chapter, we simplify the search process for you. By sticking to the basics, you'll learn how to

- Use Twitter's advanced search feature
- Tap Google and Bing to augment your search
- Explore other Twitter tools that can enhance the search process
- Ask for help from the Twitterverse to do research, social media style

It's very unlikely that you'll use Twitter as your sole research tool. But, used in combination with other resources, these strategies will rev up your search.

Poke and Pry with Purpose: Twitter's Advanced Search

"Research is formalized curiosity. It is poking and prying with a purpose."

—*Zora Neale Hurston*

Searching on Twitter requires some poking and prying. There is no guaranteed process; even the experts have to experiment a bit to find what they want on Twitter. There are essentially three entry points for search in Twitter:

- **The search box** on the right panel at your home page: This tool works best when you know a person's username or want to see @mentions.

- **The Find People text link** near the top of your Twitter home page: Use this for looking up names and companies you are interested in.

- **The Advanced Search feature** at http://search.twitter.com/advanced: Although it's the most helpful of Twitter's various search options, this link is not readily findable at the site. Here, you'll find options to search for words, exact phrases, hashtags, and more, as seen in figure 30.1.

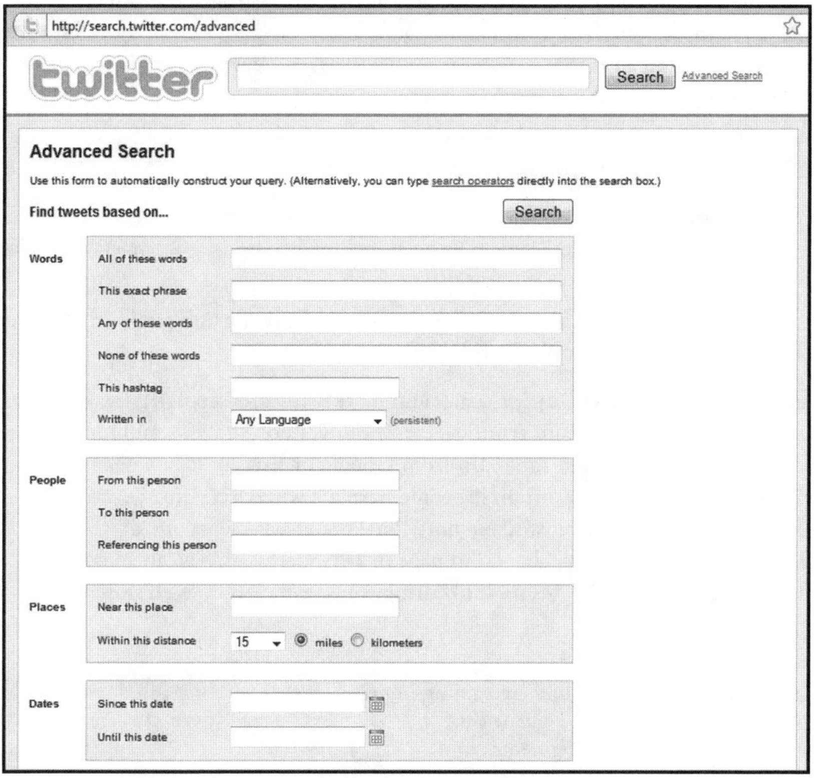

Figure 30.1: Twitter's Advanced Search feature.

Let's say you're looking for jobs in healthcare in the Seattle area. At http://search.twitter.com/advanced, next to "Any of these words," enter "healthcare medical." Next to "This hashtag" enter "jobs" (the word "jobs" works better than "job"). Next to "Near this place," enter "Seattle." Change the "Within this distance" default to "50" miles. Click "Search." Experiment with this tool and you'll find lots to pursue.

> **Tip:** For further ideas on using Twitter's Advanced Search feature, see Ann Smarty's post at http://tinyurl.com/searching-twitter.

Tap Google, Bing, and LinkedIn to Augment Twitter Searches

"Research is the act of going up alleys to see if they are blind."

—*Anonymous*

Both Google and Microsoft's Bing recently inked deals with Twitter to integrate status updates into their search results. This means when you search for something that could be aided by real-time observations, you'll find tweets from other users who are there. For example, what's happening at a job fair, conversations from a professional conference, the latest interviewing questions being asked, and anything else that could lead to insights and insider information.

If you can't find what you're looking for using Twitter search, try similar keywords using Google or Bing. In addition, consider these ideas:

- **Help phrases:** At Google.com, enter the search string "I need help with [your need]." For example, "I need help with finding contacts at Pelco Manufacturing."

- **Top lists:** Google "Twitter, follow, [your field], [your industry]" (fill in your field and industry in place of the bracketed phrases).

For finding insider contacts, career coach and market research expert Rebecca Bosl of acceleratejobsearch.com reminds us to not overlook the 50+ million users at LinkedIn. "You can search LinkedIn from Google or Bing to locate people in your target companies. In addition, if people have a Twitter account, beyond their LinkedIn profile, they will most likely note the Twitter handle in one of these places: personal Web site, Facebook fan page or personal page, VisualCV.com, online resume, company Web site, LinkedIn groups, association Web sites, or company Web site."

> **Tip:** Real-time search engines are gaining in popularity. If you don't find what you're looking for with Google or Bing, try sites like Collecta (www.collecta.com) or TweetMeme (www.tweetmeme.com).

Explore Other Twitter Tools for Finding Stuff

"Research is what I'm doing when I don't know what I'm doing."

— *Werner von Braun*

Here are a few sites, at-a-glance, compiled by Barbara Safani (@BarbaraSafani; www.careersolvers.com) of Manhattan-based CareerSolvers. These tools can help you locate and connect with companies, recruiters, and people in your industry who are discussing industry trends and job leads. They can also help you find more people to follow and build community with.

- **Tweep Search** (www.tweepsearch.com): Searches Twitter bios for keywords.

- **TweetBeep** (www.tweetbeep.com): Like Google Alerts for Twitter, TweetBeep sends alerts that mention you, your target companies, or anything of interest, with hourly updates.

- **Tweet Scan** (www.tweetscan.com): Also works like Google Alerts and searches tweets based on keywords.

- **Trendistic** (www.trendistic.com): Allows you to view popular trends discussed on Twitter.

- **Twubble** (www.crazybob.org/twubble/): Lets you search the users your friends are following and pick those you want to follow.

- **Twemes** (www.twemes.com): Follows tweets that have embedded tags that start with a # character (in other words, the hashtag symbol).

- **Twellow.com** (www.twellow.com): The Yellow Pages of Twitter, with more than 6 million users.

- **Just Tweet It** (www.justtweetit.com): A directory for Twitter users organized by category. You can add your name to the directory.

- **Monitter** (www.monitter.com): See tweets from the entire Twitterverse containing keywords you request.

- **TwitteRel** (www.twitterel.com): Find users with similar career interests.

A couple of our favorites from this list include

- **Tweep Search** (http://tweepsearch.com): We've had great success finding people and companies with this tool. Search for "recruiter Dallas" if you're looking for Dallas-based recruiters. Or search "Pepperidge Farms" if you're looking for employees of, or people involved with, that particular company (substitute your target company, of course).

- **Twellow** (http://twellow.com): Both a search engine and directory of Twitter users with six million entries, Twellow analyzes tweets and sorts them into categories, such as employment agencies, job search, internships, and more.

- **Monitter** (http://monitter.com): Also described in chapter 21 on interviewing, this site can feel more like a fire hose than a stream because it generates all the tweets on Twitter (not just those of people you're following) containing the keywords you ask it to return. For example, "How do cover letter" (albeit disjointed since it's not a complete sentence) returns tweets relevant to writing a cover letter. Or "programming jobs Phoenix" returns a feed of jobs in Phoenix.

> **Tip:** Find something you like? Many sites offer an RSS feed, so you can sign up to have the relevant information continually delivered to your phone or computer.

Research, Social Media Style

"It's not what you know, but who you know that counts."

—*Anonymous*

Social media is shifting the way we research. It used to be that a job seeker might hole up in front of a home computer, mouse in hand, and plug keywords into search engines to dig up data on companies. Today, although a mouse, keywords, and search engines are still important, those tools are augmented by the "social media encyclopedia" that now exists in the form of online networks such as Twitter, LinkedIn, and Facebook.

Twitter is like having hundreds of help-desk attendants from the Library of Congress at your disposal. Just ask, and you can have rich resources at your fingertips. For example, let's suppose you are considering a position in another part of the country about which you are not very familiar. Career coach Jan Melnik suggests tweeting general questions, such as these:

---

yourname Who are some of the most respected employers in Omaha?

---

yourname Anyone know which manufacturers in the San Diego area are hiring? Esp. in aerospace?

---

yourname I'm a teacher, furloughed, and thinking of a relo to the West Coast... what are job prospects for educators?

---

yourname Can anyone suggest a good contact at (company name) and how best to approach for a win-win conversation?

---

yourname Looking to transition career from consumer goods sales into pharma... any contacts you'd recommend?

The proverb about who you know being more important than what you know applies here. With Twitter, you now "know" thousands of people who might be able to help answer your questions.

Tip: Don't be discouraged if you ask a question of the Twitterverse and don't get an immediate response. It's possible that your tweet was overlooked. Try asking the question several times, using different wording, and at different times of the day.

Create a list of the questions you need answered and the people you'd like to know. Choose one new research tool or idea from this chapter that could help with that solution and experiment with it. And, if by chance that tool wasn't the answer, turn the page to find a plethora of apps that will likely do the trick!

CHAPTER 31

TWITTER APIS: THERE'S AN APP FOR THAT!

"The Twitter client landscape is evolving rapidly. Like the browser wars from the early Internet days of the 1990s, it's both exciting and dangerous. By trying different tools, you become a pioneer — with an arrow in your back but with great stories to tell."

— *Greg Dourgarian, Staffing Talk Blog, November 2009**

Friends and family of iPhone users frequently joke that their loved ones have been afflicted with a unique illness specific to iPhone ownership: an altered perspective of the world in which an app exists to "fix" whatever problem is encountered, from finding out what's playing on the jukebox to being reminded to take daily medication and making dinner reservations. Apple's iPhone App Store commercials are obviously paying off, as ubiquitous users echo its pithy tagline in answer to any dilemma: "I'll bet 'There's an app for that'!" Without question, the iPhone community has helped evangelize Twitter, spawning growth in the number of Twitter users and driving demand for new mobile apps. And, no longer exclusive to iPhone aficionados, Twitter users from all walks of life and technology platforms now have access to a suite of software applications that can enhance their user experience.

The list of Twitter API services and options is lengthy and ever-changing. Many services are run and hosted by startup companies. Attempting to identify the most useful APIs for a roundup is similar to trying to buy the best computer now that will last you for the next three years, or trying to pick only one of Baskin Robbins's 31 flavors to eat for the rest of your life: It's particularly challenging because your needs may change over time, and product offerings change with predictable regularity!

For these reasons, this chapter provides you with a broad overview of available APIs by category. Rather than overload you with an exhaustive list of what's available at the time this book goes to press, we've chosen a sampling of popular tools. And, at the end of the chapter, we'll show you where to go for updates on the latest and greatest tools as applications and services continue to evolve.

---

*www.staffingtalk.com/2009/11/comparison-of-twitter-clients-for.html

Desktop Twitter Clients

Many messages on Twitter are posted through sites other than Twitter. Figure 31.1 shows how Twitter displays which application was used to post; note the time stamp (4 minutes ago) and the "from Seesmic" beneath the tweet, meaning that @chandlee used the Seesmic API to post this tweet.

> **Need to Know:** Applications that enable you to use Twitter through alternative client hosts or in innovative ways are called *Application Programming Interfaces*, also known as *APIs* or *apps* for short. An alternative client host, such as TweetDeck or HootSuite, interfaces with Twitter and enables you to tweet without logging in to Twitter.

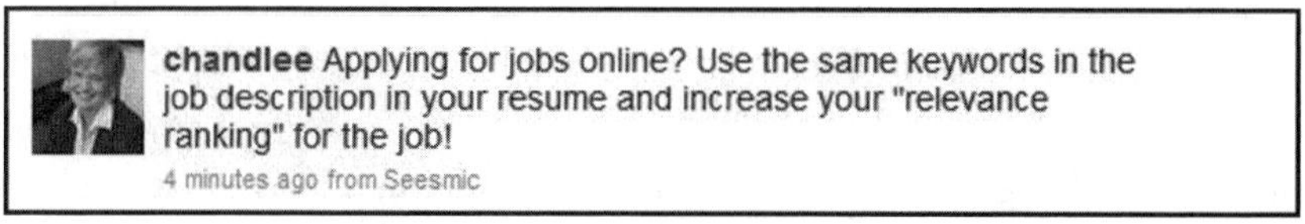

 chandlee Applying for jobs online? Use the same keywords in the job description in your resume and increase your "relevance ranking" for the job!
4 minutes ago from Seesmic

Figure 31.1: How Twitter shows you the source of a tweet.

You can use the following applications at your desktop or mobile window to Twitter. Through the desktop applications, you can create, customize, and view multiple columns of users. They allow you to customize viewing and notification preferences, shorten URLs, and post directly to Twitter. Bonus: These applications also interface with other social networks, such as Facebook or LinkedIn, allowing you to communicate across platforms using one browser.

- **TweetDeck** (http://tweetdeck.com): A user favorite.
- **Seesmic** (http://seesmic.com): Similar to TweetDeck in many ways, and the first to introduce integration with Twitter lists.
- **HootSuite** (http://hootsuite.com): A desktop client similar to TweetDeck and Seesmic, with the added benefit of a tweet scheduler to arrange for tweets to go out at specified times.
- **Echofon** (http://echofon.com): Available exclusively for Mac and mobile users; an iPhone App is also offered.
- **Brizzly** (http://brizzly.com): This multifeatured client browser enables you to monitor multiple Twitter accounts at once (a must if you use one Twitter account in your day job and another to manage your job search).

URL Shorteners: 140-Character Conservation Tools

Twitter gives you just 140 characters per status update, which can be problematic if you have a long URL that you want to include in your tweet. Enter URL shortening apps, which enable you to transform URLs of 100+ characters to as few as 20. Here are three of the most popular:

- **Bit.ly** (http://bit.ly): A crowd favorite, particularly because it enables you to track how many clicks a link receives. The downside to using bit.ly is that the links expire over time.

- **Ow.ly** (http://ow.ly): Ow.ly is the URL shortener tool for HootSuite, but it can also be used separately. Ow.ly-shortened links also expire over time.

- **TinyURL.com** (http://tinyurl.com): A no-frills shortening tool. You cannot track statistics on your links, but they never expire.

To use these apps, log on to the site and follow the simple directions (for example, at http://bit.ly, paste your long URL into the blank field and then click Shorten; you can also set up an account, which will enable you to tweet from bit.ly).

Finding Conversations on Twitter

As discussed in chapters 14 and 15, engaging others in conversation is a great way to build your personal Twitter community. Joining in discussions of trending topics (represented by the keywords and hashtags at the bottom of the Twitter login page or in your Twitter sidebar) is one effective technique to engage others; finding out what people are saying about topics of interest to you is another. Three APIs that allow you to search and add to the conversation are

- **Retweet** (http://retweet.com): News by the people, for the people (but not to be confused with Twitter's retweet feature).

- **Tinker.com** (http://tinker.com): A site for researching and discovering the "top stories" on Twitter and Facebook.

- **TweetMeme** (http://tweetmeme.com): Your source for searching and retweeting the "hottest stories on Twitter."

Finding New Friends with Shared Interests

Chapter 13 provides strategies for the art of attracting followers and creating a following. Another quick way to do this is to find people who want to talk about the same things you do.

There are many Twitter APIs that are designed to help you expand your reach and increase others' awareness of what you do. These include directories categorized by location and field. Here are a few of our favorites:

- **Twellow** (http://twellow.com): Similar to the Yellow Pages, this directory allows you to search for users by area of expertise, profession, or other designated keyword. One recruiter we spoke to called it her favorite for searching candidate bios.

- **Mr. Tweet** (http://mrtweet.com): Mr. Tweet is a personal networking assistant that will help you find influencers and others with your shared interests to follow. You can also recommend people or get recommended to increase your area of influence.

- **WeFollow** (http://wefollow.com): This user-powered search directory allows you to search for people to follow by keywords, location, and sphere of influence. You can also add yourself, your location, and five of your own interests to the directory. (Once you join, you must confirm a tweet to send out to Twitter announcing your selections.)

TWEETFEEL: WILL YOU LOVE IT?

Researching Employers on the Basis of What Others Say

Want to source out how others feel about a particular company before you apply? Check out TweetFeel (http://tweetfeel.com). This API scans message content for emotions and rates messages on a ☺ or ☹ scale that allows you to see positive— or negative—reputations in a flash. You can also customize your searches in TweetFeel so that you decide what you want to see and eliminate any mentions you feel are erroneous to your evaluation.

Timing Is Everything: How to Get Your Tweet Across at the Right Time

In job search—as in relationships—timing can be everything. Statistics routinely show that Tuesday is the most productive day for hiring managers and recruiters because many job seekers apply for positions on Sunday night and Monday.

Some applications that allow you to schedule your tweets ahead of time include HootSuite and SocialOomph (http://socialoomph.com). These sites have many cool features from list creation (HootSuite) to the ability to send automated direct messages to new followers (SocialOomph).

WHAT'S THE OPTIMAL TIME TO TWEET?

In June 2009, the Web site Hubspot released a report on "The State of the Twittersphere." Findings included the fact that office hours during the U.S. work week were the most popular time to tweet, with spikes in early morning (9 to 10 a.m.), mid-afternoon (3 to 5 p.m.), and just before bed (11 p.m. to midnight). British Internet content consultant and SEO expert @malcolmcoles did his own research and found that 4:01 p.m. is the best time to tweet if you want it to be seen.

Tweet O'Clock (http://tweetoclock.com) will tell you when specific Twitter users typically tweet, giving you a greater likelihood of your tweets or @replies being seen. According to Tweet O'Clock, the optimal times to tweet us are as follow:

- @chandlee: 10:35 a.m. on Wednesdays (EST)

- @ceocoach: 9:10 a.m. on Fridays (EST)

- @susanwhitcomb: 3:10 p.m. on Thursdays (PST)

Backing Up Your Tweets

Backing up and saving your Twitter stream is good hygiene—as wise as flossing your teeth. Why? Because Twitter has a time limit on how long it displays tweets, which can make them unsearchable after only a few days. Even if you don't think you'll need access to past tweets, you may change your mind later. You may want to look up a link to a job posting you replied to, remember the name of a networking contact, or data-mine the tweets for some other purpose, just as one of our successful job seekers did. Mark Buell (@mebuell) landed his job after submitting his Twitter stream as a writing sample during the interviewing process (to learn more about Mark's successful search, see appendix C).

Here are two ways to archive your tweets:

- Use one of the apps listed in a well-researched ReadWriteWeb.com blog post on how to archive your tweets: www.readwriteweb.com/archives/10_ways_to_archive_your_tweets.php. Some of the more straightforward apps in this list are Tweetake, Tweetscan, BackupMyTweets, and TweetBackup.

- To keep track of all of your tweets moving forward, set up an RSS feed of your tweets (viewable on sites that enable you to view and receive content from RSS feeds, such as Google Reader). To grab your feed, go to your personal Twitter account page (http://twitter.com/yourhandle).

  On the right-hand menu, below the avatars/pictures of people you are following, you will see the small RSS icon and a text link labeled "RSS feed of [yourusername's] tweets." Click on this link. A new page will appear, with the words "Subscribe to this feed using...." Click the drop-down arrow that displays options such as Bloglines, MyYahoo!, and Google. Choose your option and then click Subscribe Now. You're done!

Technical APIs

Use these APIs to save time and enhance your Twitter experience. (See chapter 27 for more strategies on how to get the most out of Twitter in 15 minutes a day or less.)

Applications That Distribute Content Across Sites

In addition to some of the desktop Twitter clients mentioned earlier in this chapter (TweetDeck, Seesmic, HootSuite), these apps help you share content across other social media platforms:

- **Twitterfeed** (http://twitterfeed.com): If you have a blog, this app will automatically list your posts on Twitter and Facebook.
- **Digsby** (http://digsby.com): Aggregates IM, e-mail, and social networks. You can also use it to post updates on Twitter.

> **Tip:** Looking for fun and interesting apps? Visit www.igorhelpsyousucceed. com/2009/11/twitter-apps for "25 Twitter Apps You Never Knew Existed."

Social Media APIs

Some job seekers—especially those seeking positions in social media—choose to develop multimedia campaigns as part of their job search. This can include photos (@litmanlive sent a cake to his 500th follower and put a picture of it on Twitter) and video (@albiedrzycki used Twitter to publicize his musical cover letter video through YouTube and landed on CNN).

Popular APIs for posting photos include Twitpic (http://twitpic.com), TweetPhoto (http://tweetphoto.com), and yfrog (http://yfrog.com), which also enables you to post video. Video-sharing APIs include TwitVid (http://twitvid.com), Twiddeo (http://beta.twiddeo), and TweeTube (http://tweetube.com).

Tools to Evaluate Your Twitter Influence

To evaluate your efforts, consider one of these Twitter tools:

- **Twitalyzer** (http://twitalyzer.com): Defines your popularity on Twitter, as scored by number of followers, number of times you've been retweeted, or mentions by others. It also measures "generosity," meaning how often you retweet.
- **Twitter Grader** (http://twittergrader.com): Twitter Grader measures the power, reach, and authority of a Twitter account, including how much a user engages with others. Only those users who have used the tool before receive a "grade."

- **TweetLevel** (http://tweetlevel.com): Ratings on influence, popularity, trust, and level of engagement from Edelman, a leading independent global PR firm.

- **Klout** (http://klout.com): Similar to the Online Identity Calculator™ mentioned in chapter 6, Klout measures your "influence across the social Web" and classifies you into one of four quadrants: are you a casual user, a climber (increasing your usage), a connector, or a persona (digitally distinct)?

- **TweetEffect** (http://tweeteffect.com): This cool tool lets you find out which of your Twitter updates made people follow or leave you.

NOW WHERE DID I PUT THAT?

An API to Save Your Favorites

This one is for the closet research nerds or those who have a tendency to misplace things (your authors have their hands raised!). FavStar.fm (www.favstar.fm) allows you to track and maintain records of your favorite Twitter messages (simply highlight the star next to tweets you like), see most popular "favorites" on Twitter, and check out favorites of other Twitter users. It's like having your own Twitter bookmark.

Mobile Apps

We end this chapter where we began—by briefly discussing APIs that allow you to connect with Twitter via your mobile phone. Many users exclusively connect with Twitter via mobile devices, especially because they can receive direct messages as text messages. New York new media content guru Rob Blatt uses this feature so frequently that he doesn't even keep phone numbers of his Twitter friends—they simply text by DM instead.

As we go to press, the race to release new APIs for mobiles continues. Here is a sampling of APIs available for mobile platforms:

- **Android:** TwiDroid (http://twidroid.com/) and Seesmic Android (http://iseesmic.com/seesmic_mobile/android/)

- **iPhone:** There are numerous "apps for that," but Tweetie (http://tweetie.com) is a crowd favorite. TweetDeck and HootSuite also have a free iPhone app; Seesmic is in the process of developing its own.

- **BlackBerry:** Seesmic (http://seesmic.com/seesmic_mobile/blackberry/), UberTwitter (http://ubertwitter.com), and Social Scope (http://socialscope.net)

Finally, no list of mobile apps is complete without Foursquare (http://foursquare.com), a geolocation API that allows friends to display their locations, earn points for visiting locations, and receive badges for trying new things. Foursquare is widely used in urban areas.

Want the Latest and Greatest?

Visit sites such as oneforty (http://oneforty.com) and TwitDom (www.twitdom. com) for a comprehensive list of emerging and favorite APIs, from desktop browsers and mobile apps to content-, time-, and reputation-management tools.

CHAPTER 32

PARTING TWEETS OF WISDOM
FROM SAVVY JOB SEEKERS

We close this section of the book with advice from our distinguished dozen (a baker's dozen!)—the savvy and successful job seekers you met in chapter 5. In 140 characters or fewer, here are their parting words of wisdom, along with their Twitter avatars and bios.

bianalog Be creative. Most applicants send a generic resume & cover letter. Do something unique, yet professional & tailored to the company culture.

dbirdy Be part of the community first and don't be scared to toot your own horn occasionally. Brand yourself as well; it's easier than you think.

doughamlin Give it time. Have a personality.

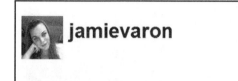

jamievaron Don't just find a way to stand out. Find a way to show employers what you can offer.

JenHarris09 Be yourself, be unique and stay connected someway, some-how...EVERY day.

JBordeaux Treat the job market as a singles bar. Authentic people draw attention; neediness repels it. Twitter is the largest singles bar on Earth.

JustJon	**Name** Jon **Location** White Plains, NY **Web** http://www.justjo... **Bio** Coder, Modder, Gamer, Blogger, Lego Builder, RonFez.Net Webmaster 719 1,132 68 following followers listed

JustJon Be friends with everyone. Talk to everyone. Put yourself out there. And most of all, smile.

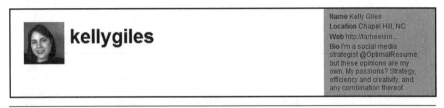

kellygiles	**Name** Kelly Giles **Location** Chapel Hill, NC **Web** http://tarheelsin... **Bio** I'm a social media strategist @OptimalResume, but these opinions are my own. My passions? Strategy, efficiency and creativity, and any combination thereof.

kellygiles If you wouldn't say it or do it to someone in real life, don't say it or do it on Twitter!

litmanlive	**Name** Michael Litman **Location** London **Web** http://litmanlive... **Bio** Social meeja bod, part time blogger and gamer. Loves infographics, sushi and Forest. Not an expert or a guru.

litmanlive Look through your last ten tweets and ask yourself: Would I hire me? Tweet things that will be useful to others--pay it forward!

mebuell	**Name** mebuell **Location** UT: 45.341545,-75.797885 **Bio** Communications Manager for www.cira.ca. Likes social justice, the North, snowboards, and mountain bikes (and wine). IABC and CPRS member.

mebuell Get out there and market yourself. No one is going to do it for you.

Shannonyelland	**Name** Shannon Yelland **Location** Vancouver, bc **Web** http://www.seedth... **Bio** Online Marketing Manager at www.activestate.com. Google Analytics, SEO, SEM and SMM geek. Coffee lover & power walker.

Shannonyelland Ask for help, help others, tell people you are looking for a job, and tell them exactly what your ideal job would be.

Stephen_Moyer	**Name** Stephen Moyer **Location** Geneseo, NY **Web** http://www.linked... **Bio** Recruiter @ Whiting Consulting, amateur photographer and I like to cook!

Stephen_Moyer Twitter is free--follow, retweet, engage, and entertain those that follow you and you are bound to find some help with your job search.

warrenss	**Name** Warren Sukernek **Location** Seattle **Web** http://bit.ly/wssbio **Bio** Partner & VP of Strategies at Lift9. I blog at Twittermaven.com. I love the Red Sox & Jets. I know, weird combination.

warrenss Build it before you need it. Don't wait until you need a job to network on Twitter.

Be sure to read these job seekers' expanded stories in appendix C.

SECTION 7

APPENDIXES

A. 140 Tweet Tips from Career Experts

B. Chapter Contributor Bios

C. The Distinguished (Baker's) Dozen: Stories from Successful Twitter Job Seekers

140 TWEET TIPS FROM CAREER EXPERTS

We extended an invitation to the Twitter community of career experts to submit their best career and job search tips, in tweet-fashion of 140 characters or fewer. We received more than 400 tips; space limitations allow us to present just 140 of them here (you can see the remainder at www.twitterjobsearchguide.com).

We encourage you to follow our "Tweet Tip" career experts as well as other guest contributors to this book on Twitter, which you can conveniently do by visiting http://tweepml.org/Twitter-Job-Search-Guide/.

Using Twitter in Your Job Search

HRCoachRenee Twitter is all about authenticity. Go to http://search.twitter.com and search for your unique "thing" or industry/niche.

Attitude

CIO_Coach Stay positive in your tweets even if you are discouraged on any given day in a job search--a former or future employer may read your tweets.

CIO_Coach Use attention-grabbing headlines to maximize readership; e.g., Companies are looking for Benefit-Bringers not Skill-Slingers.

Etiquette

KellyeCrane Avoid asking a new Twitter pal for more than one favor. You don't want to turn a supporter into someone who avoids you!

LaurieBerenson When posting tweets, always ask yourself: Would I want a potential employer to read this? Could this hurt my candidacy?

paulcopcutt Do not drop in and out of tweeting. Constantly work at communicating your personal brand.

resumeguru Offer value--offer proof--cite examples on Twitter. You have to *earn* an employer's attention, not just show up.

tomfUVA To ensure professionalism during job search, tweet as if your grandmother was reading your posting!

Connecting with Employers and Hiring Managers

DaisyWright If you are job searching via Twitter, ensure your tweets contain buzzwords that hiring managers use.

DaisyWright Twitter is the new ad agency--recruiters use it to search for passive candidates. If you're not on Twitter, you won't show up on their radar.

expatcoachmegan Tweet your expertise. If employers read your last 15 tweets, what would they say about you?

kevindonlin CareerXRoads 2009 HR survey: 12% of people hired via job boards, 27% via referrals. Get referred: follow target recruiters + employees.

paulcopcutt Is the hiring manager you are trying to reach going to be on Twitter? Check the demographics.

paulcopcutt What are your target hiring managers doing in their spare time? What do they tweet about?

PhyllisShabad Sr. execs can accrue career & job search assets via tweets to peers on ExecTweets.com. Keep it business centric & widen contacts off-Tweet.

wendygelberg Use Twitter to gain access to people you wouldn't otherwise have access to.

wendygelberg Older workers: Use Twitter to communicate your expertise and to offset negative age stereotypes; show you understand new technology & tools.

twitjobsearch Search for jobs with TwitterJobSearch.com. It grabs all of the valid jobs from Twitter and makes them easily searchable.

robynfeldberg Target ideal companies & find their recruiters. Tweet: "Top-ranking pharma sales rep looking 4 new challenge. Who does Pfizer's recruiting?"

Positioning Yourself for Your Job Search

BeverlyHarvey Put your field of expertise in your Twitter bio and include a link to an online LinkedIn profile, Web portfolio, resume or blog in your bio.

CharlotteWeeks If making a career change, make your bio and tweets about your future goal, not past career.

DailyCareerTips Best profiles tell me who you are, what you bring to the table and what you're looking for.

hireimaging Use your real name in Twitter bio. Transparency about who U R & what you do grows your foundation & helps show your value proposition.

JaneRoqueplot If you're unemployed, tweet about the project you'd like to be working on.

MegGuiseppi Revisit your Twitter bio whenever your job search focus and target change.

resumeservice Using Twitter for job search? Be ready w/ more than tweets (link to resume, VisualCV, blog, LinkedIn, email, tel #, etc.).

resumeservice To outdistance other #job candidates, promote via Twitter bio what you're offering instead of what you're *seeking*.

Following Your Interests

barbarasafani Follow the tweets of companies you admire or would like to work for and retweet their tweets.

BeverlyHarvey Follow accounts dedicated to job listings in a specific field - @journalism_jobs (Jobs in journalism), @PRSAjobcenter (Jobs in PR, comm. & mktg).

CFOCoach Follow recruiters and HR, and then read between the lines in their posts.

joanolson Follow industry leaders on Twitter & reply to posts--helps you become known, stay in the loop & find out who's hiring.

mediagirl007 Use Twitter to follow recruiters or companies of interest and learn of networking events!

PassportCoach Why look where everyone else is looking? Be innovative! Explore myriad possibilities in new fields and locations.

shannonckelly In college? Learn about jobs & internships with employers interested in your school w/ highlights from their job boards.

shannonckelly Don't miss an event. There are up-to-date posts on time/location. You may even discover a new one!

JanetCranford Use http://search.twitter.com to locate people in your field; and be sure to include relevant keywords in your bio to help them find you.

Relationship Management

careerplanning If you have a more personal Twitter account, create another one to be used solely for your job searching endeavors.

carolinarains Tweet your daily job search goals so that followers will know what specific actions can help you.

coachclaire Job Searching Tip: Be more interactive with your LinkedIn contacts by importing them to Twitter.

DaisyWright If you don't want your boss to know you are scouting the market, don't publicize your job search on Twitter. Use Direct Messages instead.

DaisyWright Nurture your Twitter relationships so you can make 'warm tweets' instead of 'cold calls' when you are ready to start your job search.

MAXyourCAREER Team job search on Twitter by cross-following 5 other job searching friends -- share ideas, encouragement, accountability, prayers.

StacySwearengen Have a visible Twitter link on your Web page so potential clients have a quick, easy way to communicate with you.

Using Twitter for Networking and Visibility

AndreaSantiago Use @ replies, DM etc 2 converse & build rapport & credibility over time. Don't bombard others w/job inquiries, interview requests, etc.

barbarasafani Twitter is like a big noisy party. You can't listen to every conversation; pick a few related to your profession or industry each time you visit.

careerrocketeer Create public lists of top thought leaders to follow using Twitter lists and share them with your industry to enhance your personal brand.

CharlotteWeeks When someone starts to follow you, send a PERSONAL (not canned) direct message.

CharlotteWeeks Make 4 of every 5 tweets about something else (conversation, sharing a link, etc.), & 1 of 5 about you.

CIO_Coach Make the first move - initiate engaging conversations through DM or open tweets with new contacts in your industry to become known to them.

HRCoachRenee Just a Few Hashtag Ideas-Use for chats #blogchat, #brandchat, #smallbizchat, #PRchat (try www.TweetChat.com to make it easier to chat).

KellyeCrane Find someone with similar interests to you and follow who they're following. Great way to expand your network.

KrisPlantrich Use Twitter to publicly thank those for help in your job search. Thanks and recommendations go a long way here!

KrisPlantrich Be curious! Tweet with those you might not normally interact with; they might be UR next opportunity – or U might be theirs.

wendyterwelp Take 5 to send a direct message (DM) to one or more on your follow list.

JeanCummings Be the one who responds to questions with links to helpful blogs or articles, not with a sales pitch or self-promotion: "givers gain!"

Using Twitter for Personal Branding and Social Media

billiesucher Before you hit update or send, ask yourself, does this tweet reflect well on me and my brand?

coachclaire Personal Branding: Always have a great picture & bio, and use your link well: Link to blog to show expertise or LinkedIn account.

KellyeCrane Show your expertise by responding to others' tweets with your insights. Demonstrating thought leadership will build your reputation.

expatcoachmegan Videoblogging on Twitter: unprofessional presentation and/or unclear message will hurt rather than help your personal brand.

MackCollier Getting on Twitter is NOT a strategy; Twitter is a tactic to execute a social media strategy.

MegGuiseppi Practice the 3 Cs of Twitter personal branding: Clarity - Consistency - Constancy.

myreinventure Do NOT start tweeting/blogging until you know your personal brand. Messaging needs to be tight, clear & consistent.

Using Social Media for Your Career

KrisPlantrich #Employment background checks include social networking. Make sure UR words work for you on Twitter, FB, Plaxo, MySpace etc.

careerfolk #jobseekers, use your LinkedIn profile as your Web site, integrating your resume into Twitter.

LouiseGarver Stand out from other applicants by providing hiring managers with valuable info through LinkedIn while reminding them to view your resume.

mediagirl007 Join "groups" on LinkedIn that relate to your work industry. Discussions here often mention open positions BEFORE they are posted elsewhere.

myreinventure Infuse your LinkedIn profile & headline with compelling differentiators that sell to your target audience and their influencers.

myreinventure Promote your online ID by subscribing to a blog in your area of thought leadership. Post comments on the blog & they become part of your permanent online ID.

RWDigest Once posted online, information never really disappears. Think twice before you write that status update or post that photo!

wendyterwelp 73% of executives find jobs through social networks. Use yours wisely. Online, it becomes your permanent record.

Using Twitter: General Tips

AndreaSantiago Proofread all your tweets! Nothing is a bigger turn-off than blatant misspellings & grammar errors (not including abbreviations, etc)

EidolonCS Edit auto-generated Tweets so that they're in your own voice. If your auto-generated Tweet is generic, it will look generic to the audience following you

cherylminnick Make sure your photo is a good-quality photo of you, not your dog!

dbashaw Keep your tweets professional, purposeful, powerful, and positive.

CIO_Coach Include a link in a tweet to a blog post or article you've written to demonstrate thought leadership, gain readership, and retweeting.

hireimaging Info best not shared on Twitter: home address, phone #s, kids' names, health details, places where U spend time. Fuzzy details = privacy.

HRCoachRenee To get followers, put your Twitter address everywhere: biz card, stationery, email sig, blog, Web site, Facebook, articles, ezine, ads...

KellyeCrane Have fun! Avoid TMI, but let some of your personality shine through. It's how real relationships are built.

Resume_Writer Twitter can be buggy. Check your direct message box frequently so you won't miss anything sent to you privately.

stephaniezonars Say it and they will come. Tweet provocative ideas and relevant resources and people will follow you.

stephaniezonars Search for and follow leaders in your industry who tweet to gain from their wisdom and to increase your own followership.

Job Search Tips: In a Nutshell

mypromotion Job search in four easy steps. 1. Know what you have to offer. 2. Know the market. 3. Have a plan for success. 4. Get and stay connected.

mypromotion Five things every job seeker must consider and deliver: 1.value statement 2.resume 3.profile 4.intro/cover letter 5.online presence.

Staying Focused and Motivated

DailyCareerTips It isn't always a terrible thing to lose a job. Sometimes it's the kick you need to move on.

DawnBugni #Jobseekers: Knowing where you want to go is equal to or more important than telling where you've been.

DawnBugni #Jobseekers: It's good to have Plan A for reemployment. It's even better to have Plan B, Plan C.... Work 'em all. Don't limit to one.

ErinKennedyCPRW Job search is a full-time job. Get up every day, make a plan & stick to it. The more action "U" take, the more "reaction" you get from others.

mypromotion Be unrelenting in pursuit of your next job. You and you alone are the catalyst for what you will accomplish.

RWDigest Use "The Rule of 5" in your job search. Do 5 things each day to reach your job search goal. THAT you do is more important than WHAT you do.

Keeping Up Appearances

annemariecross #Jobseekers: it's not always the best worker who gets the job; it's the person who adopts the best job search strategies.

KellyeCrane Be sure you don't appear desperate (which is never attractive). Saying "OMG, am I ever going to get a job?!" probably won't help your cause.

DawnBugni #Jobseekers: Don't forget to smile. That comes through on the phone too. Exude positive energy & remember, it's all about them.

Positioning Yourself for the Job

DawnBugni #Jobseekers: You've got 2 believe what U bring 2 an employer is special & you've got 2 sell it. If not U, who?

myreinventure You might need to update your skills or broaden your knowledge to ease your transition. Take a course or professional development training to round out your skills.

myreinventure When reinventing, network with professionals in desired field & cultivate mentors. These individuals will become your cheering section and potential colleagues.

Researching Leads and Employers

careerliz Research recruiters on LinkedIn and Twitter. You will be amazed at what you might have in common! This info can help you grow relationships.

KCCareerCoach Use Google Alerts to track current job trends. Transition your skills to meet new workplace needs.

KCCareerCoach Where are jobs? Follow the money! Gov't grants to contractors; states spending stimulus $$$; recession hot brands. Tweak your career goals.

MAXyourCAREER Can't find a job? Rent what you do an hour at a time. Just divide your annual salary by 2000 hours to get your minimum hourly rate.

myreinventure Use reference librarians (town or college) to flesh out list of target companies/industries-a free, useful resource for targeted job search.

resumeexpert #Jobseekers, use spoke.com & zoominfo.com to find company insiders and direct your cover letters to hiring managers.

KBitschenauer Be curious! Follow links in blogs, newsletters, ebooks, reports, Web pages--even footers--to find new gems of information.

Little Things That Make a Difference

davidheiser Be sure to communicate with important contacts about more than just your job hunt. Otherwise they'll feel like they're being used.

DailyCareerTips Think about who you have said thank you to at work. Send an email today thanking someone. cc: their boss.

DawnBugni #Jobseekers--Copy & paste job postings into Word docs & save. No guarantee it'll still B up when U interview & may contain needed info.

JanMelnik Accelerate your job search efforts between Thanksgiving and New Year's--you'll stand out and outshine your competition that's slacking off.

KCCareerCoach Anticipate job offer? Check your credit report FAST. Bad info can keep you from getting job--credit checks are common employer practice now.

KCCareerCoach Mother knows best? Advised son to do thank-you card after job interview. He was one of 9 hired out of 300 applicants.

mypromotion Be patient with HR & recruiters. They are not in the same kind of hurry as you. Keep lines of communication open.

Addressing Awkwardness/Gaps in Experience

elisabethspark Redirect pot'l employers to a current expression of ur professionalism & expertise to reduce concerns re: neg. info they may learn online.

teenarose One way to overcome being coined "overqualified" is to state you are looking for a better balance between work and personal life.

Networking Tips

CharlotteWeeks Consider meeting Twitter contacts in person for coffee, lunch, or an informational interview.

DailyCareerTips Trying to network? Use current events to help. Talk about, for ex., the World Series Game. Don't say you hate one team (they may love it!).

LaurieBerenson More effective to ask people who they know in a certain space versus who might be hiring. Broader question brings broader results.

JaneRoqueplot Ask questions for advice about your job search strategy. Everyone benefits & you remind your network you're job searching.

teenarose When starting a career, establish relationships with those who might be able to help you, as well as those you can help.

WalterAkana No matter how good your resume, the secret to career success is earning trust & connecting w/ your community. How are you earning trust?

WalterAkana Job seekers raise your credibility: Develop your professional point of view & talk about *that* when networking w/ colleagues.

wendyterwelp Take 5 to send a card on an unexpected holiday like Groundhog Day. Update your tweet peeps on the latest.

wendyterwelp Make a networking plan and stick to it. Connect with 5 people per week. Only 1 per day! Tweets count.

Personal Branding Tips

DailyCareerTips Your brand isn't just what makes you different. It's what's the same about you every time--what can your brand users count on?

paulcopcutt Make your bio a personal brand statement about what you do, for whom, and why you are different.

expatcoachmegan Personal Branding is not all about you--it's about the value you create in the lives of OTHERS (using your unique strengths).

JanMelnik Create a blog related to your subject-matter expertise, update regularly, convey real value, and periodically tweet tinyURL links.

LouiseGarver Buying a personal domain name helps build personal brand and helps with job search.

myreinventure Don't underestimate the power of your e-mail sig's brand messaging. Include your differentiation in every communication that leaves your desk.

myreinventure Google yourself regularly & track your results. What do people find? As you track your results, notice if volume and relevance increase.

savvycindy Consistently exuding a professional image is a powerful and strategic business tool in the workplace.

WalterAkana Your professional skills are the "what" that you bring to clients. It's "how" you use them that makes you stand out!

WalterAkana A way to figure out your brand value: Complete this sentence: "You can always count on me to _____."

Resume Tips

careerplanning Consider including your Twitter information on your resume right after your e-mail address.

ErinKennedyCPRW Add your LinkedIn profile to your resume. Ask former employers/old colleagues to post a recommendation 4 you (4 potential employers to view)

Jobacle Use a unique URL for each Web resume you send out by using the URL-shortening service bit.ly - that way you'll know who viewed it and when.

LouiseGarver Survey from Accountemps indicated that 3 out of 4 executives said they would not read a resume with typos.

mypromotion Anyone out there not a "team player or results-oriented"? When writing your resume sell your features and benefits, not the generic stuff.

resumeexpert A too-long #resume can encourage age bias with details going back 20+ years. Roll up old experience into value proposition instead.

RWDigest Make sure every item on your resume is unique to YOU. If it could be said about anyone else w/your job title, revise it. Use $, #, & %.

career_coach Demonstrate knowledge of current trends in the area of technology and social media. Do this in your key skills or summary areas.

Interviewing Tips

ErinKennedyCPRW If you are worried about interviewing style/questions, role-play/practice with a friend to prepare you and quell your nerves.

JanMelnik Be able to answer the question "why should we hire you?" concisely when doing interview prep.

APPENDIX B

CHAPTER CONTRIBUTOR BIOS

Social media is about community and connection, real-time conversation and resources, sharing and support. In the true spirit of Twitter, some of the career industry's brightest minds stepped up to the plate to share their best advice on how to make your job search soar. Their bios are listed below. As with our Tweet Tip Career Experts from appendix A, we encourage you to follow these thought leaders, which you can conveniently do by visiting http://tweepml.org/Twitter-Job-Search-Guide/.

Jason Alba (@jasonalba)
A popular blogger and vocal evangelist for career management, Jason Alba created JibberJobber.com to help job seekers organize and manage their job search. He wrote *I'm on LinkedIn—Now What???* and the *LinkedIn for Job Seekers DVD* (www.LinkedInForJobSeekers. com). You can see his other "for job seekers" videos, including *Twitter for Job Seekers*, at www.JibberJobber.com/ceo. A favorite of the media, he has been quoted widely on technology and the job search, including CIO.com, the *New York Times*, the *Wall Street Journal*, and many regional and local papers and magazines.

Laura Allen (@la15SecondPitch)
Laura Allen once closed a 5.5 million-dollar deal from a cold call. That's when she learned the true value of brevity. She cofounded 15SecondPitch.com in 2002 to train individuals to pitch themselves rich. She works with job seekers to help them do three things: 1. Figure out what makes them remarkable as a candidate, 2. Decide where they'd like to work, and 3. Craft a clear, concise, and compelling 15SecondPitch that makes hiring managers pick up the phone and call. An engaging speaker, Laura has been featured on NY1's "Employment Report," the *Wall Street Journal*, and *Adweek*.

William Arruda (@williamarruda)
Dubbed the Personal Branding Guru by the media and clients, William Arruda is the founder of Reach, the global leader in personal branding. He is one of the most sought-after speakers on personal branding and social media. His client list reads like the pages of *Fortune* magazine: Adobe, Cisco, IBM, L'Oreal, Microsoft, Morgan Stanley, and Starwood Hotels are just a few. William has appeared on BBC TV, the Discovery Channel, and Fox News Live, and he has been featured in *Forbes, Time,* and *Entrepreneur*. His book, *Career Distinction,* is a careers bestseller. You can connect with him at www.williamarruda.com.

Jacqui Barrett-Poindexter (@ValueIntoWords)

Jacqui Barrett-Poindexter, President, Career Trend, collaborates with professionals in career transition and individuals desiring to ignite their existing careers. A Master Resume Writer, Jacqui has a BA in Writing and 15 years of corporate experience. An intuitive researcher, she unearths clients' stories, applies an inventive approach to content/design, and originates branded resume and social media profiles. In addition to radio and television interviews, Jacqui has contributed to the Career Management Alliance member newsletter, ExecuNet's Career Smart Advisor, and the *Wall Street Journal*. Jacqui, whose Twitter name is @ValueIntoWords, is listed on many "Best People to Follow on Twitter" lists for job seekers.

Kim Batson (@CIO_Coach)

Kim Batson is the CIO Coach and President of Career Management Coaching.com, partnering exclusively with Senior Technology Executives to position them for extraordinary career and business success. A Certified Personal Branding, Job Search, and Online Identity Strategist, and Certified Career Management and Leadership Coach, Kim has a background in sales, management, technology, and recruiting with Fortune 100 experience. Kim's clients gain outstanding results with a uniquely developed personal branding program, powerful resumes/biographies, and the latest techniques in career and job search strategies. Recognized for exceptional presentation, communication, and relational skills, Kim is a keynote speaker and thought leader in the careers industry.

Rob Blatt (@robblatt)

You want to podcast? Rob Blatt can help! An Emmy- and Oscar-winning audio engineer, Rob is an expert in producing audio and video for the new media marketplace. A content strategist, audio engineer, and Web producer, he has a unique blend of hands-on experience with theatre companies, newspaper dailies, and broadcast documentary facilities.

Nancy Branton (@Branton_Careers and @LeadersCoach)

Coach, trainer, and consultant Nancy Branton is well-versed in talent management, leadership development, performance management, career development, career transition, outplacement, and job search. President of People Potential Group and Director of Leadership Coach Academy, she is the author of *The People Management Primer™: Coaching Leaders to Be Principled Leaders That Create Thriving Workplaces.* Nancy holds a PCC with the International Coach Federation (ICF) and an M.A. in Industrial Organizational Psychology. She is a Certified Leadership & Talent Management Coach, Certified Career Management Coach, Certified Job Search Strategist, Certified Personal Branding Strategist, and Certified Life Coach, and is qualified to administer 100+ assessments.

Sue Brettell (@SueBrettell)

Sue Brettell is the go-to creative passionista for personal branding design and copy. A Preferred Personal Branding Strategist with Reach, she focuses on branded new media and CMS design for dynamic professionals and executives driven to make a positive impact in the world. Sue is creatively versatile, tech savvy, innovative, and intuitive, with exquisite attention to detail. She combines years of training and experience in multidisciplinary design, publishing, and personal development to provide well-crafted visual identities and copy that effectively leverage her clients' unique value propositions. A visionary e-preneur, Sue lives in Suffolk, UK, and has clients around the globe.

August Cohen (@Resume_Writer)

August Cohen is an award-winning, triple-certified resume expert and career coach dedicated to supporting professionals in achieving their employment goals. Leveraging the talents she acquired in her successful six-figure corporate career, August directs determined job seekers in all aspects of modern career management, from powerful branded resumes to focused interview practice sessions. August serves in leadership roles for several career associations and frequently participates in industry conferences and workshops to keep abreast of issues and trends that could affect her clients. Additionally, she holds BA and MS degrees from the University of Arkansas and is Six Sigma White Belt certified.

Kirsten Dixson (@kirstendixson)

Kirsten Dixson is a personal branding consultant who is an authority on building credible online identities for career and business success. She's the coauthor of *Career Distinction: Stand Out by Building Your Brand* (Wiley), facilitates the personal branding certification programs for Reach, works with high-achieving individual clients, and delivers corporate personal branding programs. Kirsten serves as a media resource and speaker on career technology topics. She has been interviewed on *The Today Show* and quoted in the *New York Times, Wall Street Journal, Boston Globe, Real Simple, More, Advertising Age*, and CIO.com. Learn more at www.kirstendixson.com.

Alison Doyle (@AlisonDoyle)

Alison Doyle is a job search expert with many years of experience in human resources, career development, and job searching. Alison focuses on writing about online job searching, job search technology, social media, and professional networking providing expertise and advice to both job seekers and those interested in news about the field. Alison, who is the About.com Job Search Guide (jobsearch.about.com), has covered job searching for About.com (a New York Times Company) since 1998. She is the author of *Internet Your Way to a New Job: How to Really Find a Job Online* (2009) and the *About.com Guide to Job Searching* (2006).

Wendy Gelberg (@wendygelberg)

Wendy Gelberg is the founder of Gentle Job Search/Advantage Resumes and author of *The Successful Introvert: How to Enhance Your Job Search and Advance Your Career.* She is a certified career coach and resume writer whose expertise is in helping people who are uncomfortable "tooting their own horn." Designated the Introverts Job Search Expert for www.job-hunt.org, Wendy gives workshops, coaches individuals, and writes on all aspects of the job search process, including how to leverage social networking for career success. She has been featured in CNN/Fortune.com, *Money Magazine, Woman's Day, CareerBuilder*, and numerous other books and publications.

Robyn Greenspan (@RobynGreenspan)

Robyn Greenspan is Editor-in-Chief at ExecuNet, the leading business network for senior executives, where she sets and drives the editorial content strategy across ExecuNet's publications and webinar programming. She also writes and produces the company's annual *Executive Job Market Intelligence Report.* Greenspan originated the series of proprietary research reports, "Dealing with Your Digital Dirt," which raised international awareness of online reputation management, how executive recruiters use the Internet to find facts beyond the resume, and what executives can do to enhance their digital profiles. She holds a dual Master of Science in Counseling and Human Resources Development.

Katharine Hansen (@KatCareerGal)

Katharine (Kathy) Hansen, Ph.D., creative director and associate publisher of Quintessential Careers, is an educator, author, and blogger who provides content for Quintessential Careers, edits its newsletter *QuintZine,* and blogs about storytelling at A Storied Career. Kathy, who earned her Ph.D. from Union Institute & University, authored *Tell Me About Yourself, Dynamic Cover Letters for New Graduates, A Foot in the Door, Top Notch Executive Interviews,* and *Top Notch Executive Resumes;* and with Randall S. Hansen, Ph.D., *Dynamic Cover Letters, Write Your Way to a Higher GPA,* and *The Complete Idiot's Guide to Study Skills.*

Mark Hovind (@markhovind)

Mark Hovind, CEO of JobBait.com, helps six- and seven-figure executives find a job by sending letters directly to hiring decision makers. His success rate is 85 percent in 90 days for those who do it right, and half of his clients get multiple, simultaneous job offers. As a GM, COO, and CEO with experience managing hundreds of employees, Mark knows what decision makers want, and what executives must say to get the traction they deserve. His "value proposition" letters get six times more responses than resumes. Mark's monthly reports on the "Job Market Hot Spots" are used by thousands to maximize their odds.

Susan Ireland (@SusanIreland)

Susan Ireland is the author of Ready-Made Resumes software and four job search books, including *The Complete Idiot's Guide to the Perfect Resume.* Her books and software are sold to individual job seekers and licensed to government and college career centers. Trained in resume writing by the late Yana Parker (author of *The Damn Good Resume Guide*), Susan founded a certification program for professional resume writers in 1991. Program graduates comprise Susan Ireland's Job Search Team, which serves clients of all occupations and levels of employment. Information about Susan's products and professional services can be found on her Web site: www.susanireland.com.

Susan Joyce (@JobHuntOrg)

Susan P. Joyce has been tweeting since November 2008, generating 4,000+ tweets and followed by 15,000+ (through December 2009). President of NETability, Inc., Susan has been editor/publisher of Job-Hunt.org since 1998. Laid off twice, Susan founded NETability in 1995 after her last layoff. Her background includes service as an officer in the United States Marine Corps, and subsequent employment in Harvard University's Personnel Office, a compensation consulting firm, and a technology company. She earned a BA and an MBA. Widely quoted in books, Web sites, and publications like *Time, Fortune,* the *New York Times,* and the *Wall Street Journal,* Susan has been helping people leverage technology for job search since 1995.

Michael Kelemen (@animal)

Based in Toronto, The Recruiting Animal worked as a busboy and taxi driver before drifting into recruiting and a brilliant career as a pioneer of recruiter blogging. In January 2004, he cofounded the Canadian Headhunter blog. In April 2005, he became a partner in Recruiting.com. In April 2006, he founded RecruitingAnimal.com and, in October 2006, his group blog, RecruitingBloggers.com. In March 2007, he started The Recruiting Animal Show, the first online call-in show about recruiting in world history. The Recruiting Animal is currently at work on *Don't Call Us We'll Call You: A Job-Hunting Guide for the Mediocre.*

Abby Kohut (@Absolutely_Abby)

A leader in corporate staffing for 15+ years, Abby Kohut has held positions from recruiter to senior director with Kaplan, Inc.; Alpharma; Sabert; and Continuum Health Partners. She is currently President of Staffing Symphony, a staffing consulting company. A frequent speaker and popular blogger (www.AbsolutelyAbby.com), Abby delivers engaging onsite presentations and answers questions from job seekers on her biweekly www.CareerWakeUpCalls.com. She was a guest for Career Corner on SOMA TV and a speaker for Job1usa.com on WTOD Radio. Abby is a LinkedIn Open Networker (LION) who tweets on job search strategies. Her book *Absolutely Abby's 101 Job Search Secrets* is available at www.101JobSearchSecrets.com.

Cindy Kraft (@CFOCoach)

Cindy Kraft is America's leading Career and Personal Brand Strategist for Corporate Finance Executives. Known as "the CFO-Coach," Cindy is a Reach Certified Personal Branding Strategist and Online Identity Strategist, Certified Career Management Coach, Credentialed Career Master, Certified Professional Resume Writer, and Job & Career Transition Coach. She partners with CFOs and Senior Finance Executives to repackage and position themselves to land the job they want. Cindy can be reached via e-mail (cindy@cfo-coach.com) or phone (813-655-0658) or through her Web site (www.cfo-coach.com).

Jessica Lee (@Jessica_Lee and @APCOjobs)

Jessica Lee is a Senior Employment Manager for APCO Worldwide, a global PR firm headquartered in D.C. Like most upscale HR pros, she spends half of her time on recruiting and the other half on ER, training, and other HR stuff. When she's not hammering a candidate to determine Motivational Fit, she's updating her spreadsheet to determine her lifetime "time to hire" and "cost per fill." Jessica is also the editor of Fistful of Talent, a featured blog on workforce management.

Jeff Lipschultz (@JLipschultz)

Jeff Lipschultz is a founding partner of A-List Solutions, a recruiting firm in Dallas–Fort Worth. He enjoys blogging about the challenges of finding the best jobs as candidates and finding the best employees as companies. Jeff also blogs about employment trends and being a good manager. He is a featured writer on www.job-hunt.org. Jeff has a bachelor's and master's degree in Mechanical Engineering from the University of Wisconsin and University of Illinois–Chicago, respectively. He has a Master of Business Administration from Southern Methodist University with a focus in Marketing. Jeff is a charter member of the Drucker Society of Dallas.

Jan Melnik (@janmelnik)

Author of seven career/business books, Jan Melnik, MRW, CCM, CPRW, and Career Thought Leader, is president of Absolute Advantage, a career-management firm she founded in 1983. Melnik has been featured in numerous publications, is a regular career expert on NBC, and speaks frequently at colleges and libraries. She holds two undergraduate degrees in business and is a master's degree candidate at Wesleyan University. Her slogan is, "Be inspired. It's your career. It's your life." She helps clients coast-to-coast with career strategies, resumes, and coaching services and high school/college students with college and job search. On Twitter @janmelnik; via Web at www.janmelnik.com.

Chris Perry (@CareerRocketeer)

Chris Perry, MBA, is a Gen Y brand and marketing generator, an ambitious entrepreneur, and a career search and personal branding expert. Chris is the founder of Career Rocketeer (www.CareerRocketeer.com), its partner efforts (including Launchpad), and other online career services and communities (including MBA Highway). He launched all of these services as an entrepreneurial effort to better serve the growing unmet needs of career seekers—both students and professionals—during these technologically dynamic and challenging economic times. Chris also offers career search and personal branding workshops and presentations to a variety of audiences.

Lindsey Pollak (@lindseypollak)

Author, speaker, and blogger Lindsey Pollak specializes in Generation Y career and workplace issues. In addition to being Campus Spokesperson for LinkedIn, she authored *Getting from College to Career: 90 Things to Do Before You Join the Real World.* She writes a career advice blog at www.lindseypollak.com/blog and contributes columns to FastCompany.com and The Huffington Post. Her media appearances have included NBC Nightly News with Brian Williams, the *New York Times,* the *Wall Street Journal,* the *Washington Post, BusinessWeek,* CNN.com, and NPR. A popular speaker, she has delivered keynotes and workshops for Yale, Harvard, Columbia, Merrill Lynch, Time Inc., and many others.

Karla Porter (@karla_porter)

Karla Porter is the Director of Workforce Development and Human Resources at the Greater Wilkes-Barre Chamber, in Pennsylvania. Formerly, she worked as an Operations Manager turned HR Generalist in charge of super high-volume, full-cycle, third-party unassisted corporate recruiting, a change she made out of frustration at current recruiting practices and a desire to bring top-quality talent into the organization. Using social media, she reduced cost per hire by 40 percent in one year. Porter frequently speaks on job search, recruitment and retention strategy, relationship building, and the use of new media in HR and recruiting.

Barbara Safani (@barbarasafani)

Barbara Safani, owner of Career Solvers, has more than 15 years of experience in career management, recruiting, executive coaching, and organizational development. Barbara partners with both Fortune 100 companies and individuals to deliver targeted programs focusing on resume development, job search strategies, networking, interviewing, salary negotiation skills, and online identity management. She is the author of *Happy About My Resume: 50 Tips for Building a Better Document to Secure a Brighter Future* and *#JOBSEARCHtweet,* and her work is featured in dozens of career-related publications.

Dan Schawbel (@danschawbel)

Dan Schawbel is the leading personal branding expert for Gen-Y and the author of the bestselling career book, *Me 2.0: Build a Powerful Brand to Achieve Career Success* (Kaplan, April 2009). Dubbed a "personal branding guru" by the *New York Times,* Dan was named by *BusinessWeek* as one of 20 people entrepreneurs should follow on Twitter. His Personal Branding Blog is ranked in the top 20 marketing blogs by *Advertising Age.* The publisher of *Personal Branding Magazine®,* he is frequently quoted in outlets such as the *New York Times,* NPR, the *Wall Street Journal,* and ABC News. More at www.personalbrandingblog.com I www.studentbranding.com.

Marshall Sponder (@webmetricsguru)

Marshall's www.WebMetricsGuru.com, an industry blog about Web analytics, social media, and search marketing, is considered prophetic by Aberdeen Group and an influential blog on Web metrics in the analytics community. Marshall is an emeritus director at the Web Analytics Association, a member of SEMPO's research committee, and previously Senior Web Analyst, Monster Worldwide, and Senior Web Analyst, IBM.com. Marshall maintains his own Analytics Consultancy, NOW-SEO; freelances at Porter Novelli, a major PR firm; and writes a monthly column for Entrepreneur.com on leveraging online marketing technologies that help businesses succeed in a challenging economy. As the author of ArtNewYorkCity.com, Marshall covers the New York art world along with his own art. In addition, he is part owner of the Blogspeedway.com blog network and is a chat moderator for Search Engine Workshops and World Resource Center.

Mark Stelzner (@mstelzner and @jobangels)

Mark is the founder of Inflexion Advisors, applying 16 years of experience in the implementation of HR transformational initiatives. Over his career, Mark has brought more than $3 billion worth of value to his clients and employers. More info: www.inflexionadvisors.com. Mark is also the founder of JobAngels, a grassroots nonprofit dedicated to helping people get back to work, one person at a time. More info: www.jobangels.org. A highly sought-after voice in the industry, Mark has been featured by the *Wall Street Journal,* the *New York Times,* CNN, and NPR. His blog, "Inflexion Point," can be found at www.inflexionadvisors.com/blog.

Donna Sweidan (@careerfolk)

Donna Sweidan is a career coach, professional speaker, author, and social networking specialist. She has helped thousands of job seekers and career changers to find their path and overcome the obstacles in their way. She assists clients to identify their strengths, articulate their value, and successfully navigate the job market. Donna speaks and writes on a range of issues related to the job search, including social media and the psychological aspects of career management, and her job search support group has been featured in the *New York Times* and on CNN. Prior, she was Director of Career Services for The New School.

Wendy Terwelp (@wendyterwelp)

Wendy Terwelp has helped thousands of clients get hired faster and be rock stars at work since 1989. A recognized expert on networking, both online and off, Wendy has been featured in the *Wall Street Journal,* the *Washington Post,* the *Chicago Tribune,* the *Philadelphia Inquirer, Fast Company, The Business Journal,* CareerBuilder.com, Monster.com, and more, as well as numerous radio shows. She has published hundreds of articles on the Web and in print and literally wrote the book on networking, *Rock Your Network® for Job Seekers.* Get career tips and learn more at www.knocks.com. Follow on Twitter: @wendyterwelp.

Harry Urschel (@eExecutives)

Owner of e-Executives, a professional search firm specializing in senior technical to senior executive Information Technology professionals, Harry has more than 20 years of experience in the technical placement field and was a top international producer for the largest specialized search firm in the world. He has trained and managed large, top-performing recruiting teams, as well as helped hundreds of people into new careers. He coaches job seekers, teaches an eight-week class on job transition, and writes a blog for job hunters at www.TheWiseJobSearch.com. A graduate of Michigan Technological University, Harry resides with his wife and three children in Eden Prairie, Minnesota.

Bill Vick (@BillVick)

Bill Vick is a coach, headhunter, serial entrepreneur, author, vlogger, publisher, big biller, speaker, and recruitment industry consultant. Vick went from sales/marketing management with Fortune 500 companies such as Revlon and Max Factor to the computer and software industries where he launched a chain of computer stores and helped take a software company public. For the past 20 years, he has run his own retained executive search business, and along the way created a software company focused on software for recruiting and staffing firms and founded Recruiters OnLine Network (RON), a top 100 Web site. More: BillVick.com, EmploymentDigest.com, and BoomersNextStep.com.

The Distinguished (Baker's) Dozen: Stories from Successful Twitter Job Seekers

Biana Bakman (@bianalog)

Career field: Social media

Location: New York, NY

Formula for success: Building connections through Twestival and other social media events led to a job offer.

Did you make your objective and employment status a topic for discussion on Twitter, or did you keep it to yourself? At the time of my job search, my Twitter bio read, "If you like it, you should put some benefits on it...medical, dental, and vision please," or something along those lines. Obviously Beyonce's song "Single Ladies" was my inspiration for this. Luckily, the employer that ultimately hired me thought it was funny and gave me very generous health benefits from the outset.

What was the tweet or Twitter marketing campaign that made a difference for you? I was at the New York City Twestival event (#nyctwestival), texting (not tweeting). I tweeted about that, which prompted a Twitter user named @davekerpen to send a humorous reply. Dave began following my Twitter updates, and I later learned that he was a fellow Boston University alum.

> **Need to Know:** *Twestivals* are a series of events organized by volunteers around the world that bring people together offline for a great cause. Learn more at http://twestival.com.

Several weeks of job hunting then went by, filled with networking events, attempts at writing cover letters, and numerous anxiety attacks. I volunteered to help out at "Social Media for Social Change" and somehow ended up with the job of selling raffle tickets. I tweeted about that, which prompted another reply from @davekerpen. We conversed a bit about our respective experiences at BU. He finally tweeted

"@bianalog What year did you graduate? I'm old but still know a lot of people at BU. And check out our firm if you're highly motivated." That was the tweet that ultimately led to my job offer.

What's your advice for current job seekers using Twitter? Twitter is a place to be your best self. Think of Twitter as a forum to show potential employers how you add value to your community and how you would add value to their organization. You want to be conversational, but beware of being too open and/or silly. Mind you, I am often guilty of being very open and very, very silly, but in my case, it opened the doors to landing my next job!

Desiree Kane (@dbirdy)

Career field: Executive assistant
Web site: http://heroesrising.wordpress.com/
Location: Charlotte, NC
Formula for success: Twitter led to local face-to-face networking, which led to a new job with a 25 percent salary increase.

Did you intentionally set out to make Twitter an integral part of your job search or was it happenstance? I sent out hashtag-heavy tweets about once a month, saying

---

Looking to leverage my awesome #transportation #trucking #logistics & #supplychain tweeps to find #employment in #Charlotte NC. Suggestions?

---

followed by a second tweet

---

7 years exp in #administration in #operations dept of #logistics #transportation & #supplychain companies, mainly #intermodal #3PL. Pls RT

So the short answer is yes, I was intentional. All in all, Twitter was a tool to get my name in the hat initially. It was part of a larger-scale, social media–fueled job search.

What was the tweet or Twitter marketing campaign that made a difference for you? In the end, my job found me. I did not apply for it. The recruiter contacted me after seeing one of my tweets. He clicked on the link in my Twitter profile that directed him to LinkedIn. From there, he went to my online resume at www.visualcv.com, which offered more specific information. By way of my LinkedIn profile, he got my Google voice number and called me for prescreening. Six weeks later, he called me for a first interview, and then two weeks later, I had a signed job offer with better benefits, better pay (a 25 percent increase), and a better location.

What's your advice for current job seekers using Twitter? You have to be vocal about your job search, but 100 percent of your tweets cannot be geared toward that. Just like any other style of networking, you must be actively contributing before asking for anything.

Doug Hamlin (@doughamlin)

Career field: Public relations, Web development
Web site: http://doughamlin.com/
Location: Minneapolis, MN
Formula for success: Applied directly for position based on a tweet.

What was the tweet or Twitter marketing campaign that made a difference for you? Here's the exact tweet:

Weber Shandwick Minneapolis looking for mid-level html developer and PSD slicer. Plus you get to work with me. DM or @ me for more info.

What's your advice for current job seekers using Twitter? Be yourself. Twitter is about relationships, so blindly begging for a job isn't going to work. I can't tell you how many people from Twitter have become friends in real life; if I'm ever looking for another job, this circle of people will be invaluable. And show me your personality in your tweets; no one wants to hire a drone.

Jamie Varon (@JamieVaron)

Career field: Graphic design and communications
Web site: www.alifeintranslation.com/
Location: Rome, Italy
Formula for success: Created "Twitter Should Hire Me" marketing campaign. After receiving big press and an interview with Twitter, started her own entrepreneurial venture and moved abroad.

What was the tweet or Twitter marketing campaign that made a difference for you? I created a Web site, TwitterShouldHireMe.com, that included a presentation on how companies can use Twitter and how I could help them with their marketing. The campaign received a great deal of press, including a profile in *Fortune Magazine*.

What came out of all that press? I had lunch at Twitter headquarters after my self-designed job search marketing campaign received thousands of hits. Although I did not receive a job offer, the experience gave me a great deal of confidence. After receiving strong interest from several other employers, I decided to start my own graphic design business—and relocated to Rome since I could work from anywhere!

What's your advice for current job seekers using Twitter? Life isn't about getting by or waiting for time to pass. It's about running towards the things that mean something to you.

Jen Harris (@JenHarris09)

Career field: Marketing/social media strategy (freelancer)
Web site: http://caffeinatedmarketing.com
Location: Idaho
Formula for success: Received leads for new opportunities from Twitter community within minutes of being laid off.

Did you intentionally set out to make Twitter an integral part of your job search or was it happenstance? In October of last year, Twitter was the only lifeline to "my kind"…you know, the geeky ones who were on Twitter! I tweeted that I had just been laid off and needed a date for breakfast, lunch, and afternoon coffee the next day. Less than an hour later, I had three appointments for the next day and a job offer.

What was the tweet or Twitter marketing campaign that made a difference for you? I let people know where I was when I had some downtime between meetings. I had at least six impromptu coffee shop meetings, one leading to a $400 gig that happened simply because people knew that I was drinking coffee at Thomas Hammer and eating a bagel!

What's your advice for current job seekers using Twitter? Don't ask for the sale. No one likes to be pitched (i.e., listen to how great you are). If you are honest, share your knowledge, share others' knowledge, and have honest conversations without being a jerk or too polarizing, they will soon ask you "Do you have a resume? DM me your email." Bingo!

John Bordeaux, Ph.D. (@JBordeaux)

Career field: Knowledge management and innovation for national security and education
Web site: http://jbordeaux.com
Location: Lorton, VA
Formula for success: Engaged in simple conversations without agenda, which ultimately led to work redesigning the failed U.S. education system, working alongside leading professionals in innovation, public policy, and social change.

Did you intentionally set out to make Twitter an integral part of your job search or was it happenstance? Every day was spent looking for work, but not in the usual way. Instead of plastering the Internet with my CV, I used the time to develop and share some ideas, including formalizing a blog (http://jbordeaux.com), taking it from a blog I called DrFuzzy to something more businesslike. I opened a consultancy and announced my availability for both contracts and job offers.

(Note: Read John's insightful post about his job search journey at http://jbordeaux.com/a-year-ago/.)

What was the tweet or Twitter marketing campaign that made a difference for you? I engaged in simple conversations without agenda, both on Twitter and face-to-face. Searching for new colleagues, I made new friends, from Harvard professors to Silicon Valley entrepreneurs. I was chatting on Twitter and blogging—not about my situation or needs, but about my ideas.

I had coffee meetings with fascinating people—with no agenda other than "we should talk." Conversations arose from shared ideas, and the lack of agenda let us wander through fields of inquiry, often ending with nothing more than additional names and the promise of more coffee.

Still, I had a job interview almost every week. And I landed contracts. With one exception, each of these came directly from social media and colleagues/friends I had never "met" in real life.

What's your advice for current job seekers using Twitter? Treat your job situation as private information. Don't offer it; wait for the opening. (And before opening that door, test it gently.) When you send a message, you are both interrupting a loud cocktail party and whispering to people who are following you. Be professional; your messages are searchable—consider not just the people currently following you at that moment. You will not be hired based on Twitter alone, but this one tool will help you find connections into networks that do not yet realize they need you. Be generous, be kind, be real.

Jon Lazar (@JustJon)

Career field: Software programming
Web site: www.justjon.net
Location: White Plains, NY
Formula for success: Volunteered for Twestival charity event in Manhattan, which led to new friendships and a job offer.

Did you intentionally set out to make Twitter an integral part of your job search or was it happenstance? It was a mix. I was already active on Twitter when the startup I was working for was slowly going under. The signs were all there, so I began feeling out new opportunities. I saw a tweet looking for volunteers to help with the NYC Twestival Web site, so I volunteered. At the Twestival meetings, I met the cofounder of KlickableTV, where I now work.

How vocal were you about your job search on Twitter? My job search was a passive search. I was making contact with people I thought could assist in my future employment, but I never had to fully expand to a full-scale job search.

What was the tweet or Twitter marketing campaign that made a difference for you? At the beginning of last year, I had a minimal social media footprint. The Twestival meetings became my window to the world, showing me how much more was really available in my chosen field. After the Twestival event, I attended tweet-ups where I've learned a lot about the current state of technology and startups in New York City. In the process, I met some amazing people and made some good friends. It was these relationships that led to my job at KlickableTV.

What's your advice for current job seekers using Twitter? Make friends, talk to everyone, and connect with people in the industry you want to be with. Even if you aren't talking business with them, you are bonding with them, so when an opportunity arises, they will recognize you as someone who may be able to fill the position.

Kelly Giles (@kellygiles)

Career field: Social media strategist
Web site: www.tarheelsintransit.wordpress.com/
Location: Chapel Hill, NC

Formula for success: Thoughtful questions led to a new friendship on Twitter, resulting in clarity on career direction and a job lead that turned into an offer.

How vocal were you about your job search on Twitter? I didn't hide the fact that I was job searching, but that wasn't the only thing I tweeted about. My bio explained that I was "deciding between law school and the real world." Other than that, I tweeted about job search and career articles, but I didn't send pleas for help. That's one of the biggest mistakes I see job seekers make on Twitter. Instead of showing their expertise and developing relationships, they create profiles with no information, and their only tweet is something like, "Looking for a job. Can you help me?"

What was the tweet or Twitter marketing campaign that made a difference for you? There were two tweets that made a big difference for me. The first was one of my earliest ones, and it introduced me to the connection that would help me land my job. I tweeted about how UNC–Chapel Hill's (my alma mater) career services office should teach personal branding. A career coach at Bowdoin College named Sherry Mason (@sherryfm) reached out to me, asking what else I thought they should do.

We messaged back and forth, and I learned that Sherry was a lawyer turned career counselor. She took an interest in my situation and really counseled me through the law school decision (and I decided it wasn't for me).

The second important tweet was the introduction to my current employer, Optimal Resume. Sherry, knowing my interest in Web 2.0 job searching and my desire to stay in North Carolina, introduced me to @optimalresume, who was Optimal Resume's chief operating officer. Within the week, I went to lunch with the CEO and COO, and a few days later, I had a job offer.

What's your advice for current job seekers using Twitter? The power of Twitter will be in whom you follow and who follows you. It's the only place where you can make a direct, organic connection with people you want to know. It starts by following people. I advise job seekers to follow people based on two criteria: industry and geographic location. Figure out what you want to do and where you want to do it. Then follow people who are doing what you want to do in the location you want to be. But the goal is to get them to follow you back. How do you do that? Tweet interesting content of your own: industry-related articles, commentary, etc. But most important, engage with them. Retweet their tweets, ask questions, send comments, share information. Build a relationship. When you take this approach, networking becomes organic. That's where Twitter is uniquely powerful in the job search.

Michael Litman (@litmanlive)
Career field: Public relations
Web site: www.litmanlive.co.uk/
Location: London, UK

Formula for success: Build presence, get noticed, get hired. Was recommended by a friend for a job on the basis of tweets, which led to an invitation to hire.

Did you intentionally set out to make Twitter an integral part of your job search or was it happenstance? It wasn't intentional, but I did make myself available on Twitter and network with who I thought would be the "right" people to get myself into the very small niche of social media PR in London. I thought it would be great to find a job via Twitter, and it came off. Someone I had intermittently tweeted with previously was, a few months later, hiring for a suitable position. I was recommended by a mutual friend for the position, and the rest, as they say, is history.

What was the tweet or Twitter marketing campaign that made a difference for you? The tweet that made a personal difference was Mashable linking to my post on "How to use Twitter to find your next job" (www.litmanlive.co.uk/2009/01/how-to-use-Twitter-to-find-your-next-job/). *Just that one single tweet took my blog down for 24 hours. It was a nervy time; I felt absolutely helpless. The traffic numbers continued to skyrocket for up to three months later.*

What's your advice for current job seekers using Twitter?
Be useful. If you see an interesting link, don't keep it to yourself; share it with your followers. They will then share it with their network and it becomes a big domino effect. Always think, "What would someone else think if they saw my tweets?"

Be yourself. Write about the things that interest you. That way, people will follow you for who you are. Don't try and pretend to be an expert in an area you're not— you'll get found out and that will be that!

Be different. Have your own views on current affairs, social media issues, online news, and the thoughts from A-listers/social media rock stars. Don't just say what everyone else is saying; that doesn't make you unique and stand out. But don't be controversial just for the sake of it. If you feel passionate about something, have an opinion and make it heard. Don't be afraid to say what you think. That's what makes you who you are.

(When @litmanlive reached 500 followers, he sent a cake to his newest friend. Read the story and see a picture of the cake here: www.litmanlive.co.uk/2008/11/reaching-500-Twitter-followers-does-it-mean-anything/)

Mark Buell (@mebuell)
Career field: Corporate communications
Location: Ottawa, ON, Canada
Formula for success: Applied directly for a position based on a tweet. Submitted personal Twitter stream as a writing sample, which helped land a job offer.

What was the tweet or Twitter marketing campaign that made a difference for you? After I shared my Twitter writing sample, my employer reviewed my Twitter account. This is an important point for job seekers to understand: Employers are looking at the whole. It's not just any one moment that makes an employer want to hire you—it's your entire record.

What's your advice for current job seekers using Twitter? Identify the thought leaders and key stakeholders in the industry you want to work for. Engage them. And be direct and upfront about what you want to do.

Shannon Yelland (@Shannonyelland)

Career field: Online marketing
Website: www.seedtheweb.com
Location: Vancouver, BC, Canada
Formula for success: Updated Twitter profile (and other profiles listed on Twitter background) indicating availability for job opportunities.

How vocal were you about your job search on Twitter? I did not keep it to myself, nor did I spam everyone all the time. I mixed in my tweets about job search here and there. The most important thing I did was to update my Twitter profile to say I was looking for a job, and then I updated my other profiles that were listed on my Twitter background.

What was the tweet or Twitter marketing campaign that made a difference for you? I tweeted here and there about my search, and I shared my experiences through the process. I tweeted about updating my profile, interviewing, coming across jobs other people might be interested in, and, finally, landing a new job.

What's your advice for current job seekers using Twitter? Integrate your Twitter strategies with Facebook, LinkedIn, and your blog if you have one. Specifically:

- Facebook and LinkedIn now have Twitter apps, so when you update your Twitter feed, it automatically updates within your profiles. Also, add your Twitter feed on the sidebar of your blog (again, if you have one).

- Update your profile in Twitter settings to say outright that you are looking for a job.

- If you don't have a blog, link your Twitter profile to your public LinkedIn profile.

- Be very clear on all of your profiles that cross-link to Twitter that you are looking for a job. If you don't tell anyone, no one will help or refer you. Twitter, and all social media, is about helping others—you will be surprised. If you do have a blog, link to it from your Twitter profile and make sure the "About" page on your blog states, clearly near the top, "Currently looking for career opportunities."

- Leverage your blog. If you don't have one, consider starting. If you do, and it's on a topic relevant to your search, put more effort into compiling great posts that show your expertise during this time. It is *very* important. I had multiple comments from potential employers that it actually helped me stand out of the crowd and convince them that I had the skills they were looking for.

- Pay attention to your tweets. I also had feedback that after I went for an interview, everyone at the company checked out my Twitter stream and it convinced them that I should be shortlisted for the job. That's great validation of Twitter working for me during my career transition.

  Make sure your tweets during your job hunt reflect mostly your career expertise. Ask yourself, "Did I post valuable tweets that show my passion on the topic?" If you comment on others' blog posts or research topics to make yourself better on the job, let others know. Avoid filling your Twitter stream up with everyday stuff that doesn't matter (your potential boss doesn't care if your cat threw up or if you are having a martini on a sunny deck).

- Set up TweetBeep.com alerts and Google Alerts with keyword phrases that match the title of the job you want (and the city, or you'll get too many alerts). This was the only way I looked for positions.

- Help others who are looking for a job on Twitter. They will help you back and more people will, too, because they see you helping others.

Stephen Moyer (@Stephen_Moyer)

Career field: Recruiting
Web site: www.linkedin.com/in/stephenmoyer
Location: Wilkes-Barre, PA; relocating for new job in Geneseo, NY
Formula for success: A soon-to-graduate college senior followed and engaged thought leaders worldwide and became an emerging thought leader and a sought-after talent in the process.

What was the tweet or Twitter marketing campaign that made a difference for you? I was in my final semester as a psychology major at Wilkes University and wanted to pursue a career in recruiting but the only interview opportunities I found through traditional, on-campus search methods were in human resources. I was doing an internship at the time at the Wilkes-Barre Chamber of Commerce and my supervisor, Karla Porter (@Karla_Porter), was a power Twitter user. She encouraged me to explore Twitter as a networking tool, and so I shifted my Twitter usage from a purely social tool to a more professional platform.

I started following the major recruiters on Twitter and began engaging them by responding to their tweets and offering my opinions on questions they posted. When they took a look to see who I was, they saw that my bio said I wanted to be a recruiter. I was later invited to be a guest on a radio show about why I wanted to be a recruiter. The exposure from that landed me my first interview with a recruiting firm. I had another interview that also resulted from Twitter (this one turned out to be my new position)—a recruiter contacted my internship supervisor (Karla) and asked her to pass along a recruiting job opportunity to me to see if I was interested. I checked out the recruiter's profile on Twitter and then called her. From the time I started on Twitter to the time I accepted an offer took just 10 weeks.

You were open to relocation and networked with recruiters in the UK and Canada, as well as the U.S. What advice would you give someone who wants to stay in the same geographic location? I'd recommend they not limit themselves to the people they follow based on geography. Go ahead and follow people worldwide who are industry leaders. Getting your name out there is important. You can tell people later that you want to stay local or mention on your Twitter bio that you're looking in a specific geographic area.

What's your advice for current job seekers using Twitter? Be persistent. You can't join Twitter and expect to have results in a day. However, developing a quality following and retweeting, engaging, and entertaining those followers will definitely help you out.

Warren Sukernek (@warrenss)

Career field: Social media marketing
Web site: http://twittermaven.blogspot.com/
Location: Seattle area, WA
Formula for success: Advertised availability for employment and leveraged Twitter for in-person networking.

What was the tweet or Twitter marketing campaign that made a difference for you? I tweeted to my community of approximately 2,800 followers that I was laid off and was seeking opportunities. I was laid off in December, in the middle of the holiday season, but found a job in just 22 days. To get there, I had 250 responses and leads, 20 interviews, and four job offers within three weeks. For the full story of my search, see www.slideshare.net/warrenss/tweet-your-way-to-a-new-job-1974286.

I ran an integrated campaign that included blog posts, tweets, and requests of friends to help. Many of them gave me recommendations on LinkedIn, tweeted, and wrote blog posts about me.

What's your advice for current job seekers using Twitter? Build it before you need it.

INDEX

A

access via Twitter, 22–23
accomplishments, 48–49
accounts
    multiple accounts, 71–72
    setup, search engine optimization, 66–67
active participants, 6
advanced search feature on Twitter, 189–190
AIM (audience, intended impact, messaging)
  model for sharing information, 167–168
Alba, Jason, 150, 153, 218
Alexander, Dan, 16
Allen, Laura, 57–60, 218
alternative client hosts, 195
Android apps, 200
APIs (Application Programming Interfaces), 194
    backing up tweets, 198
    content distribution, 199
    creating lists with, 186
    current list of, 201
    desktop Twitter clients, 195
    evaluating Twitter influence, 199–200
    finding conversations, 196
    finding followers, 196–197
    mobile apps, 200–201
    photos and video, 199
    saving favorite tweets, 200
    scheduling tweets, 197–198
    URL shorteners, 196
applying for posted jobs, 116
apps. See APIs
archiving tweets, 198
Arruda, William, 35, 37, 126, 150–151, 218
assets
    aligning with market needs, 113
    assessing, 112–113
    personal branding, 114
attitude advice, 207
audience, knowing, 166–167
automatic retweeting, 98–99
availability of usernames, checking, 66
avatars, 73–74
awareness of niche, building, 161

B

backgrounds
    benefits of, 75
    custom, 77–82
    hiring designer for, 82–83
    modifying standard, 76–77
    resources, 83–84
backing up tweets, 198
Bakman, Biana, 32, 202, 226
Baldas, Tresa, 104
Barrett-Poindexter, Jacqui, 99, 180, 219
baseline, establishing, 37–38
Bateson, Mary Catherine, 112
Batson, Kim, 156, 219
Bedbury, Scott, 49
Belasco, David, 133
best practices
    networking, 145–146
    job search, 29–30
Bieber, Justin, 105
Bing, integration with Twitter searches, 190
bio. See Twitter bio
Bit.ly, 196
BlackBerry apps, 200
Blatt, Rob, 25–27, 200, 219
blocking followers, 89
blogs, finding, 96
Bodett, Tom, 12
Bolles, Richard Nelson, 64
Bordeaux, John, 32, 203, 229
Boyd, Stowe, 43, 56–58
brand statements, 44, 50
Brand to Land Plan, 43–46
Branded Value Proposition (BVP), 44, 51
    in cover letters, 135
    questions for identifying, 53–54
    as sales pitch, 51–53
    in Twit-Fit resumes, 126–127
    Twitterizing, 54
brands. See also personal brands
    career brands, 44, 48
Branton, Nancy, 171, 219
breaking news, researching, 11–12
Brettell, Sue, 75, 219
Brice, Fanny, 166
Brin, Sergey, 56

Brizzly, 195
Brogan, Chris, 22
Bronman, Jeff, 21
Buck, James, 105
Buell, Mark, 32, 198, 204, 232
Burg, Bob, 88
buying motivators in accomplishments, 49
BVP. *See* Branded Value Proposition

C

Campbell, Anita, 16
CAR format for accomplishments, 49
career brands, 44, 48
Career Collective, 180
Career Hub, 180
Career Thought Leaders, 180
Carnegie, Dale, 51
Cashmore, Pete, 183
Cohen, August, 155, 157, 220
Colbert, Stephen, 139
Cole, Beth, 81
colors, modifying, 76–77
Colton, C.C., 97
Colvin, Kris, 78
communications plans, developing, 38–39
companies. *See also* employers
    finding reputations of, 197
    targeting in job searches, 114
    on Twitter, 17, 179
connections, finding, 7–8
content
    attracting followers with, 88
    sources for, 96
content distribution APIs, 199
conversations, finding, 196
copyright issues, 107
Corcodilos, Nick, 141
corporate culture, researching, 11–12
cover letters, 132–138
Covey, Steven, 127–128
Creative Commons, 107

D

Day-Tight Twitter Job Search Blueprint, 173–174
Dayton, Adrian T., 106
deleting tweets, 91, 106
designers, hiring, 82–83
designing custom backgrounds, 80–82
desktop Twitter clients, 195
Dickman, Matt, 151
Dig Your Well Before You're Thirsty (Mackay), 18

digital dirt, 36. *See also* online identity
    overcoming, 9–10, 39–40
    protection from, 106
Digsby, 199
direct messages (DM), 26–27, 91
directories, searching, 30, 179. *See also* lists
discretionary authenticity, 164
    AIM model, 167–168
    amount of information in tweets, 166
    inside jokes, 166
    knowing your audience, 166–167
    length of tweets, 165
    tips for, 168
    what not to share, 164–165
diversity on Twitter, 16
Dixson, Kirsten, 35–37, 94, 150, 153–154, 220
DM. *See* direct messages
D'oliveira, Ruben, 79
Donne, John, 150
Dorsey, Jack, 2
Dourgarian, Greg, 194
Doyle, Alison, 220

E

Echofon, 195
elevator pitches, 60
Emerson, Ralph Waldo, 12
employers. *See also* companies
    advice from experts, 214–215
    BVP as sales pitch to, 51–53
    connecting with, 208
    directories of, 179
    impact of tweeting on, 19
Employers Recruiting on Twitter list, 179
endorsements, gaining, 116
Enelow, Wendy, 180
engagement, 25–26, 95
etiquette advice, 207–208
evaluating Twitter influence, 199–200
events, transformation of, 22
experience gaps, advice, 215
External F.I.T., 42
extroverts, tips for, 155, 157–158

F

Facebook, 23–25
favorites, 91, 200
FavStar.fm, 200
feeds, 176, 179
Ferrazzi, Keith, 89
15-minutes-a-day Twitter schedule, 171–174
Filigheddu, Luca, 102

Fisch, Karl, 21
Fletcher, Louise, 180
floating page, designing backgrounds around, 80–81
Follow Friday, 103
followers, 85–86
    attracting, 87–89
    blocking, 89
    building list of, 16–17
    finding, 196–197
    knowing your audience, 166–167
following, 10
    interests, 209–210
    selecting who to follow, 86–87
following up interviews, 142
font usage, legal issues, 82
Four Questions, 141
Foursquare, 200
Fowler, Gene, 126

G

Gale, Porter, 16
Gallant, Deborah, 159
gaps in experience, advice, 215
Gelberg, Wendy, 155–156, 220
Gerber, Michael, 22
Giles, Kelly, 32, 204, 230
Godin, Seth, 154
Google, integration with Twitter searches, 190
googling yourself, 37–38
Gracián, Baltasar, 132
Greenspan, Robyn, 220

H

Hamlin, Doug, 32, 175, 203, 228
handles, 12
Hansen, Katharine, 221
Hansen, Mark Victor, 16
Harris, Jennifer, 32, 203, 228
hashtags, 8, 91
    searching for, 140, 177–179
headhunters. *See* recruiters
Hemingway, Mariel, 16
hex value, 76
hidden job market
    connecting to, 9
    targeting companies in, 114
hiring managers, connecting with, 208
HootSuite, 195, 197, 200
Hovind, Mark, 52, 113, 132, 221
Hsieh, Tony, 12
Hubspot, 198

Huffington, Arianna, 16, 184
Hurston, Zora Neale, 189
Huxley, Aldous, 98

I

image usage, legal issues, 82
immediacy of information, 15
influence, 172–173, 199–200
information curators, 183
insider contacts, finding, 9
integration
    online/offline activity, 89, 151–153
    search engines/Twitter searches, 190
    Twitter/other social media, 153–154
Internal F.I.T., 42
International Directory of 400+ Twitter Job Feeds list, 179
interviewing as S.O.S. consultant, 117
interviews
    advice from experts, 217
    following up, 142
    pre-interview research, 139–140
    seeking advice about, 140–141
introverts, tips for, 155–157
iPhone apps, 194, 200
Ireland, Susan, 177, 221

J

job boards, 177
job description for Twit-Fit resumes, 129–131
job leads
    advice, 214–215
    employer directories, 179
    finding, 8–9, 17, 175
    hashtag searches, 177–179
    sources of, 176–177
job search experts, finding, 30
job search information, finding, 8
job searches
    advice from experts, 180, 213–215
    aligning assets with market needs, 113
    applying for posted jobs, 116
    assessing assets, interests, priorities, 112–113
    developing ROI relationships, 115
    gaining endorsements, 116
    interviewing, 117
    as marketing, 116–117
    personal branding, 114
    psychological aspect of, 117–119
    researching T.O.P. issues, 115–116
    targeting specific companies, 114

job searches with Twitter
    additional tools for, 191–192
    advanced search feature, 189–190
    advice from experts, 207–217
    advice from job seekers, 202–205
    best practices, 29–30
    for extroverts, 157–158
    for introverts, 156–157
    jump-start tips, 30–31
    myths about, 28–29
    personal branding and, 41–42
    recruiters' advice, 120–124
    retweeting and, 101–102
    search engines and, 190
    tweeting questions in, 192–193
JobAngels, 178–179
Joel, Mitch, 153
Johnson, Steven, 22
Jolly, Tom, 16
Joyce, Susan, 64, 179, 221
Just Tweet It, 191

K

Kane, Desiree, 32, 202, 227
Kelemen, Michael, 221
Kennedy, Erin, 70
Kerrigan, Robert, 85
Klein, Jon, 16
Klout, 200
knowing your audience, 166–167
Kodak's social media guidelines, 107–109
Kohut, Abby, 120–121, 222
Kraft, Cindy, 159, 222
Kroc, Ray, 120

L

laughter, fostering, 12
Lazar, Jon, 32, 204, 230
leads. *See* job leads
learning, fostering, 12
Lee, Jessica, 66, 122–123, 222
legal issues. *See also* digital dirt
    image and font usage, 82
    law keeping pace with technology, 104–105
    ownership of tweets, 107
    public nature of tweets, 105
    social media guidelines, 107–109
LinkedIn
    comparison with Facebook and Twitter,
        23–25
    integration with Twitter searches, 190
    Twitter versus, 18

Lipschultz, Jeff, 123, 159, 222
Listology, 161
Listorious, 183
lists, 181–186. *See also* directories
Litman, Michael, 32, 204, 231
location, including in account settings, 72
Love, Courtney, 105

M

Mackay, Harvey, 18
managing online identity, 36–39
Manishin, Glenn, 106
market needs, aligning assets with, 113
marketing, job searches as, 116–117
Mason, Sherry, 231
Master F.I.T., 42
Matwyshyn, Andrea, 104
McLeod, Scott, 21
Melnik, Jan, 139, 192, 222
Meyer, Paul J., 89
micro-bio. *See* Twitter bio
microblogging, 11
Milken, Michael, 9
mobile apps, 200–201
Monitter, 140, 191–192
Mooney, Heidi Richards, 172
Morris, Clayton, 181
motivation, advice from experts, 213
Moyer, Stephen, 33, 205, 234
Mr. Tweet, 197
multichannel strategy, 95
multiple Twitter accounts, 71–72
myths about Twitter, 15–19, 28–29
MyTweeple.com, 87, 186

N

names. *See also* usernames
    checking availability of, 38
    selecting, 68–69
networking
    developing ROI relationships, 115
    value of Twitter in, 18
networking with Twitter, 144–145
    advice, 210–211, 215–216
    best practices, 145–146
    for extroverts, 157–158
    for introverts, 156
    niche marketing, 159–163
    professional association networking,
        146–147
    Roger Smith Hotel example, 148–149
networks, expanding, 10

niche marketing, 159–163
niches, 160
N.O.S.E. model, 93–95
noteworthy, writing tweets, 93
Nutshell Mail, 27

O

offline activity, tying to tweets, 89, 151–153
on-brand, writing tweets, 93–94
oneforty, 201
160me. *See* Twitter bio
online identity, 36–39. *See also* digital dirt;
    personal brands
Online Identity Calculator, 37–38
organizing Twitter streams. *See* lists
Osler, William, 170
oversharing, avoiding, 168
Ow.ly, 196
ownership of tweets, 107

P–Q

Page, Larry, 56
passive participants, 6
patterns
    in branding, 48
    tiling in background, 78
    tying to accomplishments, 48–49
people
    searching for, 12
    selecting who to follow, 86–87
    types on Twitter, 16
Perry, Chris, 179, 223
persona, attracting followers with, 88
personal brands, 9, 44
    advice from experts, 211, 216–217
    assets, 114
    authenticity of, 42–43
    benefits of, 43
    Brand to Land Plan, 43–46
    broadcasting, 9–10
    custom backgrounds. *See* backgrounds
    developing, 38
    job searches and, 41–42
    managing, 36–39
    niche marketing and, 162
    online identity, 36–39
    patterns in, 48
    refining, 47–50
    resources for information, 55
    Twitter bio, 58–60
    writing on-brand tweets, 93–94

personal tweets versus professional tweets, 19. *See
    also* discretionary authenticity
Peters, Tom, 41
Phil Rosenburg's Jobtweets Twitter list, 179
photos
    APIs for, 199
    uploading, 73–74
pitches. *See* Twitter bio
Pollak, Lindsey, 144, 223
Porter, Karla, 123–124, 223, 234
positioning for job search, advice, 209, 214
posted jobs, applying for, 116. *See also* job leads
pre-interview research, 139–140
priorities, assessing, 112–113
professional association networking, 146–147
professional tweets versus personal tweets, 19
Profile page, search engine optimization (SEO),
    64–66
profiles for Twit-Fit resumes, 129
psychological aspect of job searches, 117–119
publicly personal information, 26
Pulver, Jeff, 14

R

RandsinRepose blog, 125
rebranding yourself, 9–10
recommendations. *See* endorsements
recruiters
    advice from, 120–124, 180
    contacting, 8–9
    search engine usage, 36
    on Twitter, 17
Recruiting Animal, 121
Reed, Janelle, 81
refining personal brands, 47–50
relationships, 25–26, 210
@reply, 27, 91
reputations of companies, finding, 197
researching. *See also* searching
    advice from experts, 214–215
    corporate culture, 11–12
    for interviews, 139–140
    online identity, 36
    T.O.P. issues, 115–116
    via social media, 192–193
resources for information
    branding, 55
    custom backgrounds, 83–84
    tweet content, 96
ResumeBear.com, 168
resumes, 217. *See also* Twit-Fit resumes
Retweet, 196

retweeting (RT), 10–11, 91, 97–103
right-side graphics on custom backgrounds, 81
Roger Smith Hotel, 148–149
Rohn, Jim, 51
ROI relationships, developing, 115
Roppo, James, 105
Rosen, Peter, 86
Rosenburg, Phil, 179
RSS feeds. *See* feeds
RT. *See* retweeting
Rumford, Rodney, 28

S

Safani, Barbara, 191, 223
Sagolla, Dom, 2
sales pitch, Branded Value Proposition (BVP) as, 51–53
Salpeter, Miriam, 180
Sandwich, 4th Earl of, 132
Sarno, David, 16
saving favorites, 200
Schawbel, Dan, 19, 105, 223
scheduling tweets, 172, 197–198
search engine optimization (SEO), 64–74
search engines
    integration with Twitter searches, 190
    for job leads, 176–177
    recruiter usage of, 36
searching, 8. *See also* job searches; job searches
    with Twitter; researching
    directories, 30, 179
    for hashtags, 140, 177–179
    for job search experts, 30
    for lists, 183–184
    for people, 12
Seckel, Al, 16
Seesmic, 195, 200
Seesmic Android, 200
Senge, Peter, 21
SEO (search engine optimization), 64–74
serendipity, cultivating, 10–11
Share, Jacob, 179
sharing
    fostering, 12
    what not to share. *See* discretionary
        authenticity
Shelley, Mary Wollstonecraft, 181
shortened URLs, 73, 101, 196
shorthand, 91–92
Siedell, Tim, 12
Simmers, Bill, 79
Simmons, Kathy, 43

Simpson, Brian, 148
single-stream strategy, 95
Sirkin, Marc, 16
Smarty, Ann, 190
social media, 4, 150
    advice from experts, 211–212
    comparison of Facebook, LinkedIn, Twitter, 23–25
    Kodak's guidelines, 107–109
    personal branding and, 41–42
    researching via, 192–193
    trend-following statistics, 21
    tying tweets to, 89, 153–154
Social Scope, 200
SocialOomph.com, 172, 197
Solis, Brian, 101
Southey, Robert, 133
Sponder, Marshall, 147, 172, 224
Starbucker, Terry, 11
statistics, trend-following, 21
Stelzner, Mark, 178–179, 224
Stone, Biz, 139, 144
Strayer, Susan, 179
Sukernek, Warren, 33, 205, 235
support groups, finding, 7–8
Sweidan, Donna, 117, 224
syndicated feeds. *See* feeds

T

targeting companies in job searches, 114
terminology, 90–91
Terwelp, Wendy, 146, 224
text colors, selecting, 77
text messaging, Twitter compared to, 15. *See also*
    direct messages
thanks for retweeting, 102–103
themes in accomplishments, 49
tiling patterns in background, 78
time management, 170–171
    Day-Tight Twitter Job Search Blueprint, 173–174
    15-minutes-a-day Twitter schedule, 171–174
time requirements for tweeting, 15–16, 26–27, 89
Tinker.com, 196
TinyURL.com, 196
Tolkien, J.R.R., 188
T.O.P. issues, researching, 115–116
Totaro, Rob, 17
Tozzi, John, 56
traditional retweeting versus automatic retweeting, 98–99
transformation of events by Twitter, 22

trend-following statistics, 21
Trendistic, 191
Trout, Brett, 106
Twain, Mark, 138
Tweep Search, 191
TweepML, 186
Tweet O'Clock, 198
Tweet Scan, 191
TweetBeep, 191
TweetDeck, 26, 195, 200
TweetEffect, 200
TweetFeel, 197
Tweetie, 200
TweetLater, 172
TweetLevel, 200
TweetMeme, 196
TweetMyJobs.com, 176
TweetPhoto, 199
tweets, 2, 90
    attracting followers with, 88
    backing up, 198
    deleting, 91, 106
    how often to send, 89, 166
    impact on employers, 19
    job search questions in, 192–193
    length of, 165
    ownership of, 107
    professional versus personal, 19
    retweeting, 10–11
    saving favorite, 200
    scheduling, 172, 197–198
    sources for content, 96
    tips for writing, 93–95
    tying to offline activity, 89, 151–153
    tying to social media, 89, 153–154
    what not to share. *See* discretionary
      authenticity
    writing for retweeting, 100–101
TweeTube, 199
Twellow.com, 191, 197
Twemes, 178, 191
Twestivals, 226
Twiddeo, 199
TwiDroid, 200
Twit-Fit resumes, 125–131
Twitalyzer, 199
TwitDom, 201
Twitpic, 199
Twitter
    benefits of, 7–12
    best practices, 29–30
    comparison with Facebook and LinkedIn,
      23–25

    ease of use, 18
    importance of, 20
    integration of online and offline activity, 89,
      151–153
    integration with other social media, 153–154
    myths about, 15–19, 28–29
    power of, 22–23
    shorthand, 91–92
    terminology, 90–91
    tips from experts, 212–213
    what not to share. *See* discretionary
      authenticity
Twitter bio, 58–62, 73
Twitter Grader, 199
Twitter name. *See* names
Twitter persona, attracting followers with, 88
TwitteRel, 191
Twitterfeed, 199
TwitterJobSearch.com, 176
Twitterviews, 139
TwitVid, 199
Twubble, 191

U–V

UberTwitter, 200
unfollowing people, 89
URL shorteners, 73, 101, 196
Urschel, Harry, 122, 224
usernames. *See also* names
    checking availability of, 66
    selecting, 69–72
value propositions, 9
Varon, Jamie, 32, 203, 228
Vick, Bill, 121–122, 225
video, APIs for, 199
Voltaire, 166
von Braun, Werner, 191

W–Z

Web address in Twitter profile, 72–73
WeFollow, 197
What the Hashtag?!, 178
Where to Find Your Job on Twitter list, 179
Whitcomb, Susan, 127
Wilson, Woodrow, 134
worksheets, Twitter bio, 62
Wyse, Lois, 87
Yelland, Shannon, 33, 91, 205, 233
yfrog, 199
Zarrella, Dan, 65, 100
Ziglar, Zig, 144
Zittrain, Jonathan, 6